CODE
RED

CODE RED

How to Protect Your Savings
from the
Coming Crisis

JOHN MAULDIN and
JONATHAN TEPPER

WILEY

Published by John Wiley & Sons, Inc., Hoboken, New Jersey.
Published simultaneously in Canada.

For general information on our other products and services or for technical support, please contact
our Customer Care Department within the United States at (800) 762-2974, outside the United
States at (317) 572-3993 or fax (317) 572-4002.

Wiley publishes in a variety of print and electronic formats and by print-on-demand. Some material
included with standard print versions of this book may not be included in e-books or in print-on-
demand. If this book refers to media such as a CD or DVD that is not included in the version you
purchased, you may download this material at http://booksupport.wiley.com. For more information
about Wiley products, visit www.wiley.com.

Library of Congress Cataloging-in-Publication Data:
Mauldin, John.
 Code red : how to protect your savings from the coming crisis / John Mauldin and Jonathan Tepper.
  pages cm
 Includes bibliographical references and index.
 ISBN 978-1-118-78372-6 (cloth)—ISBN 978-1-118-78363-4 (ebk)—
 ISBN 978-1-118-78373-3 (ebk)
  1. Money—United States. 2. Saving and investment—United States.
 3. Currency crises—United States. 4. Financial crises—United States.
 I. Tepper, Jonathan, 1976- II. Title.
 HG540.M38 2014
 332.024—dc23

               2013035536

Printed in the United States of America
10 9 8 7 6 5 4 3 2 1

*This book is dedicated to
our mothers.*

*Mildred Duke Mauldin (1917–and still going)
No matter what life throws at her, she perseveres with grace
and a smile. One can grow up with no greater example of the
importance of showing up no matter what. She makes life better
for everyone who has ever known her.*

*Mary Prevatt Tepper (1945–2012)
She was a wonderful mother and a saint
who helped thousands of poor and needy
through Betel International.*

This debilitating spiral has spurred our government to take massive action. In poker terms, the Treasury and the Fed have gone "all in." Economic medicine that was previously meted out by the cupful has recently been dispensed by the barrel. These once-unthinkable dosages will almost certainly bring on unwelcome aftereffects. Their precise nature is anyone's guess, though one likely consequence is an onslaught of inflation. Moreover, major industries have become dependent on Federal assistance, and they will be followed by cities and states bearing mind-boggling requests. Weaning these entities from the public teat will be a political challenge. They won't leave willingly.

—*Warren Buffett*
Berkshire Hathaway 2008
Letter to Shareholders

Contents

Acknowledgments

We would gratefully like to acknowledge those who have helped us throughout the writing of this book. David Zervos provided the title of the book through his many humorous and insightful market commentaries. Our agent, Sam Hiyate at the Rights Factory, helped make this book happen. Our friends and reviewers of early drafts provided invaluable criticism. Charlie and Lisa Sweet of Mauldin Economics provided aggressive editing, which was needed. Evan Burton at Wiley helped bring this book to publication and into your hands.

Jonathan Tepper would like to thank his colleagues at Variant Perception, who provided many ideas and useful advice. Keir McGuinness and Jack Kirkland contributed their vast knowledge and deep insights to the chapter on commodities, gold, and real assets. Ziv Gil and Zvi Limon of Rimon Funds provided comments and criticisms and many interesting conversations and great times in Tel Aviv.

John Mauldin would like to thank his colleagues at Mauldin Economics for their support and insight, and especially Worth Wray. His business partner, Jon Sundt at Altegris Investments, has been patient. There are many people whose ideas have been foundational in my thinking but I would especially like to thank my friends Rob Arnott, Martin Barnes, Kyle Bass, Jim Bianco, Ian Brenner, Art Cashin, Bill Dunkelberg, Philippa Dunne, Albert Edwards, Mohammed El-Erian Niall Ferguson, George Friedman, Lewis and Charles Gave, Dylan Grice, Newt Gingrich, Richard Howard, Ben Hunt, Lacy Hunt, John Hussman, Niels Jensen, Anatole Kaletsky, Vitaly Katsenelson David Kotok, Michael Lewitt, Paul McCulley, Joan McCullough, Christian Menegatti, David McWilliams, Gary North, Barry Ritholtz, Nouriel Roubini, Tony Sagami, Kiron Sarkar, Gary Shilling, Dan Stelter, Grant Williams, Rich Yamarone, and scores of other writers and thinkers who have all been influential in my thinking.

Let me finally say that finishing this book would not have been possible before the end of the decade without the work and continual prodding of Jonathan Tepper. He is the best co-author any writer could have, especially one that is already overcommitted.

Any faults and omissions from the book, and we are sure there are many, are exclusively our own.

Introduction: Code Red

When Lehman Brothers went bankrupt and AIG was taken over by the U.S. government in the fall of 2008, the world almost came to an end. Over the next few weeks, stock markets went into free fall as trillions of dollars of wealth were wiped out. However, even more disturbing were the real-world effects on trade and businesses. A strange silence descended on the hubs of global commerce. As international trade froze, ships stood empty near ports around the world because banks would no longer issue letters of credit. Factories shut as millions of workers were laid off as commercial paper and money market funds used to pay wages froze. Major banks in the United States and the United Kingdom were literally hours away from shutting down and ATMs were on the verge of running out of cash. Bank stopped issuing letters of credit to former trusted partners worldwide. The interbank market simply froze, as no one knew who was bankrupt and who wasn't. Banks could look at their own balance sheets and see how bad things were and knew that their counterparties were also loaded up with too much bad debt.

The world was threatened with a big deflationary collapse. A crisis that big only comes around twice a century. Families and governments were swamped with too much debt and not enough money to pay them off. But central banks and governments saved the day by printing money, providing almost unlimited amounts of liquidity to the financial system. Like a doctor putting a large jolt of electricity on a dying man's chest, the extreme measures brought the patient back to life.

The money printing that central bankers did after the failure of Lehman Brothers was entirely appropriate in order to avoid a Great Depression II. The Fed and central banks were merely creating some money and credit that only partially offset the contraction in bank lending.

The initial crisis is long gone, but the unconventional measures have stayed with us. Once the crisis was over, it was clear that the world was saddled with high debt and low growth. In order to fight the monsters of deflation and depression, central bankers have gone wild. Central bankers kept on creating money. Quantitative easing was a shocking development when it was first trotted out, but these days the markets just shrug. Now, the markets are worried about losing their regular injections of monetary drugs. What will withdrawal be like?

The amount of money central banks have created is simply staggering. Under quantitative easing, central banks have been buying every government bond in sight and have expanded their balance sheets by over nine trillion dollars. Yes, that's $9,000,000,000,000—12 zeros to be exact. (By the time you read this book, the number will probably be a few trillion higher, but who's counting?) Numbers so large are difficult for ordinary humans to understand. As Senator Everett M. Dirksen once probably didn't say, "A billion here, a billion there, and soon you're talking about real money." To put it in everyday terms, if you had a credit limit of $9 trillion on your credit card, you could buy a MacBook Air for every single person in the world. You could fly everyone in the world on a round-trip ticket from New York to London. You could do that twice without blinking. We could go on, but you get the point: it's a big number.

In the four years since the Lehman Brothers bankruptcy, central bankers have torn up the rulebook and are trying things they have never tried before. Usually, interest rates move up or down depending on growth and inflation. Higher growth and inflation normally means higher rates, and lower growth means lower rates. Those were the good old days when things were normal. But now central bankers in the United States, Japan, and Europe have pinned interest rates close to zero and promised to leave them there for years. Rates can't go lower, so some central bankers have decided to get creative. Normally, central banks pay interest on the cash banks deposit with them overnight. Not anymore. Some banks like the Swiss National Bank and the Danish National Bank have even created *negative* deposit rates. We now live in an upside-down world. Money is effectively taxed (by central bankers, not representative governments!) to get people to spend instead of save.

These unconventional policies are generally good for big banks, governments, and borrowers (who doesn't like to borrow money for free?), but they are very bad for savers. Near-zero interest rates and heavily subsidized government lending programs help the banks to make money the old-fashioned way: borrow cheaply and lend at higher rates. They also help insolvent governments, allowing them to borrow at very low costs. The flip side is that near-zero rates punish savers, providing almost no income to pensioners and the elderly. Everyone who thought their life's savings might carry them through their retirement has to come up with a Plan B when rates are near zero.

In the bizarre world we now inhabit, central banks and governments try to induce consumers to spend to help the economy, while they take money away from savers who would like to be able to profitably invest. Rather than inducing them to consume more, they are forcing them to spend less in order to make their savings last through their final years!

Savers and investors in the developed world are the guinea pigs in an unprecedented monetary experiment. There are clear winners and losers as prudent savers are called upon to bail out reckless borrowers. In the United States, United Kingdom, Japan, and most of Europe, savers receive close to zero percent interest on their savings, while they watch the price of gasoline, groceries, and rents go up. Standards of living are falling for many and economic growth is elusive. Today is a time of financial repression, where central banks keep interest rates below inflation. This means that the interest savers receive on their deposits cannot keep up with the rising cost of living. Big banks are bailed out and continue paying large bonuses, while older savers are punished.

In the film *A Few Good Men*, Jack Nicholson plays Colonel Nathan Jessup. He subjects his troops to an unconventional and extreme approach to discipline by ordering a Code Red. Toward the end of the film, Colonel Jessup explains to a court-martial proceeding that while his methods are grotesque and abnormal, they are necessary for the defense of the nation and the preservation of freedom.

While central bank Code Red policies are certainly unorthodox and even distasteful, many economists believe they are necessary to kick-start the global economy and counteract the crushing burden of debt. David Zervos, chief market strategist at Jefferies & Co., humorously observes that "Colonel" Ben Bernanke, chairman of the Fed, is likewise brutally honest and just as insistent that his extreme policies are absolutely necessary.

We began to wonder what Colonel Jessup's speech might sound like if the colonel were a central banker. Perhaps it would go something like this (cue Jack Nicholson):

> You want the truth? *You can't handle the truth!* Son, we live in a world that has unfathomably intricate economies, and those economies and the banks that are at their center have to be guarded by men with complex models and printing presses. Who's gonna do it? You? You, Lieutenant Mauldin? Can you even begin to grasp the resources we have to use in order to maintain balance in a system on the brink?
>
> I have a greater responsibility than you can possibly fathom! You weep for savers and creditors, and you curse the central bankers and quantitative easing. You have that luxury. You have the luxury of not knowing what I know: that the destruction of savers with inflation and low rates, while tragic, probably saved lives. And my existence, while grotesque and incomprehensible to you, saves jobs and banks and businesses and whole economies!
>
> You don't want the truth, because deep down in places you don't talk about at parties, you want me on that central bank! You need me on that committee! Without our willingness to silently serve, deflation would come storming over our economic walls and wreak far worse havoc on an entire nation and the world. I will not let the 1930s and that devastating unemployment and loss of lives repeat themselves on my watch.

We use words like *full employment, inflation, stability*. We use these words as the backbone of a life spent defending something. You use them as a punchline!

I have neither the time nor the inclination to explain myself to a man who rises and sleeps under the blanket of the very prosperity that I provide, and then questions the manner in which I provide it! I would rather you just said "thank you" and went on your way.

Central bankers must hide the truth in order to do their job. Jean-Claude Juncker, the Prime Minister of Luxembourg and head of the European Union at one point, told us, **"When it becomes serious, you have to lie."** We may dislike what they are doing, but if politicians want to avoid large-scale defaults, the world needs loose money and money printing.

Ben Bernanke and his colleagues worldwide have effectively issued and enforced a Code Red monetary policy. Their economic theories and experience told them it was the correct and necessary thing to do—in fact, they were convinced it was the only thing to do!

Chairman Ben Bernanke could not be further from Colonel Nathaniel Jessup, but they are both men on a mission. Colonel Jessup is maniacally obsessed with enforcing discipline on his base at Guantanamo. He has seen war and does not take it lightly. He is a tough Marine who would not hesitate to kill his enemies. He is not loved, but he's happy to be feared and respected. Ben Bernanke, by contrast, is a soft-spoken academic. You can't find anyone with anything bad to say about him personally. His story is inspiring. He grew up as one of the few Jews in the Southern town of Dillon, South Carolina, and through his natural genius and hard work, he was admitted to Harvard, graduated with distinction, and soon he embarked on a brilliant academic career at MIT and Princeton. Sometimes, when Bernanke gives a speech, his voice cracks slightly, and it is certain he would much prefer to be writing academic papers or lecturing to a class of graduate students than dealing with large skeptical audiences of senators. But Bernanke is one of the world's foremost experts on the Great Depression. He has learned from history and knows that too much debt can be lethal. He genuinely believes that without Code

Red–type policies, he would condemn America to a decade of bread-lines and bankruptcies. He promised he would not let deflation and another Great Depression descend on America. In his own way, he's our Colonel Jessup, standing on the wall fighting for us. And he gets too little respect.

Bernanke understands that the world has far too much debt that it can't pay back. Sadly, debt can go away via only: (1) defaults (and there are so many ways to default without having to actually use the word!), (2) paying down debt through economic growth, or (3) eroding the burden of debt through inflation or currency devaluations. In our grandparents' age, we would have seen defaults. But defaults are painful, and no one wants them. We've grown fat and comfortable. We don't like pain.

Growing our way out of our problems would be ideal, but it isn't an option. Economic growth is elusive everywhere you look. Central bankers are left with no other option but to create inflation and devalue their currencies.

No one wants to hear that we'll suffer from higher inflation. It is grotesque and not what central bankers are meant to do. But people can't handle the truth, and inflation is exactly what the central bankers are preparing for us. They're sparing some the pain of defaults while others bear the pain of low returns. But a world in which big banks and governments default is almost by definition a world of not just low but (sometimes steeply) negative investment returns. As we said in *Endgame*, we are left with no good choices, only choices that range from the merely very difficult to the downright disastrous. The global situation reminds us very much of Woody Allen's quote, "More than any other time in history, mankind faces a crossroads. One path leads to despair and utter hopelessness. The other, to total extinction. Let us pray we have the wisdom to choose correctly." The choice now left to some countries is only between Disaster A and Disaster B.

Today's battle with deflation requires a constant vigilance and use of Code Red procedures. Unfortunately, just like in *A Few Good Men*, Code Reds are not standard operating procedures or conventional pol-icies. Ben Bernanke, Mario Draghi, Haruhiko Kuroda, and other cen-tral bankers are manning their battle stations using ugly weapons to get the job done. They are punishing savers, encouraging people to borrow more, providing lots of liquidity, and weakening their currencies.

This unprecedented global monetary experiment has only just begun, and every central bank is trying to get in on the act. It is a monetary arms race, and no one wants to be left behind. The Bank of England has devalued the pound to improve exports by allowing creeping inflation and keeping interest rates at zero. The Federal Reserve has tried to weaken the dollar in order to boost manufacturing and exports. The Bank of Japan, not to be outdone, is now trying to radically depreciate the yen. By weakening their currencies, these central banks hope to boost their countries' exports and get a leg up on their competitors. In the race to debase currencies, no one wins. But lots of people lose.

Emerging-market countries like Brazil, Russia, Malaysia, and Indonesia will not sit idly by while the developed central banks of the world weaken their currencies. They, too, are fighting to keep their currencies from appreciating. They are imposing taxes on investments and savings in their currencies. All countries are inherently protectionist if pushed too far. The battles have only begun in what promises to be an enormous, ugly currency war. If the currency wars of the 1930s and 1970s are any guide, we will see knife fights ahead. Governments will fight dirty—they will impose tariffs and restrictions and capital controls. It is already happening, and we will see a lot more of it.

If only they were just armed with knives. We are reminded of that amusing scene in *Raiders of the Lost Ark* where Indiana Jones, confronted with a very large man wielding an even larger scimitar, simply pulls out his gun, shoots him, and walks away. Some central banks are better armed than others. Indeed, you might say that the four biggest central banks—the Fed, Bank of England (BoE), European Central Bank (ECB), and Bank of Japan (BoJ)—have nuclear arsenals. In a fight for national survival, which is what a crisis this major will feel like, will central bankers resort to the nuclear option; will they double down on Code Red policies? The conflict could get very messy for those in the neighborhood.

Providing more debt and more credit after a bust that was caused by too much credit is like suggesting whiskey after a hangover. Paradoxical as the cure may be, many economists and investors think that it is just what the doctor ordered. At the star-studded World Economic Forum retreat in Davos, Switzerland, the billionaire

George Soros pointed out the contradiction policy makers now face. The global financial crisis happened because of too much debt and too much money floating around. However, according to many economists and investors, the solution may in fact be more money and more debt. As he said, "When a car is skidding, you first have to turn the wheel in the same direction as the skid to regain control because if you don't, then you have the car rolling over." Only after the global economy has recovered can the car begin to right itself. Before central banks can be responsible and conventional, they must first be irresponsible and unconventional.

The arsonists are now running the fire brigade. Central bankers contributed to the economic crisis the world now faces. They kept interest rates too low for too long. They fixated on controlling inflation, even as they stood by and watched investment banks party in an orgy of credit. Central bankers were completely incompetent and failed to see the Great Financial Crisis coming. They couldn't spot housing bubbles, and even when the crisis had started and banks were failing, they insisted that the banks they supervised were well regulated and healthy. They failed at their job and should have been fired. Yet governments now need central banks to erode the mountain of debt by printing money and creating inflation.

Investors should ask themselves: *if central bankers couldn't manage conventional monetary policy well in the good times, what makes us think that they will be able to manage unconventional monetary policies in the bad times?*

And if they don't do a perfect job of winding down condition Code Red, what will be the consequences?

Economists know that there are no free lunches. Creating tons of new money and credit out of thin air is not without cost. Massively increasing the size of a central bank's balance sheet is risky and stores up extremely difficult problems for the future. Central bank policies may succeed in creating growth, or they may fail. It is too soon to call the outcome, but what is clear (at least to us) is that the experiment is unlikely to end well.

The endgame for the current crisis is not difficult to foresee; in fact, it's already under way. Central banks think they can swell the size of their balance sheet, print money to finance government deficits, and keep rates at zero with no consequences. Bernanke and other bankers think they have the foresight to reverse their unconventional policies at the right time. They've been wrong in the past, and they will get the timing wrong in the future. They will keep interest rates too low for too long and cause inflation and bubbles in real estate, stock markets, and bonds. What they are doing will destroy savers who rely on interest payments and fixed coupons from their bonds. They will also harm lenders who have lent money and will be repaid in devalued dollars, if they are repaid at all.

We are already seeing the unintended consequences of this Great Monetary Experiment. Many emerging-market stock markets have skyrocketed, only to fall back to Earth at the mere hint of any end to Code Red policies. Junk bonds and risky commercial mortgage-backed securities are offering investors the lowest rates they have ever seen. Investors are reaching for riskier and riskier investments to get some small return. They're picking up dimes in front of a steamroller. It is fun for a while, but the end is always ugly. Older people who are relying on pension funds to pay for their retirement are getting screwed (that is a technical economic term that we will define in detail later). In normal times, retirees could buy bonds and live on the coupons. Not anymore. Government bond yields are now trading below the level of inflation, guaranteeing that any investor who holds the bonds until maturity will lose money in real terms.

We live in extraordinary times.

When investors convince themselves central bankers have their backs, they feel encouraged to bid up prices for everything, accepting more risk with less return. Excesses and bubbles are not a mere side effect. As crazy as it seems, reckless investor behavior is, in fact, the planned objective. William McChesney Martin, one of the great heads of the Federal Reserve, said the job of a central banker was to take away the punch bowl before the party gets started. Now, central bankers are spiking the punch bowl with triple sec and absinthe and egging on the revelers to jump in the pool. One day the party of low rates and money printing will come to an end, and investors will make their way home from the party in the early hours of sunlight half dressed, with a hangover and a thumping headache.

The coming upheaval will affect everyone. No one will be spared the consequences: from savers who are planning for retirement to professional traders looking for opportunities to profit in financial markets. Inflation will eat away at savings, government bonds will be destroyed as a supposedly safe asset class, and assets that benefit from inflation and money printing will do well.

This book will provide a road map and a playbook for retail savers and professional traders alike. This book will shine a light on the path ahead. *Code Red* will explain in plain English complicated things like zero interest rate policies (ZIRPs), nominal gross domestic product (GDP) targeting, quantitative easing, money printing, and currency wars. But much more importantly, it will explain how it will affect your savings and offer insights on how to protect your wealth. It is our hope that *Code Red* will be an invaluable guide for you for the road ahead.

Part One

I n the first part of this book, we will show you how we arrived where we are, what central banks are doing, how they are storing problems for the future, and how the current policies will end badly. In Part II of the book, we will show you how to protect your savings from the bad consequences of central bank policies.

Let's dive right in!

Chapter One

The Great Experiment

Like gold, U.S. dollars have value only to the extent that they are strictly limited in supply. But the U.S. government has a technology, called a printing press (or, today, its electronic equivalent) that allows it to produce as many U.S. dollars as it wishes at essentially no cost. By increasing the number of U.S. dollars in circulation, or even by credibly threatening to do so, the U.S. government can also reduce the value of a dollar in terms of goods and services, which is equivalent to raising the prices in dollars of those goods and services.

—*Ben Bernanke,*
Chairman of the Board of Governors of the
Federal Reserve Bank of the United States

President Lyndon B. Johnson once summed up the general feeling about economists when he asked his advisers, "Did you ever think that making a speech on economics is a lot like pissing down your leg? It seems hot to you, but it never does to anyone else." Reading a book about monetary policy and central banking can seem equally unexciting. It doesn't have to be.

Central banking and monetary policy may seem technical and boring; but whether we like it or not, the decisions of the Federal Reserve, the Bank of Japan (BoJ), the European Central Bank (ECB), and the

Bank of England (BoE) affect us all. Over the next few years they are going to have profound impacts on each of us, touching our lives in every way. They influence the value of the dollar bills in our wallets, the price of the groceries we buy, how much it costs to fill up the gas tank, the wages we earn at work, the interest we get on our savings accounts, and the health of our pension funds. You may not care about monetary policy, but it will have an impact on whether you can retire comfortably, whether you can send your children to college with ease, or whether you will be able to afford your house. It is difficult to over-state how profoundly monetary policy influences our lives. If you care about your quality of life, the possibility of retirement, and the future of your children, you should care about monetary policy.

Despite the importance of central bankers in our lives, outside of trading floors on Wall Street and the City of London, most people have no idea what central bankers do or how they do it. Central bankers are like the Wizard of Oz, moving the levers of money behind the scenes, but remaining a mystery to the general public.

It is about time to pull the curtains back on monetary policy making.

Even though they are separated by oceans, borders, cultures, and languages, all the major central bankers have known each other for decades and share similar beliefs about what monetary policy should do. Three of the world's most powerful central bankers started their careers at the Massachusetts Institute of Technology (MIT) econom-ics department. Fed chairman Ben Bernanke and ECB president Mario Draghi earned their doctorates there in the late 1970s. Bank of England governor Mervyn King taught there briefly in the 1980s. He even shared an office with Bernanke. Many economists came out of MIT with a belief that government could (and, even more important, should) soften economic downturns. Central banks play a particularly important role, not only by changing interest rates but also by manip-ulating the public's expectations of what the central bank might do.

We are living through one watershed moment after another in the greatest monetary experiment of all time. We are all guinea pigs in a risky trial run by central bankers: it's Code Red time.

Those of us who are of a certain age remember the great Dallas Cowboys coach Tom Landry. He would stalk the sidelines in his fedora, holding a sheet of paper he would consult many times. On it were the plays he would run, worked out well in advance. Third down and long and behind 10 points? He had a play for that.

The Code Red policies that central bankers are coming up with more closely resemble Hail Mary passes than they do Landry's carefully worked out playbook: they are not in any manual, and they are certainly not normal. The head coaches of our financial world are sending in one novel play after another, really mixing things up to see what might work: "Let's send zero interest rate policy (ZIRP) up the middle while quantitative easing (QE) runs a slant, large-scale asset purchases (LSAPs) goes deep, and negative real interest rates, financial repression, nominal gross domestic product (GDP) targeting, and foreign exchange intervention hold the line."

The acronym alphabet soup of the playmakers is incomprehensible to the average person, but all of these programs are fancy, technical ways to hide very simple truths.

In *Through the Looking Glass*, Humpty Dumpty says, "When I use a word, it means just what I choose it to mean—neither more nor less." When central bankers give us words to describe their financial policies, they tell us exactly what they want their words to mean, but rarely do they tell us exactly the truth in plain English. They think we can't handle the truth.

The Great Financial Crisis of 2008 marked the turning point from conventional monetary policies to Code Red type unconventional policies.

Before the crisis, central bankers were known as boring, conservative people who did everything by the book. They were generally disliked for being party poopers. They would take away the punch bowl just when the party got going. When the economy was overheating, central bankers were supposed to raise interest rates, cool down growth, and tighten monetary policy. Sometimes, doing so caused recessions. Taking away the punch bowl could hardly make everyone happy. In fact, at the start of the 1980s, former chairman Paul Volcker was burnt in effigy by a mob on the steps of the capitol for hiking short-term interest rates to 19 percent as he struggled to fight inflation. Central bankers like Volcker believed in sound money, low inflation, and a strong currency.

In the throes of the Great Financial Crisis, however, central bankers went from using interest rates to cool down the party to spiking the punch with as many exotic liqueurs as possible. Ben Bernanke, the chairman of the Federal Reserve, was the boldest, most creative, and unconventional of them all. With his Harvard, MIT, and Princeton background, he is undoubtedly one of the savviest central bankers in generations. When Lehman Brothers went bust, he invented dozens of programs that had never existed before to finance banks, money market funds, commercial paper markets, and so on. Bernanke took the Federal Funds rate down almost to zero, and the Fed bought trillions of dollars of government treasuries and mortgage-backed securities. Bernanke promised that the Federal Reserve would act boldly and creatively and would not withdraw the punch bowl until the party was really rolling. Foreign central bankers like Haruhiko Kuroda (BoJ); Mervyn King and his replacement from Canada, Mark Carney (BoE); and Mario Draghi (ECB) have also promised to do whatever it takes to achieve their objectives. We have no doubt that whoever replaces Bernanke will be in the same mold.

These are the days of a new breed of central banker who believes in the prescription of ultra-easy money, higher rates of inflation, and a weaker currency to cure today's ills. Their experimental medicine may have saved the patient in the short term, but it is addictive; withdrawal is ugly; and because long-term side effects are devastating, it can be prescribed only for short-term use. The problem is, they can't openly admit any of that.

Central bankers hope that unconventional policies will do the trick. If everything goes as planned, inflation will quietly eat away at debt, stock markets will go up, house prices will go up, everyone will feel wealthier and spend the newfound wealth, banks will earn lots of money and become solvent, and government debts will shrink as taxes rise and deficits evaporate. And after all is well again, central banks can go back to the good old days of conventional policies. There is no guarantee that will happen, but that's the game plan.

So far, Code Red policies have lifted stock markets, but they have not worked at reviving growth. But Code Red–type policies are like a religion or communism. If they don't work, it is only proof that they were not tried in sufficient size or with enough vigor. So we're guaranteed to see a lot more unconventional policies in the coming months and years.

How I Learned to Stop Worrying and Love Inflation

The Great Financial Crisis was a story of a huge mountain of debt that was piled too high, reached criticality, and then collapsed. For decades, families, companies, and governments had accumulated every kind of debt imaginable: credit card bills, student loans, mortgages, corporate and municipal bonds, and so on. Once the mountain rumbled, broke, and started to collapse, the landslides spread everywhere. The epicenter of the crisis was the U.S. subprime mortgage market (in fact, many foreign leaders still think it was fat, suburban, Big Mac–eating Americans who caused the global crisis), but the United States was just a small part of a much bigger problem. Countries such as Ireland, Spain, Iceland, and Latvia also had very large real estate bubbles that burst. Other countries, including Australia, Canada, and China, have housing bubbles that are still in the process of bursting. It's the same problem everywhere: too much debt that cannot be paid back in full.

(We certainly would not minimize the role of the Federal Reserve in failing to supervise the banks and especially subprime debt. By holding interest rates too low for too long and by willfully ignoring the developing bubble in the U.S. housing market, they certainly played a central role.)

When a person has too much debt, the sensible thing to do is to spend less and pay down the mortgage or credit card bills. However, what is true for one person isn't true for the economy as a whole. Economists call this principle the *paradox of thrift*. Imagine if everyone decided overnight to stop spending beyond what was absolutely necessary, save more, and pay down their debts. That would mean fewer dinners out, fewer visits to Starbucks, fewer Christmas presents, fewer new cars, and so on. You get the picture. The economy as a whole would contract dramatically if everyone spent less in order to pay down debts. But, in fact, that is exactly what happened during the Great Financial Crisis. Economists call this process *deleveraging*. And the last thing central banks want is for everyone to stop spending money and reduce their debts at the same time. That leads to recessions and depressions.

At least that was the theory proposed by John Maynard Keynes, the father of one of the most influential economic schools of thought, and it has become the reigning paradigm. It's all about encouraging consumption and reviving "animal spirits." If the economy is in the doldrums (recession), it is up to the government to run deficits, even massive ones, in order to "prime the pump." Put plenty of money into people's hands so they will go out and spend, encouraging businesses to expand and hire more workers, who will then consume yet more goods, and so on. Wash, rinse, and repeat.

Another solution if you have too much debt is to declare bankruptcy. In many countries that can be an effective way of starting over again. You put behind you debts you can't pay, offer to pay what you can, and start anew. Once again, what is good for the individual isn't necessarily good for the economy as a whole. Imagine what would happen if millions of people declared bankruptcy at the same time. Banks would all go bust, and the government would probably have to pick up the tab and recapitalize the banks. And then, before long, the government would find itself going bust.

The difference between what is right for one person and what is right for society is paradoxical. It is what logicians call the *fallacy of composition*. What is true for a part is not true for the whole. If you drive to work 10 minutes early, you might avoid traffic. If everyone drives to work 10 minutes early, the traffic jam will happen 10 minutes earlier. Central banks don't want everyone to be prudent or to go bankrupt at the same time. They would simply prefer everyone to remain calm and carry on spending.

If you want to avoid everyone's ceasing to spend—or, worse yet, everyone's going bankrupt at the same time—the only way to make the debt go away in real terms is through inflation. Inflation is the Ghostbusters of debt. It wipes debt out over time. For the sake of simplicity, imagine that you owe $100,000. If inflation is 2 percent, it will take about 30 years to cut the value of the loan in half. But if the rate of inflation doubles to 4 percent, it will take just 18 years to halve the value of the loan. And if inflation doubles again to 8 percent, you will halve the loan in 8 years!

Inflation is just what the doctor ordered for an economy with too much debt. By ratcheting up inflation, central bankers can erode debt quickly and quietly. But while inflation is the friend of debtors, it is the enemy of savers; so for central bankers to come out and say they're in favor of inflation would be like the pope's announcing one day that he's not Catholic. That isn't going to happen.

Inflation is a subject that divides economists because it means different things to different people. Not all inflation is bad. Inflation is generally considered to be problematic when the broad price level of most goods and services starts to go up because too much money is chasing too few goods. The increase in the price of a haircut is bad inflation. The method of cutting hair is no different than it was in the 1930s or the 1950s, yet it is vastly more expensive to get your hair cut today. (I [John] pay 200 times more for a haircut today than I did when I was a kid.) However, an increase in the price of a Picasso or de Kooning is considered to be normal, or "good," inflation. The higher prices are merely a reflection of more wealthy people in the world chasing fine art. They reflect the scarcity of the goods for sale and the laws of supply and demand at work. And who complains about the asset inflation of a rising stock market or rising home values?

Then there is good deflation and bad deflation. The deflation of falling telegraph, telephone, or Internet prices is viewed as good. Better technology means that prices fall because we can do the same things more cheaply or even nearly for free. For example, in *Money, Markets & Sovereignty*, Benn Steil and Manuel Hinds describe the second phase of the Industrial Revolution in the United States between 1870 and 1896. Prices fell by 32 percent over the period, but real income soared 110 percent amid robust economic growth, expanded trade, and enormous innovation in telecommunications and other industries.

The bad kind of deflation is different. When demand drops because people have too much debt and not enough money to spend, prices fall, too, though the cost of production does not. Jobs dry up, leaving people with even less to spend. That is the kind of deflation central bankers fear today.

Alphabet Soup: ZIRP, QE, LSAP

Let's look at how central bankers attempt to create inflation and how they help households, companies, and governments burdened with too much debt. We'll go through the main acronyms and technical terms and explain what they mean and how they affect you.

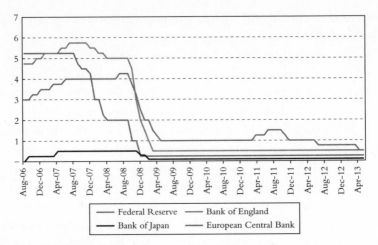

Figure 1.1   Global Interest Rates
SOURCE: *Variant Perception*, Bloomberg.

The main way monetary authorities have an impact on the economy is by setting interest rates. Interest rates determine the price at
which people will borrow and lend. In the old days, when the economy was growing quickly, central banks would raise rates. When the
economy was slowing, they'd cut rates, which meant that financing got
cheaper, credit was easier, and money was looser.

The reason the Fed cut interest rates was to stimulate the economy.
Lower rates mean lower mortgage, credit card, and car payments. They
give businesses access to cheaper capital and hopefully spur profits and
thus hiring. This puts more money into the hands of consumers. As an
example, U.S. 30-year mortgage rates recently hit a record low of 3.66
percent, down from 4.5 percent the same time last year. A number of
mortgage holders will refinance, given the much lower rates, increasing
their disposable income. That almost makes us want to buy a house or
two. Who can complain about a free lunch?

Cutting rates can only go so far until you hit zero. You can see this
in Figure 1.1. Then you're stuck with a floor. In fact, central banks cut
rates during the financial crisis, and then left them near zero and have
not raised them since. Leaving rates at or near zero is what central banks
refer to as *zero interest rate policy* (ZIRP). Currently, the United States,
United Kingdom, Japan, Switzerland, and, arguably, the Euro area are all
engaging in ZIRP.

In a ZIRP world, debtors are overjoyed and savers are screwed. Imagine borrowing at 5 or 10 percent and then suddenly seeing your borrowing costs fall to a little above zero. No matter how much debt you had before, paying very little interest every month is a lifesaver. Low borrowing costs make it easier for struggling businesses to roll over their debt and reduce the real value of debt payments. If you reduce the coupon payment on a loan, that is economically the same thing as forgiving part of the principal amount, but this forgiveness is hidden. The low rates effectively allow "zombie" households and businesses to limp along without going bankrupt.

Near-zero interest rates are, however, terrible for savers, investors, and lenders. Imagine you're a retiree, and you've been responsible and saved all your life; you've put money in the bank that you expect to pay you interest every month. You probably bought some bonds as well so you could collect coupons every quarter. In a ZIRP world, you would be getting very little every month from interest and coupon payments. You would live your retirement years with far less income than you had planned for, or you would need to work far longer in order to save more.

This is happening to retirees all over the world—it's why more and more people over 60 are still working. The Federal Reserve and central bankers are not particularly worried about savers. Most Americans are struggling with debt. In an indebted society, helping debtors beats helping savers.

Inflation is the opposite of a gift that keeps on giving. Higher inflation allows the Federal Reserve and other central banks to take real interest rates below zero. *Nominal interest rates* are the actual interest rate you get. *Real interest rates* are nominal rates minus the inflation rate. If your bank offers you 2 percent on your bank account, the nominal rate is 2 percent. So far, so simple. If inflation is 2 percent, then the real interest rate is 0 $(2 - 2 = 0)$. The interest rate is only just keeping up with inflation. If inflation is 4 percent, then the interest you are getting on your bank account isn't even keeping pace with inflation. Your real interest rate would be negative 2 $(2 - 4 = -2)$. As you can see, with rates near zero, as long as inflation is positive, central banks can create negative real rates. Even though nominal rates can be trapped at zero, real interest rates can go below zero.

When real rates are negative, cash is trash. Negative real rates act like a tax on savings. Inflation eats away at your money, and is in effect a tax by the (unelected!) central bankers on your hard-earned money. Leaving money in the bank when real rates are negative guarantees that you will lose purchasing power. Negative real rates force savers and investors to seek out riskier and riskier investments merely to tread water. It almost guarantees people don't save and stop spending. In fact, Bernanke openly acknowledges that his low interest-rate policy is designed to get savers and investors to take more chances with riskier investments. The fact that this is precisely the wrong thing for retirees and savers seems to be lost in their pursuit of market and economic gains.

Simply by opening their mouths, central bankers can affect not only today's interest rate, but tomorrow's *expected* interest rate as well. If Bernanke (and his successors) or Mario Draghi of the ECB promise to keep interest rates near zero until kingdom come, investors will generally take them at their word. By promising to keep rates low, central banks have crushed bond yields. The bond yield curve tells the story. The yield curve is the structure of interest rates for bonds for today, tomorrow, and the day after tomorrow. By plotting a line for each bond maturity, you can see what expected rates are out into the future: 2 years, 5 years, 10 years, and 30 years. The U.S. government can now issue 10-year debt for less than 2 percent yield. This is below the rate of inflation. It implies the Fed has been successful at keeping rates below inflation all the way out to 10 years.

Lots of big economists such as Paul Krugman, Ben Bernanke, Gauti Eggertsson, and Michael Woodford, have provided the intellectual underpinnings that justify Code Red policies (the list of names is actually quite long). They argued that if unconventional monetary policy can raise expected inflation, this strategy can push down real interest rates even though nominal rates cannot fall any further (i.e., they can't fall below zero). Read their research and bear that in mind when these same economists say they don't want to create inflation.

Government bonds used to offer a risk-free rate of return. You took no risk in buying them, and you were guaranteed a return. Jim Grant, the astute financial analyst, has noted that bonds have rallied so much, and the yields on government bonds are so low, that they now offer investors *return-free risk*: you're now guaranteed a loss buying government bonds. Coupons are so low that investors are not even being compensated at the rate of inflation. It is hard to see how rates can go much lower or how more fools can be found to buy the bonds. The only people who buy British, Japanese, German, or American government bonds today in any size are institutions that are legally forced to do so, like insurance companies and pension funds.

From a central banker's point of view, leaving interest rates near zero is useful, but it has given them little *direct* influence over the economy. They can control rising inflation and expectations of higher prices only indirectly. However, central banks still have more bullets in the chamber they can use.

Quantitative Easing, a.k.a. Money Printing

In addition to manipulating interest rates, central banks have the ability to increase the money supply through quantitative easing (QE). Despite all the syllables, that's just a fancy way to say money printing. When the Fed wants to print new money and expand the money supply, it goes out and buys government bonds from banks that it has designated as "primary dealers." The Fed takes delivery of the securities and pays the dealers with newly printed money. The money goes into the dealers' bank accounts, where it can then support lending and money creation by the banking system. Likewise, when the Fed wants to reduce the money supply, it sells bonds back to the banks. The bonds go to the dealers, and the money paid to the Fed simply disappears. (As you can see, both "printing" money and making money disappear happen electronically and instantly. No actual printing of currency is involved. No trees are harmed in the process.)

Banks absolutely love QE—it is a gift to them, and it's one that circumvents the congressional appropriations process. To pay for QE, the Fed credits banks with electronic deposits that are reserve balances at the Federal Reserve. These reserve balances have ballooned to $1.5 trillion, from a mere $8 billion in late 2008. The Fed now pays 0.25 percent interest on reserves it holds, which amounts to nearly $4 billion a year in the banks' coffers. If interest rates rise to 3 percent, and the Federal Reserve then raises the rate it pays on reserves correspondingly, the interest payment will rise from $4 billion to $45 billion a year—an even larger gift! And that is one of the reasons why people are so worried about what will happen if the Fed ever goes back to a normal policy regime. Will the primary dealers lose their interest bennies? Will the Fed actually raise reserve rates? Or will the Fed reduce the money supply, taking away profits of the banks? There is a reason the markets are worried, and it has to do with profits. Their profits. Stay tuned.

The Fed has done over $1.5 trillion of money printing via QE. It is set to do a lot more. See Figure 1.2 for the projected growth of the Fed's balance sheet. It resembles a Nasdaq stock in 1999, shooting to the moon. You would think that $1.5 trillion might be enough, but many respected economists and writers such as Paul Krugman and Martin Wolf are calling for even more QE. When you hear pundits calling for even more QE, you can almost conjure reruns of old *Star Trek* episodes, with Captain Kirk—make that Captain Ben—shouting, "Dammit, Scotty, you've got to give me more QE!" as the Fed tries to escape a black hole of high debt and low growth.

Every time a central bank prints money, it creates winners and losers. So far, the biggest beneficiaries of money printing are governments themselves. This should come as no surprise. (To paraphrase Captain Renault in *Casablanca*, "I'm shocked, shocked to find that money printing is going on in here!") Central banks everywhere are printing

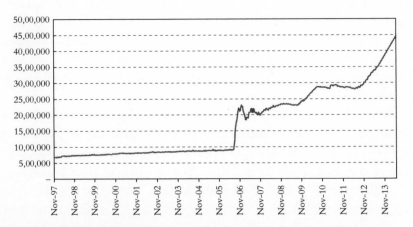

Figure 1.2   Projected Growth of the Federal Reserve's Balance Sheet
SOURCE: *Variant Perception*, Bloomberg.

money to finance very large government deficits. In fact, in 2011, the Federal Reserve financed around three quarters of the U.S. deficit; in 2012, it financed over half of it; and in 2013, it will finance most of it. Why borrow money from real savers when the central bank will print it for you?

The problem for savers and investors is that *all* the major central banks are in on the act. Take a look at Figure 1.3 and you can see that it isn't just the Fed. It is the BoJ, the BoE, the Swiss National Bank, and even the ECB that have expanded their balance sheets. In the case of Japan and England, the central banks are buying bonds outright. The Europeans are not buying bonds directly, but they've provided unlimited financing for private banks to do so. And the Swiss have been buying loads of everyone else's bonds to keep their currency from appreciating. It's a lollapalooza of money creation.

Since printing the money to buy government bonds costs nothing (given that central bank money is just bytes on a computer somewhere), governments get money for nothing and their checks for free. The central bank buys government bonds in the open market rather than from the government directly, and the pretense of an arm's-length transaction between government and central bank maintains

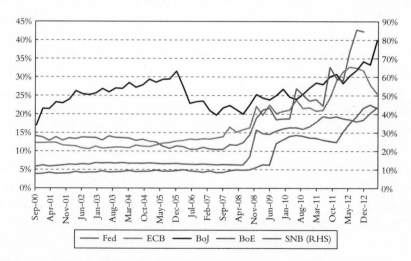

Figure 1.3   Central Bank Balance Sheets Shoot Up to the Moon
SOURCE: *Variant Perception*, Bloomberg.

the illusion of central bank independence, with all parties claiming a separation of monetary and fiscal policy. But that's just for show. By essentially issuing bonds to itself, the government appears to raise revenue miraculously, without burdening anyone else. Yet free money is like a unicorn that leaves trails of tasty chocolate droppings wherever it goes: it exists only in the realms of fantasy. (You or I might simply say, "There are no free lunches"; but as John Maynard Keynes put it, "Words ought to be a little wild, for they are the assaults of thoughts on the unthinking.")

Since there can actually be no such thing as a government raising revenue at no cost, simple logic tells us that someone has to pay. It is impossible to know in advance who will pay for a central bank's "free lunch," only that someone, somewhere will eventually pay. So governments are using quantitative easing to raise revenues without even knowing upon whom the burden will fall (let alone telling them). Compare this to raising revenue the normal way, by taxation. It is possible to know who raised the tax, when it was levied, when it is payable, and how much has to be paid. The burden of money printing, however, falls on unsuspecting victims. These are generally creditors, savers, and investors, but the costs are even more widely felt. It is easy for your local politician to deny culpability—the central bank is by design out of his control. (Well, except in Japan these days. Things like central bank independence can change when survival is at stake.)

Extremely high government spending would be difficult without central bank financing. As the book goes to press, for every dollar that the U.S. federal government spends, it borrows 40 cents (and that has been the case for some time). To put this in everyday terms, in 2012 the median American household income was $50,054. If a normal American family ran its budget like the U.S. government, it would borrow about $20,000 a year to pay for expenses. Most households would love to print money to finance their spending. By printing money, the Federal Reserve lends a helping hand to ease spending. (If the Federal Reserve is reading this, any money printing sent our way would be much appreciated. Please call for our bank account details. We promise to spend any such money immediately and thus do our part to drive up consumer spending.)

The biggest winners from the Fed's policies have been stockholders. The job of all central bankers is to keep prices stable. In the case of the Fed, it also has the job of promoting full employment in the economy. The two missions are referred to as the "Dual Mandate." However, in a Code Red world, the central banks have created a third mandate for themselves: make stock prices go up through large-scale asset purchase (LSAP) programs. Bernanke spoke directly about this in a speech in January 2011:

> Policies have contributed to a stronger stock market just as they did in March 2009, when we did the last iteration of this. The S&P 500 is up 20 percent-plus and the Russell 2000, which is about small cap stocks, is up 30 percent-plus.

He returned to the theme in a speech in 2012.

> LSAPs also appear to have boosted stock prices, presumably both by lowering discount rates and by improving the economic outlook; it is probably not a coincidence that the sustained recovery in U.S. equity prices began in March 2009, shortly after the FOMC's decision to greatly expand securities purchases. This effect is potentially important because stock values affect both consumption and investment decisions.

These remarks are vintage Bernanke. If you're an investor or speculator, the message is loud and clear: Buy stocks. We've got your back. (But let's see who takes the blame when the stock market falls next time. Just saying . . .)

The reason the Fed wants stock prices to go up is that when stocks go up, investors are happy and likely to spend more money. It is trickle-down monetary policy. QE, ZIRP, and LSAPs to the tune of $85 billion of purchases a month are pumping up the stock market, all with the hope that rich people will spend those gains, and that money will trickle down to the rest of the country. So far, no dice. (As we write this, new jobs created per month in the United States are around 150,000, so it takes about $500,000 of QE to create one job. Bravo to the Fed!! It would be far easier to simply write the unemployed checks for $100,000. That would be 80 percent cheaper.)

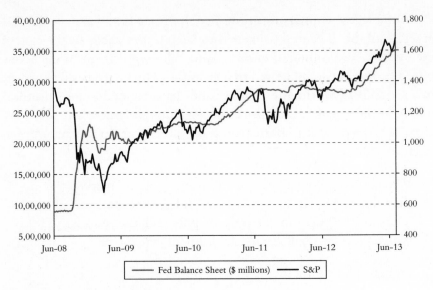

Figure 1.4   QE and LSAPs Have Been Very Bullish for Stocks
SOURCE: *Variant Perception*, Bloomberg.

The problem is that there is no clear link between developments in financial markets and the real economy. Research now points to the problem: the "wealth effect" from a rise in the stock market is quite small. Higher stock market prices tend to benefit only the few who were already wealthy. The same economists who despise supply-side economics are madly infatuated with supply-side monetary policy. Go figure. Trickle-down monetary policy indeed!

Most Americans own stocks, but only the wealthiest 10 percent of the population own significant amounts of stocks. Their retirement accounts are worth an average $277,000. But middle-income families have just $23,000 in their accounts, and the poor have nothing at all. The rich were almost all employed before quantitative easing anyway. Afterwards, they still have jobs and are richer. As for the poor, they still have very high unemployment and have not benefited in the slightest from a higher stock market.

Debasing Your Currency

In a world of zero interest rates, negative *real* rates and quantitative easing, money has less and less value. Central bankers are perfectly aware of this, and they've discussed it in public. In fact, devaluing the dollar is a very explicit goal. In a speech in 2002 Ben Bernanke admitted that creating money electronically would immediately devalue the dollar. As he argued:

> Like gold, U.S. dollars have value only to the extent that they are strictly limited in supply. But the U.S. government has a technology, called a printing press (or, today, its electronic equivalent) that allows it to produce as many U.S. dollars as it wishes at essentially no cost. By increasing the number of U.S. dollars in circulation, or even by credibly threatening to do so, the U.S. government can also reduce the value of a dollar in terms of goods and services, which is equivalent to raising the prices in dollars of those goods and services.

The Obama administration is thrilled with a weaker dollar. Christina Romer, former chair of the Council of Economic Advisers, also noted that, "Quantitative easing also works through exchange rates." She argued that the Fed could engage in much more aggressive QE to further lower the dollar, if needed. We will return later to the point that this makes it hard to object when Japan does the same thing but just twice as intensively!

While devaluing the dollar might seem like an insane idea to a normal person, it is exactly what some central banks want. Weakening your currency is a tried and tested strategy that countries have used throughout the years. Central bankers who weaken their currencies are like drag racers that inject nitrous oxide into their engines. It is like cheating and can give an economy a little extra push in the race for economic growth. The fact that is bad for the long-term survival of their engines is lost in the drive to win the race today.

Many countries rely on exports or would like to export more to grow. A weaker currency makes goods and services more appealing to foreigners. For example, a few years ago, when the pound had an exchange rate of $2.10 against the dollar, lots of British women traveled to New York for the weekend to buy handbags and eat out. But when the pound bought only $1.35 worth of goods, no one hopped from London to the United States to go shopping. On a very large scale, the same happens. For a U.S. auto maker, selling cars to foreigners gets a lot easier if the dollar is weak against foreign currencies.

When a currency appreciates, exports can be hit very hard. It's tougher to sell computers, cars, and ships to foreigners, and so most countries and their businesses want a weak currency. It is easier for a business to sell products when their currency is dropping than it is to become more productive. Politicians may say they want a strong dollar or a strong euro, but in practice the opposite is true. (Watch what they do, not what they say.)

Devaluing your currency sounds wonderful in theory. In practice, it doesn't always work out as planned. Central bankers, like drag racers, can inject nitrous oxide into their engines to get a little more horsepower. If you are the only one doing it, you'll have an edge. The problem is that if everyone is doing it, no one has an advantage. And eventually, everyone burns out their engines and no one wins. Despite the initial optimism they may inspire, in the long run currency crises can only lead to stagnation, inflation, falling standards of living, and poor growth.

Navigating a Code Red World

Whenever central bankers spike the punchbowl through money printing or currency devaluations, investors are happy. Every QE announcement has made stocks go up. Every major currency sell-off, whether it is the dollar or, lately, the Japanese yen, has lifted stock markets and commodities like oil, copper, wheat, and corn in the terms of the currency being trashed—er, we mean devalued. The policy of very low interest rates and money printing appears to have worked, up to this point. Most stock markets have doubled from the lows they hit after Lehman Brothers went bankrupt. The euphoria of investors should come as no surprise. When Nixon took the dollar off the gold standard in 1971, stocks skyrocketed. But investors should recall that the joy was short-lived. As it turned out, the 1970s were one of the worst decades for investing in stocks or bonds. Commodities did well for a while and then crashed. Investing was treacherous. The near future will likely be equally tumultuous, marked by bubbles, booms, and busts; and investors will need to be prepared.

For many investors, the last few years have been a stormy voyage. It is easy to feel like a medieval explorer sailing through uncharted waters into terra incognita beyond the edge of the map.

In a memorable (and relevant!) scene from *Blackadder*, one of our favorite comedies, Lord Melchett hands Blackadder a map and says, "Farewell, Blackadder. The foremost cartographers of the land have prepared this for you; it's a map of the area that you'll be traversing." When Blackadder opens it, he sees the map is blank. Lord Melchett smiles and adds, "They'll be very grateful if you could just fill it in as you go along. Bye-bye."

Luckily, you do not need to be without a map, or indeed to fill in an empty map as you go along. Code Red will show you how to navigate the treacherous currents ahead.

Key Lessons from the Chapter

In this chapter we learned:

- Before the Great Financial Crisis, central bankers used conventional monetary policy. Now they are experimenting with nonconventional "Code Red" policies like quantitative easing, zero interest rates, large-scale asset purchases, and currency debasement. These policies will lead to inflation in the long run.
- If you have borrowed too much, it is good to spend less and save. Central bankers, however, want everyone to keep borrowing and spending. Their policies are designed to encourage borrowing and speculation.
- The way to get people to spend their money instead of save is to create negative real interest rates on cash. Inflation in most countries is higher than interest rates, so cash is trash.

- Politicians and central bankers want to encourage exports, so they are trying to devalue their currencies and make goods and services cheaper for foreigners. Unfortunately, not everyone can devalue their currency at the same time.
- Currency wars have happened before in the 1930s and 1970s. They rarely end well for anyone, but governments pursue currency wars anyway.
- Let's review some Code Red terms:
  - ZIRPs—zero interest rate policies. Many central banks have cut interest rates to zero and can't cut them anymore. The central banks have promised to keep them near zero for years.
  - LSAP—large-scale asset purchase program. This is when a central bank prints money to buy bonds, mortgage securities or stocks.
  - QE—quantitative easing. This is when central banks expand the size of their balance sheet to influence the economy rather than through raising or lowering interest rates.
  - Currency wars—is a policy to deliberately weaken your own currency. This happens when central banks use QE and ZIRP to reduce the attractiveness of holding cash. Central banks also can "talk down" their currency and say they want it to go lower.

Chapter Two

Twentieth-Century Currency Wars

The Barbarous Relic and Bretton Woods

In truth, the gold standard is already a barbarous relic.

—*John Maynard Keynes,*
A Retrospective on the
Classical Gold Standard, 1821–1931

The farther backward you can look, the farther forward you are likely to see.

—*Winston Churchill*

Those who do not remember the past are condemned to repeat it.

—*George Santayana*

I n *Endgame*, we wrote a chapter on Japan titled "A Bug in Search of a Windshield." We argued that it was a matter of *when*, not *if* Japan would suffer a major economic crisis. There was no way of knowing when Japan's fiscal and monetary catastrophe would happen, but we knew it would come. Events have moved quickly since we wrote the book, and we are already seeing the beginning of the end. In fact, since January we've been calling 2013 "The Year of the Windshield." (*Endgame* recently came out in Japanese, just in time to let the Japanese know how screwed they really are. To all our Japanese readers: please don't shoot the messenger.)

Japan has waded further into debt and Code Red policy responses than has any other nation. The country holds clues to what will happen in the United States and Europe without a serious change in direction. Indeed, those clues can be seen as a gift to the United States and Europe—a priceless opportunity to see what happens when an uber-Keynesian policy is pursued to its logical conclusion.

It is impossible to overstate the importance of the bold experiments the Japanese government and the Bank of Japan (BoJ) are now conducting. The impact of events in Japan will be felt across the entire world over the next few years, so it is critical to look carefully at what is happening there. In the next chapter, we are going to take a very deep dive into the situation in which the Japanese find themselves today, which amounts to a death match for economic survival. This is easily Japan's economic equivalent of the Battle of Verdun or the Battle of Thermopylae. With utter determination, Japanese leaders are deploying every weapon in their economic arsenal on this frontline.

The recent volatility in Japanese markets is breathtaking but characteristic of what one should come to expect from a country that is on the brink of fiscal and economic disaster. We don't mean to be trite, but from a global perspective, Japan is not Greece: Japan is the third-largest economy in the world. Its biggest banks are on a par with those of the United States. It is a global power in trade and trade finance. Its currency has reserve status. It has 2 of the world's 6 largest corporations and 71 of the largest 500, surpassed only by the United States and comfortably ahead of China, which has 46. Even with the rest of Asia's big companies combined with China's, the total barely surpasses Japan's (CNN). In short, when Japan embarks on a very risky fiscal and monetary strategy, it is guaranteed to have a serious impact on the rest of the world. And doubly so because global growth is now driven by Asia.

Japan has fired the first missile in what future historians will record as the most significant global currency war since the 1930s when the gold standard still reigned, and the first in a world dominated by true fiat money.

We will look at how Japan got to this moment. But before we can put Japan's predicament and its response in perspective and reckon with the events that lie ahead, we must turn to history to understand how currency wars periodically begin, gather momentum, and crash down upon the world like tsunamis, inundating economies.

The 1930s: First Mover Wins

Currency wars are not new. Global monetary confrontations have happened twice before in the last century. The first time was in the 1930s when the major countries abandoned the gold standard in a free-for-all. In that episode, countries were fighting deflation and trying to revive growth during the Great Depression. A currency war was a temporary, necessary measure to fight the deflationary aspects of the gold standard. The second episode happened in the 1970s when President Nixon ended the link between the dollar and the price of gold. During that period, most countries were trying to rid themselves of the constraints of a fixed exchange rate system so governments could spend freely. The result was higher inflation, higher unemployment, and no real benefit to anyone.

We'll look at each episode in turn, but let's start with the 1930s.

The world today has striking parallels with the 1930s. The stock market crashes of 1929 and 2008 happened after years of a rapid buildup in private debt. In the 1920s, as in the 2000s, financial innovation and increasing leverage created an unstable financial system that grew too far, too fast and crashed. In the 1920s, financial innovation allowed consumers to buy radios, washing machines, and refrigerators on installment credit; and they could margin their stock market investments by up to 90 percent. The similarities don't end there. What started as a private debt crisis in both cases transformed into a government bond and currency crisis.

Most people think the Great Depression was caused by a stock market crash. In fact, the Wall Street crash of October 1929 saw stocks fall by just 26 percent—not much worse than the 20 percent crash in the fall of 2008. Believe it or not, the 44 percent fall from September

1929 to March 1931 was *smaller* than the decline after the Lehman bankruptcy, from September 2007 to March 2009.

If the 1929 crash had simply ended in 1931, we might be calling it the Almost Great Depression, but it didn't. The second leg down started with the failure of Credit-Anstalt, Austria's biggest bank, in May 1931. The bankruptcy of Credit-Anstalt started a cascade of bank runs in Hungary, Czechoslovakia, Romania, Poland, and Germany. As in the current crisis, in 1931 a European banking crisis was the catalyst for a sovereign debt crisis and currency war. The banking crisis that began in a peripheral European country in 1931 soon spread to all major global economies. Global trade plunged, international capital movements dried up, industrial production slumped, unemployment surged. The parallels with the European crisis today are eerily familiar.

The international financial system of the 1930s, dominated by the gold standard, could not cope with banking crises. After World War I, many countries had put themselves on the gold standard and had to exchange their currencies for gold at fixed prices. If countries wanted to prevent large outflows of gold and stay on the gold standard, they had to hike interest rates going into a downturn, which was economically suicidal. When the bank runs of 1931 happened, Britain was the first to take itself off the gold standard on September 19 of that year. The pound immediately fell 30 percent against the U.S. dollar. At the time, there were about 25 countries with close economic or imperial links to Britain that had tied their currencies to the sterling, so the shock waves of devaluation extended around the world to Australia, New Zealand, South Africa, and even many countries that hadn't been part of the British Empire.

Britain's move also set off a chain reaction of devaluations in Japan, the United States, France, Germany, Sweden, and Norway, among others. One country after another left the gold standard and competitively devalued. (You can see the dates for leaving the gold standard in Table 2.1.) Almost every country pushed down its exchange rate in a desperate effort to export its way out of depression.

This is a crucial point and parallel with what is happening today. Every country wants to grow its way out of its problems, and for most that means increasing exports. Moreover, they all feel that devaluing their currency is the easiest way to become competitive. Why reduce labor costs directly and so forth when a currency devaluation

Table 2.1 Returning to and Leaving the Gold Standard

Country	Return to Gold	Suspension of Gold Standard	Foreign Exchange Control	Devaluation
Australia	April 1925	December 1929	–	March 1930
Austria	April 1925	April 1933	October 1931	September 1931
Belgium	October 1926	–	–	March 1935
Canada	July 1926	October 1931	–	September 1931
Czechoslovakia	April 1926	–	September 1931	February 1934
Denmark	January 1927	September 1931	November 1931	September 1931
Estonia	January 1928	June 1933	November 1931	June 1933
Finland	January 1926	October 1931	–	October 1931
France	August 1926– June 1928	–	–	October 1936
Germany	September 1924	–	July 1931	–
Greece	May 1928	April 1932	September 1931	April 1932
Hungary	April 1925	–	July 1931	–
Italy	December 1927	–	May 1934	October 1936
Japan	December 1930	December 1931	July 1932	December 1931
Latvia	August 1922	–	October 1931	–
Netherlands	April 1925	–	–	October 1936
Norway	May 1928	September 1931	–	September 1931
New Zealand	April 1925	September 1931	–	April 1930
Poland	October 1927	–	April 1936	October 1936
Rumania	March 1927– February 1929	–	May 1932	–
Sweden	April 1924	September 1931	–	September 1931
Spain	–	–	May 1931	–
United Kingdom	May 1925	September 1931	–	September 1931
United States	June 1919	March 1933	March 1933	April 1933

SOURCE: League of Nations, *Yearbook*, various dates; and miscellaneous supplementary sources.

is so much less painful, especially for politicians? The problem is that, for one country to export, another country must be a buyer! Not everyone can be a net exporter at the same time.

In the 1930s, each country's depreciation only worsened the problems of its trading partners. Eventually, even countries that wanted to keep their currencies tied to gold were forced to devalue and leave the gold standard.

Not only were countries trying to cheapen their currencies, but they put up trade barriers and tariffs to protect their local industries. Such "beggar-thy-neighbor" policies sparked capital controls and high trade barriers that severely harmed global commerce and deepened the Great Depression. Trade barriers seem like a very appealing idea in theory, but if everyone erects them, no one wins, and everyone is worse off. The nasty combination of tariffs and competitive devaluations was disastrous for countries that didn't devalue.

For decades, the prevailing wisdom on the 1930s was that no one won in the global currency war, and everyone was worse off. Lately, heavyweights in the world of economics have forced a rethink of the era. Barry Eichengreen, one of the world's experts on the gold standard, argues that the competitive devaluations were not bad and in fact were critical for economic recovery:

> In fact, this popular account is a misreading of both the 1930s and the current situation. In the 1930s, it is true, with one country after another depreciating its currency, no one ended up gaining competitiveness relative to anyone else. And no country succeeded in exporting its way out of the depression, since there was no one to sell additional exports to. But this was not what mattered. What mattered was that one country after another moved to loosen monetary policy because it no longer had to worry about defending the exchange rate. And this monetary stimulus, felt worldwide, was probably the single most important factor initiating and sustaining economic recovery.

His conclusion that competitive devaluations were good for everyone turned conventional wisdom on its head. If you're very sick and need an operation, morphine is exactly what you need during the recovery. You wouldn't want to be hooked on it for good, but there are times that call for desperate measures.

The sooner countries left the gold standard, the sooner industrial production bounced back. The stark evidence with regard to abandoning the gold standard and returning to growth appears in Figure 2.1. The arrows indicate the dates that countries left the gold standard: in Britain and Japan that was 1931; in the United States, 1934. France didn't leave the gold standard until 1936 and was the last major country to do so. The thick lines show the evolution of industrial output afterwards. You can see that the bottom for industrial production in each country coincided with leaving the gold standard. In the currency war of the 1930s, the moment countries devalued their currencies they started growing again.

To give you a sense of how dramatic the recovery was when countries left the gold standard and reflated, consider economist Christina Romer's description of the U.S. rebound:

> Through a combination of actions, the most important of which were monetary, Franklin Roosevelt managed to turn our ocean liner of an economy on a dime. Industrial production climbed 57% in the first four months of the Roosevelt administration. And real GDP continued to grow at an average rate of nearly 10% per year between 1933 and 1937.

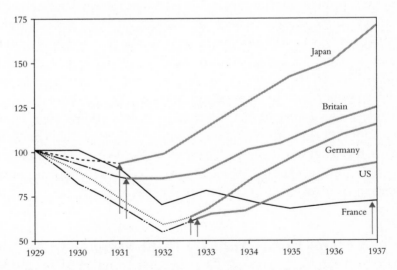

Figure 2.1 Leaving the Gold Standard and Economic Recovery
Source: Barry Eichengreen, "The Origins and Nature of the Great Slump, Revisited" (working paper), 1991.

You will not be surprised to learn that "Colonel" Bernanke, the biggest advocate of Code Red policies, is an expert on the Great Depression and came to the same conclusions as Professor Eichengreen. In a paper titled "The Gold Standard, Deflation, and Financial Crisis in the Great Depression: An International Comparison," Bernanke argued rightly that the length and depth of the deflation during the 1930s related to how long countries stuck to the gold standard. (*Note:* We know we are endangering our gold bug friends by increasing their blood pressure. But stick with us!) Deflation and economic contraction went hand in hand. After looking at economic growth and deflation in many countries, Bernanke wrote:

> In summary, data from our sample of twenty-four countries support the view that there was a strong link between adherence to the gold standard and the severity of both deflation and depression. The data are also consistent with the hypothesis that increased freedom to engage in monetary expansion was a reason for the better performance of countries leaving the gold standard early in the 1930s, although the evidence in this case is a bit less clear-cut.

In other words, the lesson from the Great Depression is that the sooner you loosen monetary policy and devalue, the sooner you recover.

Today, many central bankers are looking at the currency war of the 1930s, and the conclusions they're drawing are clear. In a speech to the Economic Club of New York in early 2013, Chairman Bernanke boasted, "In fact, the simultaneous use by several countries of accommodative policy can be mutually reinforcing to the benefit of all." Bernanke argued that, rather than call unconventional policies and devaluations "beggar-thy-neighbor" policies, they should be called "enrich-thy-neighbor" policies. That's probably taking the lessons from the 1930s a bit too far, but when it comes to unconventional policies, Chairman Bernanke believes the more the merrier.

The Euro: Today's Gold Standard

In the 1930s, the gold standard was an inflexible fixed-exchange-rate system. Today, the role of the gold standard is played by the euro.

During the Great Depression, countries faced the choice of either abandoning gold or causing domestic economic damage through monetary contraction and deflation. Today, many countries face doubts about whether they will remain in the euro and have a choice of either abandoning the European single currency or else inflicting further domestic economic damage in the form of fiscal contraction and deflation.

The introduction of the euro in 2000 was a milestone in a very long political process effecting a deeper integration of the European Union (EU). While there were economic arguments for and against creating the euro, the pure economic costs and benefits were not the main consideration. The main reasons countries joined the euro was to bind the European project further politically and symbolically. It is ironic that a project that was meant to tie European countries closer together may well be what tears Europe apart.

After the introduction of the euro, capital flowed freely; and countries such as Spain, Ireland, Portugal, and Greece imported lots of foreign goods, borrowed heavily, and built up very large unsustainable external debts in a currency they could not print or devalue. The EU periphery countries are now saddled with severe, unsustainable imbalances in real effective exchange rates and external debt levels that surpass those typically seen in the run-up to emerging-market debt and currency crises. The real effective exchange rate is the trade-weighted average of a country's currency relative to an index or basket of other major currencies, adjusted for the effects of inflation. Very simply, it measures the difference between what a Spanish euro can buy versus what a German euro can. Higher inflation would lead to the weakening of a currency, and lower inflation or deflation would lead to a stronger currency. In other words, the peripheral countries' exchange rates—adjusted for inflation—became extremely overvalued.

Previously, such undervaluations or overvaluations in real effective exchange rates would have been solved via devaluations or changes in open market prices for currencies. Now that the drachma, escudo, peseta, and lira don't exist, the possibility of devaluations does not exist either. All the burden of adjustment has to fall on wages and prices via so-called internal devaluation, or deflation. This process is hugely contractionary and poses tremendous problems, as the European periphery is now discovering. However, wages and prices in most of the periphery are not very flexible, due to the strong influence of unions in most industries. This is particularly true in Spain, Portugal, Greece, and Italy, while Ireland has shown greater wage flexibility.

The Eurozone is not an effective currency area: it functions like a modern-day gold standard, such that the burden of adjustment falls on weaker countries. Under a classical gold standard, countries that experience downward pressure on the value of their currencies are forced to contract their economies, which raises unemployment because wages don't fall fast enough to deal with reduced demand. Interestingly, the gold standard didn't work in the other direction: it didn't impose any burden on countries seeing *upward* market pressure on their currencies. This one-way-only adjustment mechanism creates a deflationary bias for countries mired in recession. In contrast to the era when countries abandoned the gold standard to remain competitive, today the euro forces adjustment in real prices and wages instead of exchange rates. But, like the gold standard, the euro has a recessionary bias, where the burden of adjustment is always placed on countries whose real effective exchange rates are weaker.

The solution from European politicians has been to call for austerity, but the public and private sectors can deleverage only by amassing large current account surpluses, which is not feasible given high external debt and low exports in the periphery. The peripheral countries need to export to help themselves; however, exports are only a small portion of their economies. So long as peripheral countries stay in the euro, they will bear the burdens of adjustment and be condemned to contraction or low growth. Just as countries that left the gold standard returned to growth, countries that leave the euro will grow again.

Unfortunately, we will see very little improvement for the European periphery as long as these countries stay in the euro. Almost all European politicians and central bankers believe that the euro is a political project and not an economic one. No matter how dire the economic news, no matter how high the unemployment rate or how painful the human cost, they do not see leaving the euro and devaluing as a solution. The peripheral countries are trapped in almost permanent contraction. As we write this, unemployment in the periphery is absurdly high. Greece and Spain have 27 percent of their people without jobs, while in Portugal the figure is 17.5 percent and in Ireland almost 15 percent. Youth unemployment tops 50 percent in some countries, and young people are leaving for other countries to find work. The most important factor for long-term future growth is a vital, educated force of young workers, and many countries are losing their "seed corn."

Policy makers seem indifferent to such catastrophic numbers. Given their attitude, it is hard to see what further economic data could change their minds. They have clearly not learned the lessons of the 1930s, and they will condemn the European periphery to remain mired in a modern Great Depression.

The 1970s: Weaker Currencies, Higher Inflation

The differences between the two currency wars of the twentieth century—the first in the 1930s and the second in the 1970s—could not be greater. The Great Depression and deflation were the primary reasons to abandon the gold standard in the 1930s. In the 1970s, governments that devalued competitively did so for very different reasons. It is extremely important to understand the differences between the two periods.

Let's look at exactly what happened in the 1970s.

After World War II, 730 delegates from the United States, Great Britain, and most of Europe got together to devise an alternative to the gold standard. They created a system called Bretton Woods (because that is the name of the resort in New Hampshire that was the place for the conference) that they hoped would provide the right measure of flexibility but also prevent competitive devaluations like those in the 1930s. In theory, under the new system the dollar was convertible into gold at $35 per ounce, and all other currencies were convertible into the dollar—though only for central banks. (To give you an idea of how inflation has eroded the value of the dollar, gold is now trading at roughly $1,300 an ounce.) The dollar effectively served as the anchor of the global financial system. At first, the system made sense, as the United States was the strongest country in the world, was the biggest creditor, and had most of the world's gold reserves. Because almost no country asked for gold in exchange for its dollar holdings, the system gave the U.S. unparalleled economic power through currency control, power that even Britain at the peak of the British Empire never had.

The United States enjoyed what economists call *seigniorage*. Counterfeiters benefit when they print money because they can exchange paper money that is worthless for real goods and services. Governments have the legal right to print money, but they enjoy the same benefit as a counterfeiter does: governments can get something for nothing. Money is backed by the full faith and credit of a country and by foreign exchange reserves, but governments have often succumbed to the temptation to issue too much money. Seigniorage allowed the United States to abuse its position at the center of the Bretton Woods system to create more dollars than it should have.

Seigniorage is the amount of real purchasing power that a government can realize by printing money. When a government prints money, it effectively borrows interest free since it receives goods in exchange for the money, even though it has to accept the money in return at some future date. If inflation has eroded the value of the money that comes back to the government, it benefits even more from seigniorage. Bretton Woods was in essence an international currency system that allowed the United States to receive seigniorage in exchange for creating more dollars for global trade.

Conventional wisdom maintains that Bretton Woods broke down because the United States tried to spend too much money on "guns and butter." According to this explanation, President Johnson overspent on social programs and on the Vietnam War. It is true that almost every year through the 1960s the U.S. government spent more than it took in through taxes. However, that alone wouldn't have caused the breakdown. The real problem was that the Federal Reserve helped the government out with a very loose monetary policy. From the creation of the Federal Reserve until 1960, the Fed had bought just $27 billion in Treasury securities, paying for them by creating bank reserves—money—out of thin air. In less than a decade afterwards, the Fed bought over $62 billion in Treasury securities—more than twice the total they had bought before. (How quaintly small that number seems now, as the Fed is doing that much in just one month!)

Inflation might have remained moderate in most countries if central banks had acted responsibly, but there was another factor at work.

Very high oil prices and high prices for food led to a vicious circle. Workers demanded higher wages to deal with higher prices because they expected lots of inflation, and firms increased prices because of rising costs. The wage-price spiral was a case of self-fulfilling expectations. All along, the Fed kept accommodating both workers and management by providing more and more money.

In the 1960s the Fed became less independent and more willing to accept higher inflation in order to get lower unemployment. Also, various Fed chairmen and governors saw their role as helping the U.S. government finance its spending. Central banks around the world were happy to create too much money, because they genuinely thought that higher inflation would mean lower unemployment rates. It may sound stupid, even insane now, but many economists in the postwar period believed in something called the *Phillips curve*. Amazingly, some recidivist economists still do. The Phillips curve posited a long-run inverse relationship between inflation and unemployment. Economists thought that lower inflation came about through a tighter money supply, and a tighter money supply meant less growth and fewer jobs. So central banks erred on the side of looser money and higher inflation. In time, everyone figured out what the game was, and simply expected higher inflation. But in the end, central banks ended up with both higher inflation *and* higher unemployment.

As the U.S. government ran budget deficits and trade deficits through the 1960s, foreign central banks began to demand more and more gold in exchange for the dollars they held. U.S. gold reserves kept falling. Eventually, the United States decided to pull the plug on Bretton Woods.

The second currency war started memorably in 1971. President Nixon interrupted the regularly scheduled broadcast of *Bonanza* on a Sunday evening to tell Americans he was devaluing the dollar. The announcement completely unlinked the dollar from gold and set off a race among other currencies to catch up. A month later, Japan floated its currency, and many other countries followed. Currency wars are usually accompanied by tariffs and protectionist measures. Just as in the 1930s, currency devaluations in the 1970s also came with trade barriers. Nixon introduced a 10 percent surcharge on imports when he made his initial announcement. Other countries followed suit.

Immediately after Nixon's announcement, every country started looking after itself. When Japan, too, floated its currency, other countries did
not want to see their currencies appreciate suddenly against the dollar or
yen. Switzerland charged a fee on deposits to discourage capital inflows.
Germany imposed capital controls to prevent the buying of marks. After
the United States, Japan, and the United Kingdom had devalued their currencies, Italy devalued the lira. Foreign leaders began to complain loudly
about the devaluation of the dollar. But the Americans didn't care. As
President Nixon famously said when the Italians complained, "I don't give
a s★★t about the lira." Not much has changed since then.

Even though Nixon ended gold convertibility of the dollar in
1971, Bretton Woods didn't really die until 1973. Many currencies still
foolishly tried to stay pegged to the dollar. It was only in 1973 that the
International Monetary Fund declared Bretton Woods dead.

What was the end result of 1970s currency devaluations? Before the
demise of Bretton Woods, the United States was the only country that
enjoyed seigniorage. After Bretton Woods, all countries enjoyed the right
of seigniorage. Most countries rapidly increased the amount of money
in circulation and used monetary policy to stimulate domestic demand
and finance government spending. As you can see from Figure 2.2,
countries like Germany that had sound money policies saw their currencies strengthen against all other currencies.

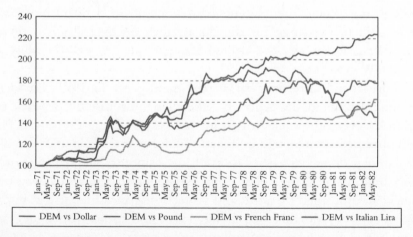

Figure 2.2   G7 Currencies vs. Deutschmark in the 1970s
SOURCE: *Variant Perception*, Bloomberg.

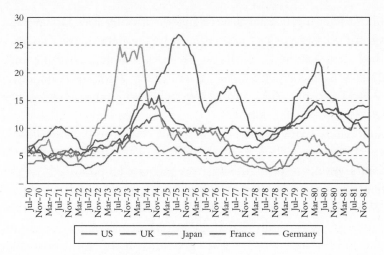

Figure 2.3 G7 Inflation Rates in the 1970s
Source: *Variant Perception*, Bloomberg.

Depreciating currencies almost always generates higher inflation down the line. In the 1970s, countries were not devaluing their currencies to escape economic contraction and deflation as they were in the 1930s. The fight between inflation and deflation is a tug of war. At first in the 1930s, deflation was winning the tug of war, but devaluations and money printing stopped deflation in its tracks. In the 1970s, there was no need for devaluations and loose money. There was no tug of war. You can see that from Figure 2.3. In the 1970s, however, countries were devaluing competitively in order not to be left behind. Inflation was very subdued in the 1960s before Nixon ended the link between the dollar and gold, but over the next decade it climbed steadily. In the 1970s, cumulative inflation was over 50 percent, and the value of the dollar was cut in half. In fact, in just a decade, inflation increased by a factor of 10, from 1.6 percent in the late 1960s to 16 percent 10 years later.

The lack of response by the Federal Reserve to rising inflation gave lie to the fiction that the central bank was independent of the government. Arthur Burns, the chairman of the Federal Reserve from 1970 through 1978, succumbed to political pressure to hold interest rates down. He openly acknowledged the fact that he would have liked to raise rates to respond to inflation but wanted to cooperate with the civil authorities. And what the government and business wanted was low rates.

Like today, interest rates were held artificially low. Given the pressures from oil, food prices, and rising wages, inflation rose rapidly. If the Fed had demonstrated a little bit of independence, crushing inflation would not have happened, and it would not have been necessary for Paul Volcker to put the country through two back-to-back recessions to break the back of inflation.

And here a word that is positive about central bankers must be made. When Paul Volcker took over the Fed in 1979 he began to seriously restrict the money supply. Interest rates rose rapidly, peaking at 21 percent. As John can personally attest, it was a difficult time to be an entrepreneur.

While Volcker is considered a hero today, an example held up to all central bankers as the paradigm of what independence should be, we should remember that it was very difficult for him personally take the path he did. He was roundly criticized from all corners and burned in effigy on the steps of the Federal Reserve. To say he was not popular was an understatement. Even though Ronald Reagan benefited from his policies, he did not reappoint him in 1987, instead choosing a bright, young free-market economist named Alan Greenspan.

If things progress along the lines of current policies of the major central banks today, we are going to need several Paul Volckers in our future. We sincerely hope that a man or woman with his independence will show up sooner rather than later.

Today versus the 1930s and 1970s

On September 27, 2010, the Brazilian finance minister, Guido Mantega, accused the United States of fomenting a "currency war." Mantega argued that emerging markets were being hurt by a rapidly weakening dollar. The phrase stuck, and the sentiment that we may be slipping into another currency war has only grown since.

Today's currency war is different from those of yesteryear. In the old days, the need to devalue currencies was related to trade imbalances and balance-of-payments crises. Today, the main driver is the Code Red policies of places like the United States, United Kingdom, Europe, and Japan. Each one is competing with the others to see who can loosen monetary policy the most via QE, ZIRP, and a weakened currency.

Mantega was right to complain. The flip side to a weakening dollar is that other currencies appreciate and become uncompetitive. In two years, between 2009 and 2011, the Brazilian real appreciated by 40 percent against the dollar, and inflation surged in Brazil. When the central bank hiked interest rates to fight inflation, foreign investors poured money into the country. Who wants zero interest rates in the United States, United Kingdom, or Europe when you can get 6 percent in Brazil? Fighting the hot-money flows pouring into the country was difficult and frustrating for Brazil.

Brazil is not the only country that has scrambled to blunt the effects of a developing currency war. To prevent a sudden decline in the competitiveness of their exports, central banks in Korea, Thailand, Brazil, Malaysia, and other emerging markets have intervened to slow the appreciation of their currencies by buying dollars. To make these interventions effective and reduce further inflows of hot money, most have allowed their money supplies to rise quickly and have reduced interest rates sharply. They could take steps to limit domestic money growth, but those are costly and do not always work. More important, they would not even need to take these steps if the United States, United Kingdom, Europe, and Japan weren't busy devaluing their currencies. Duvvuri Subbarao, governor of the Reserve Bank of India, put it best: "Every time there is quantitative easing by the Fed, that gets discussed. We all have to reckon with the spillover impact of our policies on other countries."

Emerging-market countries have to fend for themselves. Bernanke, Kuroda, and other developed-country central bankers accept no responsibility. If other countries don't like a weaker dollar or yen, too bad. Bernanke places the blame not on the United States for weakening the dollar, but on emerging countries for not revaluing their currencies or imposing capital controls. As U.S. Treasury Secretary John Connally said to foreign finance ministers in 1971, "The dollar is our currency, but it's your problem." Indeed.

Currency Wars and Japan

Will the extraordinary and desperate Code Red policies of the Bank of Japan work? In our humble view, printing money may do many things, but it won't increase Japan's long-term growth rate. Money printing will succeed at massively weakening the yen. It will ultimately raise inflation and eat away at the real value of all the Japanese government debt. Some foreign investors believe that money printing will drive up the cost of the Japanese government to fund itself. But more on Japan's specific problems in a little bit.

First, it is useful to look at what happened to Japan in the two currency wars we just reviewed. Let's look at the 1930s and then the 1970s from the Japanese perspective.

Japan's current policies under Prime Minister Shinzo Abe involve increased government spending and money printing to finance the spending. These measures bear a striking resemblance to policies that Japan tried during the Great Depression under Finance Minister Korekiyo Takahashi. Takahashi was a groundbreaking finance minister. (Recently, a book appeared that extolled his virtues: *From Foot Soldier to Finance Minister: Takahashi Korekiyo, Japan's Keynes.* Unsurprisingly, it was an immediate hit with Japanese academics.)

Takahashi took Japan off the gold standard in December 1931. He devalued the yen by 60 percent against the dollar and 40 percent on a broad, trade-weighted basis. The Japanese government ran large budget deficits on purpose in order to increase economic growth. In order to finance the spending, Takahashi made the BoJ monetize debt. In other words, the central bank printed money to pay for goods and services.

The results of the Japanese experiment in the 1930s were very positive at first. Growth returned and inflation was low. Growth of real gross domestic product (GDP) was 6.1% from 1931 to 1936, while inflation was very subdued at only 1.5 percent. The success of the Takahashi experiment led Ben Bernanke to describe him as the man who "brilliantly rescued" his country from the Great Depression. The initial dose of inflation counteracted the deflation and downturn that haunted Japan. When the economy started to grow, the BoJ reduced the money supply by selling back many of the bonds it had monetized. The BoJ managed the tug of war between deflation and inflation with great skill.

As time passed, the danger of deflation and depression receded; unfortunately, however, the Japanese government had become addicted to money printing to finance spending. You can see this in Figure 2.4.

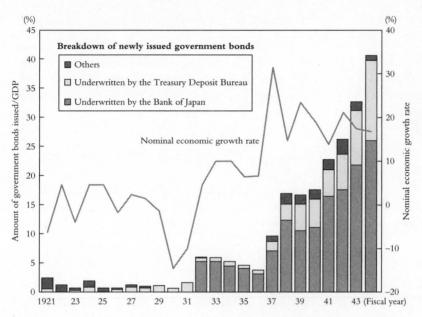

Figure 2.4   Percentage of Japanese Debt Monetized by the Bank of Japan in the 1930s

SOURCES: *Showa zaisei shi* (Financial History of Showa), edited by the Office of Financial History of Showa of the Ministry of Finance, Volume 6, Toyo Keizai, 1954; Kazushi Okawa, Nobukiyo Takamatsu, Yuzo Yamamoto, *Choki keizai tokei 1, kokumin shotoku* (Long-Term Economic Statistics 1: National Income), Toyo Keizai, 1974; *Meiji iko honpo shuyo keizai tokei* (The Key Economic Statistics of Japan in and after Meiji), the Statistics Bureau, the Bank of Japan, 1966.

(The military in particular needed it to bankroll their imperialist ambitions, and a faction of the army assassinated Takahashi, among others, in 1936.) From 1937 to 1940, growth was 5 percent, but inflation jumped to 12 percent. And once World War II started, Japanese inflation was about 50 percent a year for several years. Finally, right after the war, Japan experienced hyperinflation of over 350 percent.

If you look at Figure 2.5, you can see clearly how a little bit of money printing can lead from low inflation to a few hundred percent inflation in just a few years.

Inflation did a wonderful job of getting rid of the debt that Japan had built up during World War II. The Japanese had run up their debt to finance the war, such that debt-to-GDP was 204 percent in 1944. The extremely high levels of inflation slashed the real value of Japanese government bonds. Within two years after the end of World War II, the

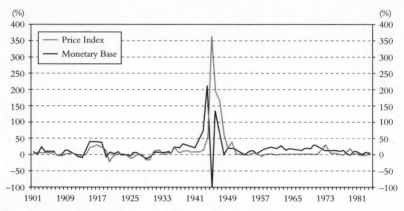

Figure 2.5   Japanese Inflation in the 1930s and 1940s
Source: Historical Statistics of Japan (1868–1985) on CD-ROM, JapanReviewNet.

debt was only 56 percent of GDP. Since the borrowing for the war was almost exclusively domestic, Japan was effectively able to inflate its way out of its debt burden.

Japan's experience in the 1970s currency war was radically different than during the 1930s. During the Great Depression almost every country in the world was experiencing deflation and depression. In the 1970s, however, many countries overheated with strong growth and rising inflation. Throw in currency devaluations and a hyperactive Federal Reserve, and you had a recipe for rising inflation. The United States and almost all western European countries had inflation rates in the high teens for much of the late 1970s. The Great Inflation ended only after severe recessions in the early 1980s and very aggressive monetary tightening.

Unlike countries that experienced high inflation in the 1970s, Japan was remarkable for how *low* its inflation was by comparison. If you look at Figures 2.6 and 2.7, you can see how Japan avoided the problems of high inflation in the 1970s. Japan's inflation peak occurred right after the end of Bretton Woods and was really a one-off event. Afterwards, inflation went straight back down toward the levels of the 1960s.

During this period, Japan was a model of restraint in its money growth and the management of its currency. Milton Friedman, one of the greatest monetary economists in the world, said the BoJ was one of his favorite examples of a successful central bank. Friedman liked Japan

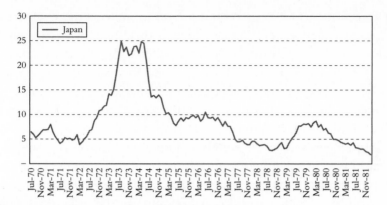

Figure 2.6   Japanese Inflation Spike in the 1970s
SOURCE: *Variant Perception*, Bloomberg.

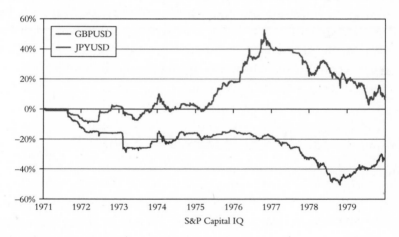

Figure 2.7   Exchange Rates against the Japanese Yen
SOURCE: Mauldin Economics, S&P Capital IQ.

because, in his view, Japan accepted that "substantial inflation is a monetary phenomenon." Another reason was that Japan didn't devalue the yen competitively, as most countries did. The yen was devalued once when Bretton Woods fell apart and then appreciated as other currencies devalued during the rest of the decade. As we talk about the coming currency wars, it is useful to remember that at one time the yen was $357 to the dollar. It rose over 40 years where one dollar would buy only 78 yen. That is an appreciation of 400 percent. It is hard to imagine the United States, the United Kingdom, or Europe allowing their currencies to appreciate by more than 400 percent in the context of today's global market. But that is exactly what happened. As we will discuss in the next chapter, Japan wants a little of that appreciation back, thank you very much.

One of the key takeaways from this overview of currency wars is that central banks have the power to stop deflation as well as to create inflation if they want to do so. They simply need to be very aggressive, devalue their currency, and monetize government spending. In almost all countries that chose to abandon the link to gold, leaving the gold standard in the 1930s arrested deflation and created inflation. Likewise, we saw that in the 1970s, competitively devaluing in a currency war could create persistently higher inflation but could offer little in the way of higher growth.

With those lessons in mind, let's fast-forward to today. Do we think we'll get inflation if we're seeing competitive devaluations and large increases in the global money supply? You bet. We've seen it before. Let's hope central banks know exactly when and how quickly to take their foot off the Code Red accelerator.

Key Lessons from the Chapter

In this chapter we learned:

- The world is in the early stages of a currency war. Other countries will follow Japan and try to weaken their currencies. No country wants to be the last one to the party and miss out on the Code Red punch.
- Political leaders deny that there is a currency war, but every country will look after its own interests. We will likely see protectionism and tariffs that will harm trade.
- There were two twentieth-century currency wars:
  - The first happened in the 1930s when countries devalued competitively after leaving the gold standard. The countries that left first grew fastest and were able to generate inflation.

- The second was in the 1970s when Bretton Woods broke down and currencies were allowed to float freely. Almost all countries tried to devalue their own currencies against others, which led to very high inflation worldwide. In the end, all major currencies were devalued against commodities, gold, and real goods and services.
- Banking crises usually lead to sovereign debt crises. Sovereign debt crises usually lead to currency crises.
- Using currency devaluations as a one-off against a big deflationary crisis like the Great Depression can help restore growth by reducing the real value of debt. Using currency devaluations when inflation is already moderate will only create more inflation and serial, beggar-thy-neighbor devaluations.

Chapter Three

The Japanese Tsunami

Starting a Currency War

I shot an Arrow into the air

It fell to earth I know not where

—Henry Wadsworth Longfellow

Alice laughed: "There's no use trying," she said; "one can't believe impossible things."

"I daresay you haven't had much practice," said the Queen. "When I was younger, I always did it for half an hour a day. Why, sometimes I've believed as many as six impossible things before breakfast."

—Alice in Wonderland, Lewis Carroll

Japanese economic circumstances were unstable when we wrote *Endgame*, much like a too-tall sandpile. A single grain of sand could cause an avalanche, but we simply did not know which grain it would be. Everyone has memories of building sandpiles at the beach. We were creators then, pitting our skills against the laws of physics, piling the sand higher and higher until gravity foiled us in a moment and sent it sliding down again. Imagine dropping one grain of sand after another onto a table. A pile soon develops. Eventually, just one more grain triggers an avalanche. Most of the time the avalanche is a small one, but sometimes it builds on itself, and one whole side of our pile slides down.

In 1987 three physicists, named Per Bak, Chao Tang, and Kurt Weisenfeld, began to play the sandpile game in their lab at Brookhaven National Laboratory in New York. Piling up one grain of sand at a time is a slow process, so they wrote a computer program to do it electronically. Not as much fun, but a whole lot faster. Not that they really cared about sandpiles the way we did as children. They were more interested in complex nonequilibrium systems.

They learned some interesting things. What is the typical size of an avalanche? After a huge number of tests involving zillions of grains of sand, they found that there is no typical number. "Some involved a single grain; others, ten, a hundred or a thousand. Still others were pile-wide cataclysms involving millions that brought nearly the whole mountain down. At any time, literally anything it seemed, might be just about to occur."

The Quake and the Sandpile

In the case of Japan, the grain of sand that finally caused an avalanche was, fittingly enough, a major earthquake. Normally, natural disasters have only a brief impact on a country's economy. Even major disasters like Hurricane Katrina rarely have a lasting effect. True, Katrina was a terrible blow for New Orleans, and it damaged many refineries and oil rigs along the Gulf Coast, but its impact on U.S. economic growth was minor and lasted only a quarter. You can't say the same thing about the earthquake that struck off the Japanese coast in 2011.

The earthquake off the Pacific coast of Tohoku was one for the record books. It was the most powerful earthquake ever known to have hit Japan. It was the fifth most powerful earthquake in the world since scientists started measuring earthquakes. It registered a whopping 9.03 on the Richter scale. The tsunami that followed the earthquake killed more than 15,000 people. By comparison, the 1994 Northridge earthquake in Los Angeles was one of the strongest ever recorded in an American urban area, and it killed only 57 people.

But the reason the Tohoku earthquake will have such a major, lasting impact on Japan's economy is that the earthquake may have ended Japan's reliance on nuclear energy. The Fukushima Dai-ichi Nuclear Power Plant, 150 miles northeast of Tokyo, was severely damaged by the earthquake and tsunami, causing one of the world's worst-ever nuclear accidents. Before the Fukushima disaster, the Japanese relied very heavily on nuclear energy, but overnight they were forced to start importing a lot more very expensive gas, coal, and oil.

Importing expensive natural gas in turn caused a deterioration of Japan's current account surplus, a broad measure of trade and investment flows. A strong yen made it impossible to offset the increased energy purchases with export sales. In 2012, the current account balance experienced the biggest fall on record and shrank to its lowest level in 15 years. The trade account showed its first deficit since 1980. For an aging country that has long relied on exports and running a large surplus, the numbers were disastrous.

Japan could not afford to see its current account balance fall. Japan has been both one of the world's largest external creditors and the world's largest domestic borrower. For decades it ran trade surpluses, selling more goods to the rest of the world than it imported. After decades of exporting, it has accumulated an enormous pile of dollars, euros, and other foreign currency reserves. At the same time, Japan is the world's largest debtor to its own citizens. The country has an insanely high government debt–to–gross domestic product (GDP) ratio, and almost all that debt is held by Japanese institutions and individuals.

The rest of this chapter will delve into the situation the Japanese face and explain why they must act in the way they have chosen (the path of "Abenomics"). If you do not understand this, you will not have the confidence to act appropriately with respect to your investments, because all along the way the mainstream media and economic cognoscenti are going to tell you that things will be fine. But things will not be fine even though there will be moments when the markets will be screaming that the mainstream is right and we are wrong. Every 5 to 10 percent move back up in the yen will be seen as "the end" of the trade and a confirmation that Japanese Code Red policies have worked. We will get calls from the press asking us if things are now different. But no, they will not be, not for a very long time.

Can the picture change? Of course. And from time to time we will post updates with our latest thinking at www.thecoderedbook.com. But for now, let's survey the challenges that Japan confronts.

The problems in Japan began a long time ago. In the late 1980s, Japan experienced the popping of one of the biggest bubbles the world had ever seen. During the ensuing 24 years of low growth and very high government spending, Japan's federal government debt has skyrocketed. Japan's public debt rose from 67 percent of GDP in 1990 to over 240 percent today, and is estimated to reach 245 percent in 2014. That is considerably more than twice the level of debt the United States or most European countries have. The news is bad. The *Financial Times* reported in March 2013: "Japan's central bank governor has told parliament that the government's vast and growing debt is 'not sustainable,' and that a loss of confidence in state finances could 'have a very negative impact' on the entire economy."

Complicating matters, Japan has been in a deflationary slump for over two decades. As you can see from Figure 3.1, while nominal

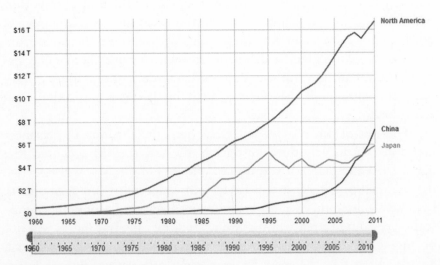

Figure 3.1   GDP: Japan Stuck in a Rut
SOURCE: Google Finance.

GDP for the US and China has continued to grow, Japan's nominal GDP has barely increased. As prices have kept falling over the years, deflation has caused the real burden of debt to grow heavier and heavier. Deflation discouraged spending—people held onto their cash, expecting even lower prices down the road. Interest rates, meanwhile, have been stuck at the zero bound, and nominal GDP has not grown. Instead, it has only bobbed up a little and then down a little, on and on, since 1995.

Banzai! Banzai!

After the earthquake, the tsunami, and the Fukushima nuclear accident, the outlook for the Japanese economy was absolutely dire. With the weighty stones of disparate problems tied around the ankles of Japan's prostrate economy, the Japanese were ready for radical new measures. Shinzo Abe, the new prime minister, campaigned and won the election in late 2012 on the promise of massive money printing and government spending. By these means the Abe administration resolutely purposed to haul the country out of deflation back to its feet again.

Among other things, Abe called for enormous quantitative easing to weaken the currency, create inflation, and finance large-scale government spending. Coupled with promised market reforms, this very Code Red strategy has been labeled *Abenomics*.

Abe's moves were revolutionary. Even though central banks should be independent from governments, Prime Minister Abe threatened to strip the Bank of Japan (BoJ) of its independence if it refused to set a 2 percent inflation target. Unsurprisingly, the BoJ put its tail between it legs and obeyed. When the conservative governor of the BoJ resigned, Abe appointed Haruhiko Kuroda. Governor Kuroda is a man so radical he makes Ben Bernanke look cautious.

During World War II, the Japanese charged into battle shouting the war cry *"Banzai!"* The Japanese equivalent of "Long live the king!" the expression literally means "Ten thousand years!" (though to soldiers on the other side it came to mean a suicidal, hell-for-leather attack). If the central bankers of the world now think they're hearing a battle cry of *"Banzai!"* from the lips of their Japanese brethren, they may not be far from wrong because the Japanese are indeed undertaking a mad charge to fight deflation and rescue their economy at all costs. As with all good suicidal charges, once the cry has gone up and the thundering charge has begun, there can be no turning back.

As we will see, the Japanese have no good choices left, but only disastrous ones. It was our contention in *Endgame* (and it is far more evident today) that the Japanese intend to monetize their monstrous debt as the only viable solution to stave off utter economic collapse. The fact that this policy will eviscerate the yen is of secondary importance to them. In fact, a weak yen will help to ameliorate, at least internally, the devastating consequences of the actions they are taking.

Three Arrows

Prime Minister Abe has committed to a "three-arrow" approach to solve Japan's problems. The three arrows in his quiver are aggressive monetary easing, more credible fiscal plans, and a growth strategy based on structural reform.

The monetary easing will be the easy part. Essentially, the BoJ is engaging in almost as much quantitative easing as the U.S. Federal Reserve has undertaken, but in a country one third the size of the United States. In short, the BoJ is embarking on one of the most aggressive injections of cash into the economy that any major developed country central bank has ever tried. Even financial analysts and economists may not have fully grasped the mind-boggling scale of what is being done. The BoJ will nearly double the size of its bond purchases, will double its money supply over the next two years, and will vastly extend the range of assets it buys to include private-sector debt. The bank said it would increase its purchases of government bonds by ¥50 trillion (about $520 billion) per year. That is equal to about 10 percent of Japan's GDP. That is a staggering amount of money printing. And that is just the opening salvo in what will surely be seen by historians as the first major offensive in the Currency Wars of the Late Teens.

Let's quickly review a few charts on the history of the yen. The first is the yen against the U.S. dollar since 1990. Yes, the yen has fallen 35 percent or so against the dollar in its recent move, but it must fall

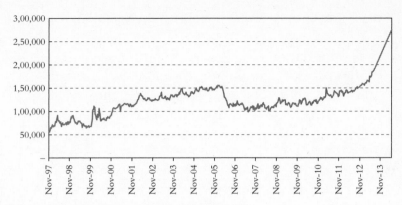

Figure 3.2 Projected Size of Japan's Balance Sheet
SOURCE: *Variant Perception,* Bloomberg.

another 20 yen to get back to where it was just six years ago. It traded at over 350 yen to the dollar when John was in school, back in the Dark Ages. The yen's four-decade appreciation of some 470 percent against the dollar puts the recent move of less than 25 yen into historical perspective.

Let's put the recent drop in the yen in context, to see what its implications are. The *Nihon Keizai Shimbun,* the main Japanese business newspaper, has reported that every one-yen fall in the yen/dollar rate will translate into a $2.7 *billion* increase in profits for the 30 largest Japanese exporters.

For every one yen the currency drops in value against the dollar, Toyota estimates that its profits will increase by $340 million. Per one-yen drop! Toyota reported $3.33 billion in profits last quarter, so that additional $340 million of profit per one-yen fall could send its profits in the second half of 2013—and its stock—to the moon.

But those profits don't just magically appear; they come from sales, which are due in large part to better terms of trade and lower costs. More to the point, those profits come from sales that might otherwise have gone to other companies based in other countries and that might have been valued instead in euros, dollars, yuan, or won. And that is why businesses and finance ministers all over the world are not happy with Japan.

Japan ran a massive trade surplus for years. More recently, it has run a large trade deficit. If you have both a trade deficit and a fiscal deficit,

Figure 3.3 The Yen vs. the Dollar since 1990
Source: Mauldin Economics, S&P Capital IQ.

either private savings has to make up the difference, or the central bank has to print massive amounts of money. That is an accounting identity; there are no other choices. Absent massive monetization, you suck all the available investment capital from your private economy. But Japan needs growth to get out of its fiscal and economic morass. That means it desperately needs more exports, since its aging population has a limited capacity to generate significant increases in consumer spending. The trend is ugly.

A rather useful analysis of the competitive relationships between Japan and its Asian neighbors was recently published by Charlie Lay at Commerzbank. In it he provides a chart generated from International Monetary Fund (IMF) data that examines export similarity with Japan. Germany is the country whose exports are most similar to Japan's, followed by Korea and Taiwan, then the United States, the United Kingdom, and France.

Charlie also asks who will buy the products Japan longs to export thanks to a weaker yen? China is becoming an ever larger part of global trade as the country continues to develop. Who exports the most to them? Japan, of course, and Japan competes directly with Korea, Hong Kong, and Taiwan for that business.

Figure 3.4 Japan's Balance of Trade Turns Negative
Source: www.tradingeconomics.com; Ministry of Finance, Japan.

As you might expect, profits in companies in Korea, Hong Kong, and Taiwan are getting hammered, as those companies have to lower prices in order to compete with resurgent Japanese firms. While the government of Japan will never publicly admit it, it will not be long until the yen reaches 120 and even higher against the dollar, although the road will get bumpier as the yen falls in value, on and on, and other countries respond. Japanese monetary policy is almost irrevocably committed to continuing to devalue the yen for a very long time at what will be an ever-increasing rate. If the yen moves back to where it was just six years ago, Germany et al. are in deep schnitzel as far as their export trade is concerned.

All central banks are increasing their balance sheets. Figure 3.7 from Capital Economics, which compares monetary bases, will help you understand the muted response of the United States and the United Kingdom to Japan's moves. How can the other central banks truly criticize Japan when they pursued the same policy, and Japan, at least in the chart, merely seems to be responding?

Meanwhile, European Union (EU) ministers, notably in Germany, have been very vocal in complaining about Japan. The European Central Bank (ECB) has an inflation mandate that theoretically limits

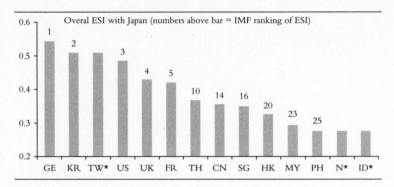

Figure 3.5 Export Overlap between Japan and Its Neighbors
SOURCES: UN Comtrade, IMF; *Commerzbank Estimates.

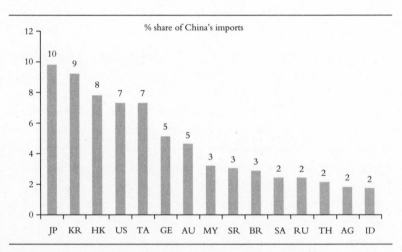

Figure 3.6 Japan and Korea Compete for the Chinese Market
SOURCE: Commerzbank Corporates & Markets.

them from undertaking quantitative easing (QE) on the scale that the United States, United Kingdom, or Japan has done. We say theoretically because when Germany joins France in a serious recession due in part to "currency tensions," we fully expect those very creative people at the ECB to come up with a "legal" way to join the QE party. And

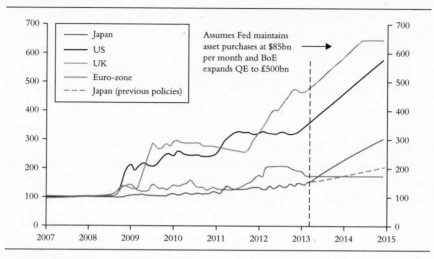

Figure 3.7 Monetary Bases
SOURCE: Thomson Datastream, Capital Economics.

everyone knows that when Draghi decides to stir things up, he does so with style and a full orchestra in accompaniment. And the Bundesbank will be playing the bass drum.

Let's Export Our Deflation

The number one export that Japan is offering is its deflation, the one Japanese product that no one wants. It is trying to push deflation on every country that competes with it for trade. It is just as if the leaders of Japan had got together and said, "We can't seem to get rid of our deflation. Let's see if we can export it."

The Abe government and the BoJ under Kuroda-san have targeted 2 percent inflation. Even with nominal GDP growth Q1 2013 of 3.6 percent (annualized), the country was in deflation. They have been trying to generate inflation for 24 years. How will they now get 2 percent inflation? One way might be to increase the cost of their imports. The problem is that Japan imports only about 16 percent of its GDP, according to recent World Bank data. And inflation created in that way would have particularly harsh effects on retirees. Energy and food (which are largely imported) and any other item that needs resources not found in

Japan will rise in cost as the value of the yen falls. Those living on fixed incomes will be hurt the most, and that is a very large and growing part of the population of modern Japan.

Bottom line: To turn the Bad Ship Deflation around, rechristen it the Good Ship Inflation, and then speed up to 2 percent inflation, the Japanese will need their currency to fall in value by about 15 to 20 percent a year. Easy enough, you might think: the yen fell that much just in the first six months of 2013.

Well, not so fast. The problem is that the Japanese have to effect that 15 to 20 percent devaluation *every* year, on a trade-weighted basis, with all their trading partners. Japan trades with the world, and what matters is the trade-weighted yen (just as the trade-weighted dollar is what makes the difference in the trade balance of the United States).

While the trade-weighted yen is down over 20 percent against the average of the currencies of Japan's key trading partners, that is not as much as it is down against the dollar. Australia and other Asian countries are just beginning to respond to Japan by lowering exchange rates and by other means, so the "easy" devaluation of the yen has already happened. The hard work is just starting, as other countries will increasingly feel forced to respond. No major country can export its deflation to the rest of the world without the rest of the world seeking to redress the balance.

For Japan to get that 15 to 20 percent-a-year currency depreciation for the next five years would be such a tectonic-plate shift for the world that it is difficult to express the magnitude of the task. That would put the yen at 200 to the dollar by 2018 or sooner. If you are Germany, can you deal with that? If you are Korea? China?

This is a nightmare scenario for central bankers worldwide. If there is a mandate, a central theme in the Handbook for Central Bankers, it is that deflation must always and everywhere be fought tooth and nail. Deflation must be given no quarter. Who wants to become the next Japan?

If deflation shows up on your watch, you have to fight it. And if your interest rates are already low, then the only tool you have in your deflation-fighting toolbox is QE.

Let us be very clear. Japan is about to unleash the most significant currency war the world has ever seen. The problem today is that politicians, labor unions, and businesses everywhere want to use exchange rates as the tool to manage their balance of trade, rather than focusing on improving their own competitiveness and manufacturing skills, not to mention controlling their own spending and fiscal budgets. The problem, as they see it, is the competition from abroad, and that competition is always judged to be unfair. Thus, the pressure on central banks to respond to Japanese QE is going to be immense.

We believe that we may be entering a most dangerous period where politicians and central bankers feel the need to "do something"; and that something will include QE, exchange-rate interventions, and protectionist policies. Think in terms of "Central Bankers Gone Wild," armed with electronic printing presses and dreaming of new, ever more creative ways to prop up the markets.

It was less than 30 years ago that the U.S. central bank willingly took direction from the government and business even though they knew better. And now, the economic theory that dominates central bank thinking supports an easy-money policy. Haven't we seen the end of this movie before?

Reform and the Demographics of Doom

The second arrow in Abe's quiver is fiscal reform. Japan's yawning fiscal deficit, if it were closed too quickly, would plunge the country into immediate and deep recession. The yen would strengthen against the dollar and other currencies, and Japan's exports would once again be damaged. Such is the paradoxical outcome if you suddenly decide to live within your means when you have been on a spending binge. For our U.S. readers, think about what would happen next year if the government were to cut $1.6 trillion (or about 10 percent) from our national budget.

Japan has a GDP that is now close to 500 trillion yen (give or take a few tens of trillions). Their most recent budget calls for ¥92.6 trillion in spending, almost evenly divided between ¥43.1 trillion financed from tax revenues and ¥42.9 trillion from the issuance of new bonds, adding to Japan's massive public-sector debt that already totals nearly ¥1 quadrillion. Say that with a straight face: 1 quadrillion. This massive debt is not a recent phenomenon—it has been accumulating for many years.

All the while, tax revenues have been going down for decades, as the country has been mired in no-growth deflation for 24 years. Revenues are now down to where they were in 1985. To put that dismal showing in context, let's look at U.S. tax revenues by way of comparison. Back in 1985, they totaled $734 billion (or $1,174 billion in constant 2005 dollars). Last year, however, U.S. tax revenues amounted to $2,450 billion in constant 2005 dollars—that is, more than double the 1985 total.

As you can see from Figure 3.8, courtesy of our friend and Japan expert Kyle Bass at Hayman Capital Management, reveals the yawning gap between revenues and expenditures. (If Japan were a stock, would you be a buyer?)

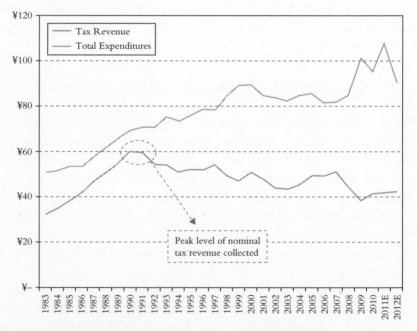

Figure 3.8 Japanese Tax Revenue and Expenditures (¥ in trillions)
Latest estimates available as of October 2011: Japan Ministry of Finance, BoJ.
SOURCE: Courtesy of Hayman Capital Management, LP.

To address the revenue shortfall, at least in part, the Abe government plans to raise taxes. Japan's current sales tax is 5 percent, due to an increase to 8 percent next year and 10 percent by 2015, although leaders will "look at economic data" in October to decide whether taxes will indeed rise. That is a large tax increase, and it will, of course, hurt consumer spending. Taking a risk by actually making a forecast that will be either right or wrong when you read this book, we look for the increase to be either outright postponed or the implementation slowed down. To do otherwise means that Abe and team mean to double down on printing, which may happen anyway. There can be no other economically consistent choices.

True fiscal reform requires significant economic growth. Japan has had none for two decades, and now conditions for growth are even more adverse. Growth in GDP comes from two (and only two) sources: growth in (working-age) population and growth in productivity.

Japan's working-age population is falling steadily as its citizenry rapidly ages. The statistics are scary. For the third year in a row, Japan's population dropped. Projections by the Japanese government indicate that if the current trend continues, the population of Japan will decline from its current 128 million to 117 million in 2030 and to 97 million in 2050. The Japanese have only 1.39 children per woman, and the number of the elderly relative to other age groups is growing faster in Japan than just about anywhere else. In 2012, sales of adult diapers surpassed sales of baby diapers for the first time. That statistic hits home the critical point: The country is facing a demographic collapse, and it is pretty hard to grow when your population is shrinking. Japan finds itself now entering in uncharted demographic territory.

Carl Weinberg of High Frequency Economics, writing in the *Globe and Mail*,[1] offers us a succinct analysis of the Japanese demographic dilemma:

The National Institute of Population and Social Security Research projects that Japan's working-age population will decline over the next 17 years, to 67.7 million people by 2030 from 81.7 million in 2010. We select 2030 as the endpoint of today's discussion because almost all the people who will be in the working-age population by 2030, 17 years from now, have been born already. Immigration and emigration are trivial. The 17-per-cent decline in the working-age population is a certainty, not a forecast. It averages out to a decline of 0.9 per cent a year. In addition, these official projections show a rise in the population aged over 64 to 36.9 million in 2030 from 29.5 million in 2010. If the labor-force participation rate stays constant, we estimate the number of people seeking work in the economy will fall to 56.5 million by 2030 from 65.5 million today and 66 million in 2010.

What happens when a nation's population declines and the proportion of working-age people decreases? In the first, simplest, level of analysis, the production potential of the economy declines: Fewer workers can produce fewer goods. This does not mean GDP must decline; productivity gains could offset a decline in the labor force. Also, an increase in the labor-force participation rate could mute the effect of a declining working-age population. However, even if the labor force participation rate were to rise to 100 per cent by 2030 from 81 per cent today (which it cannot, because some people have to care for the old and the young, and some are disabled or lack adequate skills or education), there would be fewer workers available in 2030 than there are today.

With fewer people working, the burden of servicing the public-sector debt will be higher for each individual worker. We project that the debt-to-GDP ratio and the debt-per-worker ratio will grow unabated over the next 17 years and beyond. Also, the rise of the ratio of retired workers to 32 per cent of the population from 23 per cent means that people who are still working in 2030 will have to give up a rising share of their income to support retirees. The disposable income of the declining number of workers will fall faster than the decline of production and employment. Overall demand of workers will decrease—with their disposable income—faster than output for the next 17 years at least. Demand will also fall as new retirees spend less than in their earning years.

Based on demographic factors alone, the decline of aggregate demand between now and 2030 will exceed the decline of output, creating persistent and widening excess capacity in the economy. Prices must fall in an economy where slack is steadily increasing. In addition, advancing technology will likely increase output per worker in the future. With overall demand and output falling, productivity gains will lower labor costs and add to downward pressure on prices. Disinflation and deflation are the companions of demographic decline.

Sighing yet? Weinberg's assessment is all dark storm clouds and no silver lining.

But what if you cast around creatively for reasons to be more optimistic? Japanese women participate in the labor force at just 63 percent, about the lowest female participation rate among developed nations. What if the participation rate of women happens to rise dramatically because of the 250,000 new day care jobs Abe has promised? And what if older people decide to work longer? And maybe men will do more (even though they have one of the highest participation rates now). Why, the unemployment rate could drop by, say, 40 percent.

If you make unrelentingly optimistic assumptions such as these, then you can get to a 1.5 percent growth rate (which is, we are sorry to say, not anywhere near enough). Abe has bet big that creating inflation will encourage people to stop postponing spending in hopes that things will get even cheaper. Never mind that most older people don't think like that. Or that those older people who mostly don't think like that are, in fact, the people in Japan with the most money to spend. Prospects for spurring consumer spending are thus more limited than they might be if Japan's demographics were different. Abe's program is yet another case of operating on the basis of textbook economic theory rather than grappling with the reality that is staring you in the face.

An aging population means that someone has to take care of parents as they get older. And in Japan (as in many other places), that responsibility usually falls to the women, which lowers the female participation rate in the workforce. And where will those 250,000 day care workers come from? Who is going to pay for them? Which programs will get cut to pay for those day care workers? And what about the serious need for nursing-home workers? There are far more old people in Japan than there are toddlers. And while it is just anecdotal, the problems of finding child care in Japan is a huge complaint among working-age mothers who actually want to go back to work!

Because of the demographic problems of an aging Japan, economic growth will require even greater productivity growth than seems within the bounds of possibility. Where is that going to come from? Real productivity growth (as opposed to nominal growth due to inflation) is not something you can just dial up with government policies and QE. It is incremental in nature. If you want 3 percent GDP growth in a country whose population is shrinking by 1 percent, you need 4 percent productivity growth, give or take. That just doesn't happen on a sustained basis in an already developed country.

What is one of the primary sources of increasing productivity? It is private capital investment (and yes, government can also be a source of capital and infrastructure). Yet private investment in Japan fell in Q1 2013. The growth that occurred came from currently available industrial capacity. Clearly, Abe and company have decided that the spare capacity in Japan must be utilized (which will increase productivity because of past investment) so that new investment and a new growth cycle can start.

The Hard Part: Structural Reform

But new growth will also require concerted political and structural reform, something that Japan has been reluctant to tackle in the past. They would not restructure their banks or their debt after the bubble burst in 1989, and their failure to do so has been a main cause of the economic malaise of the past 24 years. The history of Japan since 1989 has been that they avoid real reform, preferring the easier option of more government spending.

Political reform will not be easy, for reasons detailed in an essay by Alexandra Harney entitled "Japan's Silver Democracy" in a recent issue of *Foreign Affairs*:

Although this transformation has only just begun, it is already weighing heavily on Japan's national finances. It is widely known that the country's public debt levels are expected to hit 240 percent of GDP next year—higher than in Greece. But it is less well understood that a portion of Japan's debt comes from funding the national pension program. Indeed, total spending on social benefits, including health care, pensions, and nursing for the elderly, now exceeds spending in all other categories combined, including education, defense, and Japan's beloved bridge and tunnel building programs. Much of those expenses are directly related to the rising costs of caring for the elderly. Japan's total expenditures on those 65 and older tripled in the two decades before 2004 and have only continued to increase since then. Spending on families and the young, by comparison, has not increased nearly as much.

In Japan, these vital issues are subjected to very little public discussion. Particularly ahead of elections, politicians avoid addressing subjects that are sensitive for the elderly, such as the over-generosity of the pension system, the excesses and inefficiencies in the health-care system, and the economic difficulties facing young people, which dampen already low fertility rates. The reason: voter demographics. Over the last three decades, as Japan's population has aged, the percentage of Japanese voters over 60 has more than doubled, to 44 percent. By comparison, as of November 2012, only 21 percent of registered U.S. voters were over 65. Meanwhile, the share of Japanese voters in their twenties has fallen, from 20 percent in 1980 to 13 percent today.

In other words, Japan has two problems: it is rapidly aging, and its old folks will not let politicians do anything about it. The longer Japan waits to confront its aging society, the higher the cost to the economy. The country must start thinking less about elderly voters and more about young families, or its economic prospects will remain assuredly grim.

The third arrow of Abenomics is to generate growth through structural reforms. Without true structural reforms, the strategy of Abenomics really can't work. As noted earlier, generating growth will be very difficult to do because the working age population will be falling by about 1 percent a year for the next 20 years. The government is not without tools to reform the economy. For example, it is looking into deregulating the health care and energy sectors, improving the corporate tax regime, and negotiating more open trade deals. All of this is much easier said than done. It is one thing to change monetary policy, and another to make deep-rooted reforms in the economy.

In short, the Japanese government has embarked upon an economic experiment in Keynesian theory that is breathtaking in its promised scope. They are betting that they can gear up enough growth to overcome deflation and demographics, allow the country to balance its budget, find an inflation level that will allow the Japanese debt to shrink relative to GDP, make Japan even more of an export powerhouse, and increase productivity on a scale never before seen in a developed country. It leaves one to wonder whether they might not solve global warming in their spare time.

They will do all this while hoping that the rest of the world sits idly by and watches Japan take export market share through QE. Meanwhile, they're picking a fight with China over islands that are basically piles of rocks, a dispute that will cost them massive amounts in lost sales, far more than the worth of the islands, even if there is substantial oil to be found in the surrounding waters. Japan is also betting that the technology landscape in its key industries won't change too rapidly.

How could anything go wrong here?

Six Impossible Things

Abe and Japan are in an almost absurdly impossible situation. Let's look at what they have to do in the light of what we just read.

They cannot continue to grow their debt at the current rate. There is a limit. No one knows for sure what that limit is, but it is drawing nearer. And they know it. So they have to get their fiscal deficit below the growth rate of nominal GDP.

To do that, they have to achieve both real growth and nominal growth. As we keep saying, pulling off real growth in a country with a shrinking population requires productivity increases on a scale not seen in any industrial country anywhere for any sustained period of time. So they have to settle, in part, for nominal growth, which means they absolutely must generate inflation or their country will collapse into a massive debt deflation, with skyrocketing interest rates.

But 2 percent inflation implies that interest rates on Japanese bonds must be at least 2 percent, if not 3 percent or more. That is double what interest rates are now, after the recent spike in the yield of Japanese government bonds (JGBs) from 0.5 percent to 1 percent, which sent the Japanese stock market into a tailspin.

That brings us to a major dilemma, which Kyle Bass calls the Rational Investor Paradox. If you are an investor or fiduciary in Japan and you now believe the BoJ is quite serious about creating inflation, do you continue to hold JGBs? Any serious analyst would assume that interest rates will climb to at least the rate of inflation, assuming you believe that Japan can create inflation. Especially if they pursue a policy that is going to lower the purchasing power of the yen, why would you, a rational investor, want to hold long-term Japanese bonds? Why wouldn't you sell as soon as Kuroda announced the "shock and awe" policy? (The announcement certainly left us in shock and awe! And, intellectually, we knew it had to be coming!) A massive selloff is exactly what happened the day after Kuroda announced his policy. The BoJ had to step in a few days later and start buying bonds in significant quantities to hold the rate down.

If you are the Abe administration, however, your bond-marketing problem is compounded by the fact that the natural buyers of your bonds for the past 20 years have been the retirement plans of your workers. But your country is rapidly getting older, and now those pension plans and individual savers are starting to cash in those bonds in order to meet pension obligations and to live in retirement. Your major pension plans are now sellers (on net) of JGBs. Mrs. Watanabe is not going to be a buyer of bonds in retirement. She will want to sell in order to buy rice, sushi, and sake—and to help out her grandkids. She will need to pay for rising energy and health care expenses and other basic needs. In short, you are rapidly running out of buyers "at the margin," which is where markets are made.

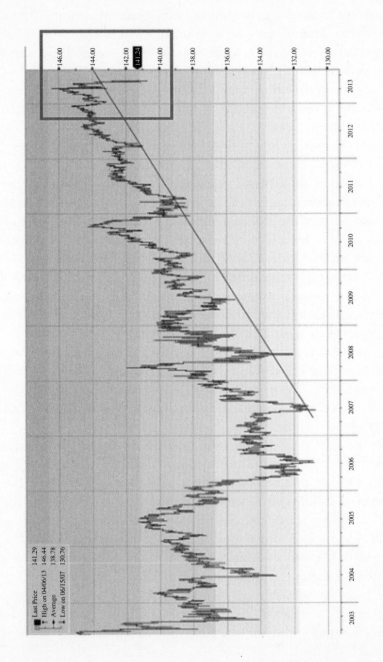

Figure 3.9 Japanese 10-Year Continuous Futures Contracts
SOURCE: Bloomberg.

It costs the Japanese government 24 percent of its revenues just to pay the interest on its debt at current rates. According to our friend Grant Williams (author of the powerhouse weekly letter *Things That Make You Go Hmmm . . .*), if rates rise to just 2.2 percent, then 80 percent of revenues will go just to pay the interest. Even at the low current rates, the explosion in Japanese debt has meant that interest rate expense has risen from ¥7 trillion to over ¥10 trillion. Note in Figure 3.10 that the Japanese government is now issuing more in bonds than it pays in interest. Somewhere, Charles Ponzi is smiling.

Now, let's get to the crux of the problem. The Japanese cannot allow interest rates to rise much more than they already have. That way leads to fiscal disaster. Yet the buyers of Japanese bonds are starting to get nervous and leave the market—a rational consequence of the drive for inflation, which remains an absolute must if Abenomics is to have a snowball's chance in Hades of working. That means there is only one real source of bond buying power left: the BoJ.

The BoJ is on its way to becoming the market for Japanese bonds. It is eventually going to have to "hit the bid" on every bond that

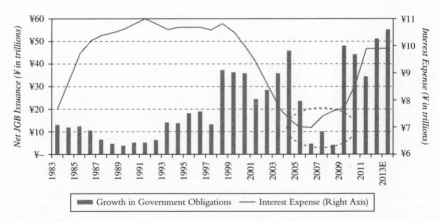

Figure 3.10 Net Japanese Government Bond Issuance and Interest Expense
NOTE: Fiscal 1983–2010 represents Ministry of Finance actual budget settlement: 2011 represents the 2011 estimated budget adjusted for the supplementary budgets, and 2012 represents the initial budget. Debt issuance represents only general JGB issuance and does not include FILP, reconstruction, compensation, or borrowings.
Latest data available as of January 2012: Japan Ministry of Finance, BoJ, Bloomberg, 2011. Estimates represent latest Ministry of Finance estimates.
SOURCE: Courtesy of Hayman Capital Management, LP.

is issued by the government because if the current policy is maintained, it will drive all buyers from the market, leaving just sellers. The pension systems will not necessarily exit their JGBs, but they will let them roll off, as they need to raise cash to meet their pension obligations. International buying of Japanese bonds will also slow to a trickle.

The BoJ is going to have to print—sorry, Kuroda-san, we meant pursue QE—to a far greater extent than it has announced in order to keep up with the demands that will be heaped upon it. We are talking about numbers that will stagger the imagination, bigger than Carl Sagan's "billions and billions." It will not be long before the word *quadrillion* starts to be used more frequently. Kyle Bass remarked that if you started counting and called out one number every second, it would take 33 million years to get to a quadrillion. A quadrillion is a thousand trillion or a million billion or a billion million. We humans simply have no way to grasp the enormity of such a number. Nor can we understand the implications when such fantastic numbers must be applied to the world's money supply.

So the solution that Abe and Kuroda have seized upon, to the applause of mainstream economists, is massive QE. Let's look at a paper recently published by UC Berkeley Professor Christina Romer, former chairwoman of the President's Council of Economic Advisers.[2]

Basically, Romer (with a direct nod to Krugman et al.) suggests that Abe and Kuroda have initiated what she calls a regime shift and that "it just might work." And then she proceeds to compare what Japan is doing to the policies of Roosevelt in the early 1930s. Quoting from the introduction:

> Last week, we witnessed one of the most exciting developments in monetary policymaking since the 1930s. The Japanese central bank staged a honest-to-goodness regime shift. The Bank of Japan went beyond vague promises and cheap talk. As I will describe in more detail later, it took dramatic actions and pledged convincingly to do whatever it takes to end deflation in Japan. The theoretical reasons why this regime shift may be important are well understood by economists. Persistent deflation and anemic growth suggest that Japan continues to

suffer from a shortfall of demand. But their policy interest rate is already at the zero lower bound. Furthermore, riskier, long-term rates are also very low—suggesting that unconventional policies such as large-scale asset purchases are unlikely to do much to further reduce nominal rates. As discussed by Paul Krugman, Gauti Eggertsson and Michael Woodford, and others, if unconventional monetary policy can raise expected inflation, this can push down real interest rates even though nominal rates cannot fall. This, in turn, can raise aggregate demand by stimulating interest-sensitive spending.

And in the conclusion she suggests that Code Red policies are the only way forward:

In a recent paper, David Romer and I discuss that such views are potentially very destructive. We show that what are widely viewed as the two largest errors in Federal Reserve history—inaction in the wake of banking panics early in the Depression, and inaction in the face of high and rising inflation in the 1970s—were both borne of unwarranted humility. Fear that policies might not work or might be costly led policymakers to conclude that the prudent thing was to do nothing. Yet there is now widespread consensus that action would have been effective in both these periods.

We have nothing to fear but fear itself: this is the heart of Keynesian thinking. And if it is good for Japan, then why not for the rest of the world?

Earlier in the paper, after discussing recent U.S. Federal Reserve policy actions, Romer writes:

But the truth is even these moves were pretty small steps. With its most recent action, the Fed has pushed the edges of its current regime. And I am sure that given the opposition in Congress and the difference of opinion within the FOMC, even those measures were a struggle. Nevertheless, the key fact remains that the Fed has been unwilling to do a regime shift. And because of that, monetary policy has not been able to play a decisive role in generating recovery. To paraphrase E. Cary Brown's famous conclusion about fiscal policy in the Great Depression: monetary policy has not been a strong recovery tool in recent years not because it did not work but because it was not tried – at least not on the scale and in the form that was necessary to have a large impact.

Wow. Double wow. Read this paper: http://elsa.berkeley .edu/~cromer/It%20Takes%20a%20Regime%20Shift%20Written%20% 28Second%20Revision%29.pdf. Absorb it. And then bookmark it and come back in five years. We will give Romer this much: she shows no unwarranted humility in this paper. She goes "all in" in backing this Japanese policy.

But we do agree with Professor Romer about one thing: this is the most serious and radical economic experiment undertaken in our lifetimes by a major economic power. And the rest of the world must pay attention. If this has succeeded in working five years from now— if Japan is growing and its debt relative to GDP is shrinking and the rest of the world has allowed the yen to drop in half, and if the people, especially the retired elderly, are better off—then let us state here and now that we will have to rethink our understanding of economics. Perhaps Abenomics stands a chance of working for the banks and large corporations, at least for a while, but those who worked and saved all their lives are not as likely to be as happy as they see their wealth eroded away.

As we will see, Japan will soon find it impossible to pay back its Godzilla-sized debt or even service the interest payments on it. The Japanese debt pile now tops one quadrillion yen. (That's 1,000 trillion yen, or one followed by 15 zeros, for those of us who are mathematically challenged.) The amount of money the central government raises yearly in taxes, however, is about ¥50 trillion. Thus, it would take all of the money raised in taxes over 20 years to pay down the debt. Japan's debt load is so great that it is essential for the interest rate the Japanese pay on it to stay very low. Every 100-basis-point (1 percent) change in the average borrowing cost is roughly equal to a quarter of the Japanese government's annual tax revenue. If Japan had to borrow instead at France's rates (which are still quite low), for instance, the interest burden alone would bankrupt the country.

Economists are split on whether the Code Red policies of the BoJ will revive economic growth and end deflation. Martin Wolf of the *Financial Times* perhaps put it most clearly: "At best, this would only work in the short run. At worst, it could destabilize inflation expectations so dangerously that it pushes Japan from deflation to ultra-high inflation, without stopping for long at any point in between."

Abe's shock and awe tactics are already having an effect. Deflationary expectations have been cut down in battle. The Japanese Cabinet Office's consumer sentiment survey found that nearly three quarters of households expect prices to rise over the next year. Retail sales are slowly increasing, as consumers want to put their money to work today rather than pay higher prices tomorrow.

A Modern Currency War

It is uncertain what the outcome will be in Japan, but what we believe (in our own display of no unwarranted humility) is certain is that Japan's Code Red, shock-and-awe monetary policy is the final grain of sand, dropped on an impossibly tall and unstable sandpile, that will start an avalanche and lead to a global currency war.

While the Japanese may be optimistic today, absolutely none of Japan's neighbors are thrilled with the rapid weakening of the yen. Across the Sea of Japan sits South Korea, one of Japan's greatest competitors when it comes to exports of flat-panel TVs, cars, microchips, and so on. Not surprisingly, South Korea has complained the most loudly about the weak yen. Very large exporters such as Samsung Electronics and Hyundai have seen their competitiveness eroded as the won increased in value by almost 30 percent in six months as the yen weakened.

Threatened with a weaker yen, South Korea already has promised that it will not stand still. South Korean government officials have threatened to impose a broad tax on financial transactions. "The recent wave of quantitative easing policies has created an unprecedented situation and makes it necessary to adopt a paradigm shift in response,"

South Korea's Deputy Finance Minister Choi Jong-ku said. The trade war between Japan and Korea is heating up and cannot end well.

Japan's Asian neighbors have plenty of reason to be fearful. A little over 10 years ago, the BoJ cut rates to zero. The yen very quickly lost about half its value, and the weakness of the yen had disastrous effects on Japan's trade competitors, including Indonesia, Thailand, Malaysia, and Korea. At first, money poured out of Japan as savers fled zero percent interest rates. Their flight led to a very big boom and spectacular bust that became known as the Asian Crisis of 1997. As Jefferies economist David Zervos wrote, "The important lesson here is that when the Japanese decide to turn the ship around and go for it, the wake generates a tsunami for ALL mercantilist nations."

Every major emerging-market country is complaining loudly about the growing weakness of the yen. India, Russia, and China have all denounced the damage that will be dealt to their exports by a weaker yen. Meanwhile, the Philippines and Thailand have protested for a different reason. They do not want too much capital entering their countries, seeking higher interest rates and stronger currencies. Yi Gang, director of China's State Administration of Foreign Exchange (SAFE), warned about the dangerous fallout from QE, zero interest rate policy (ZIRP), and large-scale asset purchase (LSAPs) in the world's advanced economies. "Quantitative easing for developed economies is generating some uncertainties in financial markets in terms of capital flows," he said, adding, "Competitive devaluation is one aspect of it. If everyone is doing super-QE, which currency will depreciate?"

In fact, it is almost impossible to find anyone outside Japan who is happy about a weaker yen. The Bank of England worked very hard to devalue the pound and has been successful in reducing the broad value of the pound against all currencies by almost a third in the past five years. Nonetheless, in an act of brazen hypocrisy, former Bank of England Governor Mervyn King said his "concern is that in 2013 we'll see the growth of actively managed exchange rates as an alternative to the use of domestic monetary policy." Translation: We'd like a weaker currency for ourselves, but please do as we say, not as we do.

The Europeans are perhaps the most schizophrenic of all when it comes to currency manipulation. (If only Europe were a real country, perhaps it wouldn't be so schizophrenic.) When investors were worried about Greece's leaving the euro and the euro's breaking up, they wanted a strong euro. However, when the yen weakened and Toyota threatened Renault's sales, the story was different. Luxembourg Prime Minister Jean-Claude Juncker warned that the shared currency is "dangerously high." He declared, "Europe is no longer willing to be the last economic player holding the toxic parcel of an overvalued exchange rate."

As criticism of Japan grew louder, the Group of Seven leading economies issued a statement in February 2013 denying that there was a currency war and affirming that there would be none in the future.

> We, the G7 Ministers and Governors, reaffirm our longstanding commitment to market-determined exchange rates and to consult closely in regard to actions in foreign exchange markets.
>
> We reaffirm that our fiscal and monetary policies have been and will remain oriented towards meeting our respective domestic objectives using domestic instruments, and that we will not target exchange rates.

As Sir Humphrey Appleby said in *Yes, Minister*, "The first rule of politics: never believe anything until it's been officially denied." The G7's denial is a sure sign that a currency war has officially started.

The "inconvenience" felt by other nations who will find their economies battered by Japanese policies is perhaps regrettable, as the Japanese will admit (at least when they attend international meetings), but it will not dampen their ardor one whit. If you live in Seoul, Paris, London, Frankfurt, or Dallas, your vote does not count. Only those voters in Tokyo, Osaka, Kobe, Kyoto, and Hiroshima will have a say. Japan is charging into battle to conduct the ultimate test of Keynes's theories, even as other nations brace for the collateral damage.

Japan intends to export its deflation, as we have seen. And with the approval of the economic cognoscenti, it is going to do so in a manner and to an extent that the world has never experienced before.

But, if you're Abe, what are your choices? They are nothing but ugly. We have to admit that if we were faced with Abe's choices, we would likely choose the same direction. The time for them to make good choices was 15 years ago. The choices that are faced by Japan today are a consequence of their previous bad choices.

Perhaps the best of a very, very ugly bad lot is that you have to try to inflate away that debt. Monetize as much as you can and just "poof" it away. You destroy your currency in the process, but you have to destroy something. And maybe your derring-do gives your exporters a boost and a competitive advantage, so you at least salvage that. Why not export your deflation? And then gamble that maybe Romer and Krugman are right. It could work! Or not. Banzai! "Damn the torpe-does, full speed ahead!

We should note that "poof" is a technical economic term we are inventing. The fact of the matter is, in very legalistic terms, the debt will not cease to exist. It will be on the books somewhere for a very long time. But if it is on the books of the BoJ, then for all practical purposes the debt does not exist. The government will be paying inter-est to itself. Poof, indeed! We should note that this is a tried-and-true mechanism for governments everywhere. Ireland recently "poofed" away their debt they borrowed from the ECB to bail out their banks by magically transforming it into 40-year bonds with the help of some very inventive legal counsel. We are sure they fully intend to pay those bonds back in 40 years. The only real requirement to poof away debt is very creative legal minds. And those the developed world has in abundance.

The government of Japan has fired the first missile in what will be the first real currency war in most of the lives of those who read this book, not the little sandbox versions we have experienced so far. There is *no* historical analogy. None. The last major currency war, in the 1930s, happened when the world was largely on a gold standard. The collapse after Bretton Woods still had a tentative link to the dollar standard. We now live in a world awash in fiat currency. Can Europe sit by and watch the yen fall 50 percent from where it is today? Will Germany allow it?

What will China do? If they respond in kind, they risk inflation. If they don't, they risk losing export sales and jobs. But as we will see in a few chapters, China has a most interesting option. It is the rest of the neighborhood that will have most of the issues. Malaysia is on a borrowing binge to finance its real estate growth. Indonesia? Taiwan? And Korea certainly can't sit idle and watch its *chaibol* (the Korean version of the Japanese *keiretsu*) get hammered, can it?

Gentlemen, They Offer Us Their Flank

Our friend, the serious raconteur Bill Bonner, tells a story of the WWI Battle of the Marne. Quoting (with a few edits):

> You remember the famous German general von Kluck, from whom we get the expression, "You dumb kluck"?
>
> Von Kluck was chasing the French down the Marne in 1914. Victory appeared close at hand; the French were pulling back. Von Kluck, who had orders to attack Paris, decided instead to pursue the French army. He was convinced they were beaten.
>
> All he had to do was keep the pressure on . . . and they would surrender.
>
> Some of his field commanders, however, noted that they were picking up very few prisoners. Normally, an army that is beaten throws off many discouraged and confused soldiers. Since there were so few, the commanders reasoned that the French army was still intact; it was merely retreating in good order and could turn and surprise the Germans at any time.
>
> The commanders were right. France's aging general, Gallieni, who was in charge of the Paris garrison, realized that the Germans were making a fatal mistake. By pursuing the troops down the Marne, rather than attacking Paris, they exposed themselves to a counterattack from the city itself.
>
> "Gentlemen," he is said to have remarked to his staff, "they offer us their flank."
>
> The French accepted the offer: they attacked. Using thousands of taxicabs, they quickly moved troops to the Marne Valley and caught the Germans unprepared. The Battle of the Marne turned the German army around and ultimately cost them the war.

The Japanese are charging the deflationary battle lines, crying *"Banzai!"* in an all-or-nothing attack. However, the action in the markets has showed us that this battle will not be one-sided. It will often get ugly. **We think the Japanese are offering us investors their flank**. In fact, John is already turning Abe's full frontal attack into an investment opportunity.

> I want to keep reiterating what I have been saying for a long time: shorting the Japanese government is the trade of the decade. That is the largest position in my personal portfolio, and it is going to get larger, as I intend to fully swap the mortgage I just took out into yen. It is my intention (more accurately styled as hope) to let Abe-san and Kuroda-san pay for a large chunk of my new apartment through their policy of destroying the yen.
>
> Will I succeed? Time will tell, but I am joined by Japanese public pension funds that have announced they will reduce their holdings of local bonds while increasing their share of both domestic and, in particular, foreign equities.

Let us clarify that: we are not suggesting you short Japanese companies or businesses but rather short Japanese government economic policies. (John is executing that trade primarily through hedge funds, although there are ways to explore that trade in a more conventional manner, which we will explore later in the book and at www.thecoderedbook.com). We think the yen will still be under pressure for some time (this is a long-term trade) and Japanese interest rates will be under pressure.

Do *not*, however, run out and short JGBs. The battle has been joined, but it is far from over. We can't with any reasonable certainty tell you how all this will play out, as we are simply in uncharted territory. But we do know we want to own assets that central banks can't print. Their actions will affect those assets, to be sure; we are going to see more volatility than we would like, but that volatility, however unsettling, creates opportunity. We will be looking in detail at that opportunity in Part II of the book.

Key Lessons from the Chapter

In this chapter we learned:

- Japan has been in a deflationary slump for over two decades. Nominal GDP has not grown. Government debt-to-GDP is now over 240 percent. Interest rates have been stuck at the zero bound. There has been no control of the fiscal deficit. The trade balance has deteriorated. The population is both shrinking and aging.

- Prime Minister Abe has committed to a "three-arrow" approach to solve Japan's problems. The three arrows in his quiver are aggressive monetary easing (QE), more credible fiscal plans, and a growth strategy based on structural reform.

- Japan is about to unleash the most significant currency war the world has ever seen. The rest of the world, especially Japan's direct competitors (Korea, China, Germany, and others) will not sit idly by as Japan takes export market share through QE.

- Japan has set a target of 2 percent inflation. But the Japanese cannot allow interest rates to rise much more than they already have. That way leads to fiscal disaster. Yet the buyers of Japanese bonds are starting to get nervous and to leave the market.

- The second arrow in Abe's quiver is fiscal reform. Japan is saddled with a yawning fiscal deficit that, if it were closed too quickly, would plunge the country into immediate and deep recession.

- True fiscal reform requires significant economic growth. Japan has had none for two decades, and now conditions for growth are even more difficult. Growth in GDP comes from two (and only two) sources: growth in (working-age) population and growth in productivity. Japan's population is actually shrinking, and its working-age population is falling even faster as the country rapidly ages.

- Real productivity growth is not something you can just dial up with government policies and quantitative easing. Japan will have a hard time significantly improving productivity.

- The Japanese are offering us investors their flank: shorting the Japanese government is the trade of the decade. Do *not*, however, run out and short JGBs.

Chapter Four

A World of Financial Repression

No nation ought to be without a debt. A national debt is a national bond; and when it bears no interest, is in no case a grievance.

—*Thomas Paine,* Common Sense

What has been will be again, what has been done will be done again; there is nothing new under the sun.

—*Ecclesiastes 1:9*

C an you imagine Julia Roberts and Gwyneth Paltrow helping the U.S. government sell bonds or Jay-Z and Justin Timberlake composing songs about Treasury bills? It would not be the first time Hollywood stars or famous musicians tried to help the government sell its debt.

The last time the U.S. government had an enormous load of debt, it used Hollywood stars to help sell government debt. The Treasury Department conducted a massive public relations campaign through radio, newspapers, and film. During World War II, war bond rallies were held throughout the country, and Hollywood stars such as Bette Davis and Rita Hayworth traveled around the country to promote war bonds. The great Irving Berlin even wrote a song titled "Any Bonds Today?" and Berlin's tune became the theme song of the Treasury Department's National Defense Savings Program.

The government also enlisted cartoon characters, actors, comedians, and musicians to encourage people to pay income taxes. Donald Duck told viewers it was their "duty and privilege" to pay income tax. Abbott and Costello appeared in advertisements to get people to pay taxes, and Irving Berlin wrote songs not only about bonds but songs about taxes like "I Paid My Income Tax Today."

While the war bond and income tax drives garnered all the press, the real reason the United States was able to borrow so much and with so little burden had nothing to do with the glitz and glamor of movie stars. The U.S. government borrowed easily because the Federal Reserve printed money to keep interest rates low. Borrowing is very easy when a central bank has your back.

How did it work in practice? As is the case today, the Treasury wanted to borrow cheaply then, and the central bank was happy to accommodate. In 1942, after the United States entered World War II, the Federal Reserve officially agreed to fix interest rates on government bonds at a low level. To maintain the pegged rate, the Fed was forced to give up control of the size of its balance sheet. Not surprisingly, the Fed bought and held all available short-term U.S. treasuries and almost all long-term government bonds.

The costs of paying for World War II pushed the national debt up sharply, from around 40 percent of gross domestic product (GDP) before the war to a peak of nearly 110 percent as the war ended. But a combination of strong economic growth, tight fiscal policies, and financial repression brought the debt back below 50 percent of GDP by the late 1950s. (Currently, our government debt has reached about 90 percent of GDP and continues climbing very sharply.)

During the war years, the Federal Reserve pegged long-term interest rates at extremely low levels so the government wouldn't have to pay much to fund itself. To make sure that inflation didn't spike, the government instituted wage and price controls. After the war, the price controls disappeared and inflation rose very quickly, averaging about 6.5 percent annually from 1946 to 1951. By the postwar price peak nine years later, wholesale prices had more than doubled, and the stock of money had nearly tripled.

Normally such high inflation would have made it much more expensive for the government to borrow money. But after being pressured by the Treasury, the Federal Reserve agreed to keep on pegging long-term government bond yields at 2.5 percent until the spring of 1951, when the Federal Reserve finally refused to print money to keep bond yields low. Because of the coordination between the Federal Reserve and the U.S. Treasury, real yields on government bonds were very negative during the years following World War II. With negative real yields, borrowers win and lenders lose. The clear winner was the U.S. government, and the loser was anyone who bought and held U.S. bonds. The combination of very low government bond borrowing costs and high inflation ate away a sizable chunk of the government's debt burden.

The same thing is happening today in almost all government bond markets around the world. Governments are winning, and investors are losing. The Federal Reserve is helping the Treasury to borrow cheaply while the government expands its deficit spending and debt accumulation. Using inflation and low bond yields this way to reduce government debt is called financial repression. And that financial repression spills over into the nongovernment markets. Banks and businesses and individuals can all borrow money at the lowest rates in several generations. Of course, savers also get the lowest rate in several generations. There are no free lunches.

Inflation and Interest Rates

As we will see in our final chapters on investing, inflation has a very close relationship to how stock markets perform over time. Indeed, one of the questions we are both regularly asked wherever we speak is something along the lines of "What do you think inflation will be?" And the answer is not easy: it depends on a number of factors that vary from country to country.

In general, the trend for the last 75 years has been one of inflation. Sometimes, in some countries, inflation has spun out of control. Very rarely have we seen outright deflation. Neither one promises good times for investors. Ever-falling inflation or low inflation is the best environment for investing.

Inflation has a significant long-term correlation with interest rates. This makes perfect sense when we recall that interest rates are simply another price: the price of borrowing money. Many prices are distorted by government policies, but none more so than interest rates. The Federal Reserve Banks directly control short-term rates and have great influence everywhere else.

In theory, the Fed's job is to use its tools to maintain a balance between maximum employment, stable prices, and reasonable interest rates. The "stable prices" goal refers to inflation. We know from his public statements that Ben Bernanke is satisfied that inflation is under control for now. His benchmark, though, is the same Consumer Price Index (CPI) whose weaknesses we discuss later. And paying attention to what central bankers say about inflation is going to become important. Japan promises to actually boost inflation up to 2 percent, and the United States and Europe promise to keep it at around 2 percent. Their commitments can change, or their ability to control inflation may take a back seat to other more pressing mandates.

For right now the Fed is engaged in a policy (quantitative easing) that is normally associated with inflation. In later chapters, we will discuss why printing money does not always immediately yield inflation in the CPI.

Today, the Federal Reserve is unofficially keeping interest rates very low so the government can fund itself. There is no explicit agreement with the U.S. Treasury as there was in World War II, but exactly the same is happening in practice. In 2013, for example, the Fed will be purchasing the equivalent of all newly issued Treasury debt through June. The government doesn't even have to worry about borrowing money. In the words of Governor Richard Fisher, the Fed "runs the risk of being viewed as an accomplice to Congress's fiscal nonfeasance."

Unfortunately, keeping interest rates artificially low via financial repression has all sorts of intended and unintended side effects that hurt you as a saver and investor. We are sure central bankers would like us to use a prettier-sounding word than *repression*, but if you are the victim of lower rates, it sounds just right. Of course, if you get a lower mortgage rate or reduced payments, then your view can change. But part of the very act of the repression itself entails a group of people meeting a few times a year to decide who wins and loses. Pardon our cynicism if we find that it is almost always the banks that win. In this chapter we'll look closely at how this form of financial repression works and what the consequences are for bonds, stocks, and your savings.

Financial Repression: Back to the Future

The book to read on the sovereign debt crisis is Carmen Reinhart and Kenneth Rogoff's *This Time Is Different*. It has been hugely influential, and almost all other books have had to refer to its thorough review of financial crises throughout history. It is an invaluable aid to understanding how large-scale crises happen and what the inevitable consequences are. Their research showed that high debt harmed economic growth. Later researchers have questioned details of their study, but none have disproven the basic thesis. Just how much debt lowers growth is still subject to debate, but dozens of articles support the view that debt is a drag on growth.[1] (In our previous book, *Endgame*, we devoted an entire chapter to outlining the key findings of Reinhart and Rogoff. For those who are interested, you can read much of that chapter at www.thecoderedbook.com.

How do you top a book as influential as *This Time Is Different*? Carmen Reinhart outdid herself with her recent scholarship. If you want to know who to read on the subject of financial repression, Reinhart wrote a series of scholarly articles outlining how governments use a wide variety of tools to reduce the real value of debt. This time she teamed up with Jacob F. Kirkegaard and M. Belen Sbrancia. They looked at economic data for countries over the past century and analyzed how governments get rid of their debt. Let's try for a summary of their research. (Again, you can find links to their work at www.thecoderedbookcom.)

After analyzing inflation and debt levels for dozens of countries, Reinhart and her colleagues found that most governments don't get rid of their debt by default. History reveals that they slowly reduce it via financial repression instead:

> Historically, periods of high indebtedness have been associated with a rising incidence of default or restructuring of public and private debts. A subtle type of debt restructuring takes the form of "financial repression." Financial repression includes

directed lending to government by captive domestic audiences (such as pension funds), explicit or implicit caps on interest rates, regulation of cross-border capital movements, and (generally) a tighter connection between government and banks. In the heavily regulated financial markets of the Bretton Woods system, several restrictions facilitated a sharp and rapid reduction in public debt/GDP ratios from the late 1940s to the 1970s. Low nominal interests rates help reduce debt-servicing costs while a high incidence of negative real interest rates liquidates or erodes the real value of government debt. Thus, financial repression is most successful in liquidating debts when accompanied by a steady dose of inflation. Inflation need not take market participants entirely by surprise and, in effect, it need not be very high (by historic standards). For the advanced economies in our sample, real interest rates were negative roughly ½ of the time during 1945–1980. For the United States and the United Kingdom our estimates of the annual liquidation of debt via negative real interest rates amounted on average from 3 to 4 percent of GDP a year. For Australia and Italy, which recorded higher inflation rates, the liquidation effect was larger (around 5 percent per annum).

There are lots of big insights in that paragraph, so let's look at them one by one.

First, Reinhart calls a spade a spade. Financial repression is a form of default and debt restructuring. It simply happens to be a more subtle way to screw creditors. While reducing your debt by 3 to 4 percent a year sounds like very little, if governments do that for a while, it really adds up:

Such annual deficit reduction quickly accumulates (even without any compounding) to a 30–40 percent of GDP debt reduction in the course of a decade. For other countries which recorded higher inflation rates, the liquidation effect was even larger. As to the incidence of liquidation years, Argentina sets the record with negative real rates recorded every single year from 1945 to 1980.

Now we're talking about really big reductions in debt. With large numbers like 30 to 40 percent in a decade, you can see why financial repression is so attractive for governments.

The financial repression tax is much higher in emerging-market economies. That stands to reason. Inflation is generally higher in developing countries than in developed ones. And higher inflation equals a higher financial repression tax. How high is that tax? Economists Giovannini and de Melo calculated the size of the financial repression tax for a sample of 24 emerging-market countries from 1974 to 1987. Their results showed that financial repression exceeded 2 percent of GDP for seven countries, and was greater than 3 percent for five countries. For five countries (India, Mexico, Pakistan, Sri Lanka, and Zimbabwe), it represented approximately 20 percent of tax revenue. In the case of Mexico, financial repression was 6 percent of GDP, or 40 percent of tax revenue.

One of the more extraordinary quotes from Reinhart's work is that for "advanced economies in our sample, real interest rates were negative roughly ½ of the time during 1945–1980." So savers and investors faced negative real interest rates and financial repression over half the time in the three and a half decades after World War II.

Much like the period of financial repression right after World War II, the 1970s was also a decade of financial repression. In fact, it was during those years that investors started calling government bonds "certificates of confiscation." When the term became popular, bonds were probably the most despised investments you could find. While the coupon on the bonds was high, inflation was always higher. Bonds were a guaranteed money loser if you were an investor. Today, inflation on government bonds is not as high as in the late 1970s, but the confiscation theme is truer now than ever. Just as in the early 1950s and the late 1970s, if you buy a government bond today, you are being repressed (that's a technical term for screwed).

Earlier in the book we explained that seigniorage is the benefit governments get from printing money and exchanging it for real goods and services. You probably won't be surprised to know that Giovannini and de Melo found that "[t]he evidence indicates that the revenue from financial repression can be quite substantial, and for several countries it is of the same order of magnitude as seigniorage." Money printing works at getting rid of debt. The most extreme examples of debt liquidation are hyperinflations. Hyperinflations in Germany, Hungary, and other parts of Europe very quickly liquidated their outstanding debts.

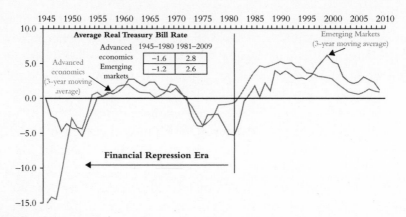

Figure 4.1 Financial Repressions since 1945

SOURCE: Carmen M. Reinhart and M. Belen Sbrancia, *The Liquidation of Government Debt,* working paper 16893.

In her writings, Reinhart lays out the mechanics of how governments quietly steal the wealth of savers and reduce their government debt. The key elements of financial repression are (1) capping of interest rates, particularly those on government debts; (2) forcing insurance companies, banks, and pension funds to buy government bonds; and (3) exerting government control over banks and Social Security funds. See Figure 4.1.

The primary way central banks keep yields low is by buying up as many Treasury bonds as they can as part of their quantitative easing (QE) programs. Figure 4.2 shows how big QE programs are as a percentage of GDP and as a percentage of total Treasury supply. As you can see, the United Kingdom has by far bought the most government bonds as a percentage of supply, while the Bank of Japan (BoJ) is buying the most as a percentage of GDP.

One of the key ways that yields are distorted is by dramatically manipulating the supply of safe assets that is available for the public to buy. For example, according to a recent Reuters article, "JPMorgan estimates that the world's central banks and commercial banks alone now hold some $24 trillion worth of bonds—or 55 percent of the entire $44 trillion universe of government, asset-backed, and corporate bonds as captured by Barclays Multiverse Global Bond Index. What's more, these players hold more than two thirds of the government bond subset, which amounts to about $25 trillion." The cumulative

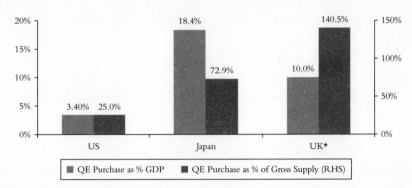

Figure 4.2 QE Purchases as a Percentage of GDP in the United States, United Kingdom, and Japan
SOURCES: Nomura, Federal Reserve, BoJ, BoE. *Based on Historical Purchases.

bond buying since 2008 by four major central banks alone—the Fed, BoJ, European Central Bank (ECB), and Bank of England (BoE)—will reach about $6.5 trillion by year-end. This year, given the latest rounds of QE from the Fed and Japan, both banks' bond buying will exceed new bond sales by their governments by at least $100 billion this year.

The best way to think about the shortage of supply is like the scramble for tickets before a Super Bowl. When supply is limited but demand is high, prices will rise to crazy levels. If you're a pension fund or an insurance company, you're struggling to get your hands on a government bond for a decent price (because the laws require you to!). In effect, you're being price gouged.

Central banks can decide what bonds they want to buy. And by buying bonds of different maturities, they can change the slope of the yield curve. (The Fed has yet to see a price or interest rate it does not want to distort.) If they want to drive down yields of two-year bonds, they can do that. If they want to lower longer end yields, they can do that, too. In fact, the Federal Reserve has resurrected a program the United States followed in the early 1960s. In Operation Twist under President Kennedy, the Fed sold shorter-dated bonds and bought longer-dated ones. It was intended to lower long-term interest rates in order to stimulate investment while propping up short-term interest rates and supporting the dollar. When Bernanke announced a bond-buying plan that was designed to flatten the yield curve, everyone called it Operation Twist. History doesn't always repeat itself, but it often rhymes.

We have already looked at how central banks monetize debts to keep yields low, but there are many other ways for governments to keep borrowing rates artificially suppressed. If you're the government, you can set all sorts of rules and regulations. You can force insurance companies to hold more government bonds and fewer stocks. You can force pension funds to invest only in government bonds, and you can force banks to hold only "low-risk" investments, which—surprise, surprise—are government bonds. Governments have many ways they can force investors' money into government bonds.

Financial repression is widespread. It doesn't matter where you look, you can see the hand of government encouraging and even forcing insurance companies, banks, and pension funds to buy government bonds. For example, the new global banking regulations, known as Basel III, will include a liquidity requirement that creates incentives to hold more government bonds on a bank's balance sheet. The impact of the change in the banking regulations is likely to boost demand for government bonds by the trillions. Countries have tried this before when they needed to borrow large amounts from financial markets. In 2009, the United Kingdom's Financial Services Authority introduced a similar measure in order to prop up the British gilt market.

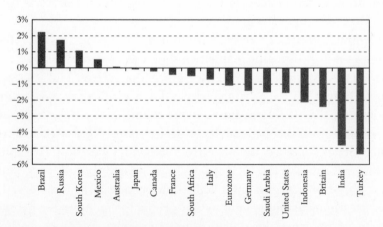

Figure 4.3　Real Interest Rates Are Almost All Negative
SOURCE: Research Affiliates, based on data from Bloomberg.

For insurers, the European Union (EU)-wide Solvency II directive will increase demand for government debt. Much like with banking regulations, under the new rules government bonds do not face a capital charge, so insurers will have a regulatory incentive to buy government bonds. The examples go on and on. France, Spain, and Ireland have forced national pension funds to buy government debt exclusively. Portugal transferred Portugal Telecom's pension plan back to the Portuguese government in 2010. The Japanese government canceled the privatization of the Japanese Postal Bank in order to keep a captive buyer for government bonds. These are just a few examples of dozens where governments have directly or indirectly controlled pension funds and banks to ensure a captive buyer for government debt.

At the risk of being cynical, we wonder just how those regulations worked out for holders of Greek bonds a few years ago. The increasing proportion of Italian and Spanish debt held by their banks is an obvious source of concern. Allowing Jon Corzine to buy European government debt as a speculation rather than short-term U.S. treasuries brought down what was a rather boring commodity brokerage firm called MF Global, and exposed to risk the assets of tens of thousands of investors. These policies were all pursued because regulators assumed that governments could not default and that government debt was 100 percent safe. We often criticize the regulators for not making sure that investment companies do not protect their customers but failed to realize that it is sometimes the very regulations that are the problem.

Taxes by Another Means

In March 2012, European leaders agreed to impose a 6.75 percent levy on insured Cypriot depositors as the price to bail out Cyprus's insolvent banking sector. Cypriots were up in arms about the "tax" on their savings. (Depositors of amounts above €100,000 may end up losing as much as 70 percent, although that figure is currently subject to intense negotiations. Unless of course your deposits were in Laiki Bank and you are completely wiped out!) Amazingly, savers in the rest of the world have faced worse hits to their savings through financial repression, yet no one has taken to the streets. Unlike the poor Cypriots, who saw their savings disappear overnight, savers in the United States, Great Britain, and China have seen their savings leak away more slowly but no less surely.

Anyone who buys government bonds or puts money into a bank these days is losing money in real terms. According to calculations of *The Economist*:

> Americans who invested in six-month bank certificates of deposit earned 3.2% between 2009 and 2012, before tax, whereas consumer prices rose by 6.6%. The financial-repression levy was therefore 3.2%. In Britain even savers who put cash in the best tax-free "individual savings accounts" (which have modest annual limits) would have earned a cumulative 11% between 2009 and 2012, during which time consumer prices rose by 13.4%. Outside that tax shelter, middle-class savers who pay a marginal tax rate of 40% would have earned a net return of 6.6%. In real terms, their savings would have declined by 6%, not far short of the original Cypriot deposit levy.

Cypriots hated the tax on their savings because it was obvious and up front, yet we have not seen people taking to the streets to protest about the tax from financial repression.

Perhaps the clearest and most memorable way to look at financial repression comes from Bill Gross, the inimitable head of PIMCO. As Gross put it, central banks are using "historically tried and true 'haircuts' that surreptitiously 'trim' an asset holder's money without them really knowing they had entered a barbershop. These haircuts are hidden forms of taxes that reduce an investor's purchasing power." He went on, "Essentially central banks and policymakers are acting like barbers. They haircut your investments. Negative real interest rates, inflation, currency devaluation, capital controls, and outright default are the barber's scissors."

Governments love financial repression for obvious political reasons. When they try to reduce the debt by raising taxes, people are up in arms. Income and sales taxes are visible and explicit. But a financial repression tax that is driven up by inflation is indirect and opaque. However, if governments cut spending to reduce debt, different political groups might protest. But financial repression cuts the debt in many cases much more effectively than either raising taxes or cutting government spending.

Will Real Inflation Please Stand Up?

Remember the Jimmy Carter years and those wonderful Dan Aykroyd spoofs of Carter saying, "Inflation is your friend!"? And if you want to go back to a more innocent era, watch propaganda newsreels from the 1930s touting the benefits of inflation. Roosevelt is portrayed as the savior bringing inflation to us all.[2]

For governments, inflation is their friend. The government and central banks contribute to higher inflation by pretending inflation is always under control. For example, throughout the Greenspan and Bernanke years, the Fed consistently chose to focus on lower inflation measures whenever doing so suited the central bank. You can see this in the semiannual monetary policy reports to Congress, specifically in the inflation forecasts made by the members of the Federal Open Market Committee. Until July 1988, inflation forecasts used the implicit deflator of the gross national product, but then the Fed switched to the Consumer Price Index. In February 2000, the Fed replaced CPI with the personal consumption expenditures (PCE) deflator. Thus from July 2004 onward, inflation forecasts have employed the core PCE deflator that excludes food and energy prices.

Using lower and lower, less comprehensive estimates for inflation has allowed the Fed to pretend that it is meeting its mandate—but by ignoring high inflation readings. In the meantime, interest rates have been kept too low, and the inflation rate has consistently remained above the Federal Funds rate.

Today, the Federal Reserve itself prefers to look at core PCE, a measure that uses chained dollars rather than a fixed basket as the CPI does. PCE and other chained inflation numbers generally yield lower inflation figures, which is why many in Congress (and the AARP) think the "chained dollars" amount to some sort of conspiracy to defraud seniors on Social Security. Retiree benefits aren't currently using chained dollars, but if Obama and Congress get their way, they will steadily lose money every year. It gets worse, though. CPI is used to calculate adjustments for income taxes. If it is too low, then incomes rise faster in real terms than cost adjustments do, and that acts as a tax increase even as your pension is adjusted lower. Even small miscalculations will add up over time to large losses for someone.

Measuring inflation is not so easy. The vast majority of readers have no idea about the rather contentious nature of the debates that go on about arcane topics such as the minutiae of how to measure some minor aspect of inflation.

Official statistics show that inflation in the United States is low; however, the average person feels inflation is rising quickly. For example, since 2002 the Big Mac has risen in price at nearly three times the rate of overall inflation. People notice that gas prices are also much higher. It is hard to argue with people who point out that prices and the cost of living are going up faster than government-reported inflation reflects. We can all see prices rising. Food, energy, tuition (try managing all that for 30 years with seven kids as John has!)—they're all going up.

So why haven't these more rapid increases shown up in the CPI? One reason is that the index itself has been modified in a variety of ways over the past 35 years. Fluctuations in home prices have been smoothed out, for example. And the index has been adjusted periodically to reflect changes in what people buy, particularly if they shift from more expensive items to cheaper ones. Such revisions to the CPI have tended to reduce the official inflation rate, on balance. Various estimates of what the annual rate would have been over the past four years if earlier methods of calculation had been continued come up with numbers in the 5 to 10 percent range. It is important to understand that there is no absolute and objective gauge of inflation. Any particular measure is simply one way of making the calculation, based on a host of assumptions.

Everyone can find personal examples showing that inflation is much higher than the government says. It leads people to distrust official data. The main problem with relying on anecdotes, though, is that our memories are selective and unreliable. As Daniel Kahneman has argued, humans have a psychological tendency known as *confirmation bias*. People with a strong opinion on a matter will seek and recall evidence supporting that belief. If you believe inflation is rampant but unreported, it's easy to find examples to support your case.

There has been a great deal written about the difficulty of measuring inflation and about the potential manipulation of inflation statistics over the past 30 years. John Williams of ShadowStats is the most noted proponent of the position that inflation is running well above the current U.S. government's number of 2 percent (for the 12 months ending February 2013).

Employing the methodology that was used in 1980 under the Carter administration, inflation would currently be about 9.6 percent (see Figure 4.4). Using the government methodology from 1990, inflation today turns out to be a little under 6 percent.

If we had kept the methodology used until 1980 for calculating the CPI and then used that number to adjust Social Security and government pensions, the U.S. government would be bankrupt today. Social Security would have gone negative in the 1990s and tripled in cost in the past 12 years (compounding at 10 percent can do that). Now, those of you living on Social Security might think a tripling of payments is appropriate, given what has happened to your budgets, but younger taxpayers would hasten to differ. (*Note:* We are not arguing that Social Security provides a livable income at current levels—different topic for another book.)

If we had used actual home prices in the CPI, inflation would have been seen as very high in the middle of the past decade. Instead, we seemed to be flirting with deflation; and if we used housing prices in 2008–2011, we would certainly have had government-reported

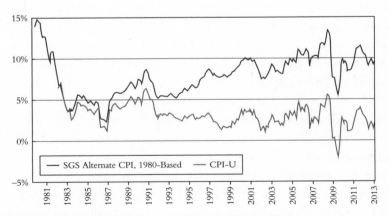

Figure 4.4   Consumer Inflation—Official vs. ShadowStats
Source: shadowstats.com.

deflation. In place of home prices, the Bureau of Labor Statistics (BLS) decided to use something called Owners' Equivalent Rent a few decades ago; and it is the largest part, a full 24 percent, of the CPI.

Something called *hedonics* is probably the most contentious part of the CPI calculation. The BLS says, "The hedonic quality adjustment method removes any price differential attributed to a change in quality by adding or subtracting the estimated value of that change from the price of the old item." This is not as mysterious as it sounds. When, for example, you replace your old computer with a new one, paying roughly what you did before, the new model you buy is always faster and more powerful than the old one. The BLS says you are getting more for your dollar; therefore, the price fell even if you paid as much or more for the new computer. Opponents say hedonics can be used to hide "true" inflation.

We do know that a lot of items have in fact gone down in price and up in quality or capacity. Cell phones are a good example. And the cost of using cells may be ready to really fall. There is a full smartphone that uses a major carrier and Wi-Fi in combination now on the market for $20 a month for all the voice, data, and text you can eat. It works on Wi-Fi in Asia, in Europe, and in the middle of the Andes. You pay basically nothing for 10 or 15 or 40 hours a week of talk time, and people can call you anywhere in the world using a local U.S. number if you are connected to Wi-Fi.

(*Fair warning:* The following will be regarded as a contentious statement by the gold bugs and hyperinflationistas out there. For some of you, to accept it would be like admitting your religious beliefs are wrong.)

The topic of those alternate inflation numbers comes up often at our tables of conversation. Over time, markets respond to actual inflation and not government statistics. In the United States, the difference is likely small, but in some countries like Argentina, the difference is large. Argentina's government can state that inflation is "only" 10 percent, but the market thinks it is 30 percent and rising.

The government calculation of inflation in 1980 or 1990 was the best they could do at the time. But it was a government calculation. There is nothing ex cathedra about either methodology. In religious terms, neither rises to the stature of the original Greek documents or

the Latin Vulgate Bible. Changing the words (the equations) in economics should not be seen as somehow equivalent to changing the
fundamental documents of a religion. There is nothing sacred about
1980 CPI methodology, and in fact we can look at it empirically and
understand that it was pretty flawed in some ways.

You might have some personal investment bias (read "quasi-
theological reason") to want inflation to be high. But that is a belief
system. It is one form of faith-based economics. (It is not a large stretch
to suggest that most economic schools require of their adherents
a measure of faith and belief.) Expectations of high inflation are for
some people a basic tenet of their belief system. Saying there is only a
little inflation must therefore be a government manipulation.

We must constantly be comparing our assumptions against what
we observe in the real world, in order to discern where our models,
with their built-in assumptions, bias our conclusions about what the
data says.

If you think *overall general* inflation is high, then you have to think
the entire world is delusional. (*Note:* Your personal inflation rate may
be much higher than 2 percent.) G7 interest rates are at an all-time
low today. That can and will change; but right now the bond market
does not see inflation as a problem anywhere in the developed world,
although Japan has now made what must be their 10th vow in the past
20 years to create inflation. This time, they may actually (for them, cat-
astrophically!) succeed. For now, however, deflation and deleveraging
are the order of the day.

We will be able to look back in 15 years to see how well we are
doing today at measuring inflation. The real surprise would come if
we *don't* change methodologies at least a few more times between now
and 2030.

Inflation Is Your Friend

Seeing inflation as some sort of religious doctrine might be amusing
if inflation were actually our friend. It may well be our friend or it
may not: we just don't know. The theology-economics parallel is probably more accurate than either side wants to admit. Both fields deal in

nebulous concepts. Both believe their work is of profound long-term significance. Neither can prove the accuracy of its claims in the short term.

Much like Christians, economists have sorted themselves into denominations over time. Central bankers, finance ministers, and certain economists function as high priests. Each church school of economic thought wants to save souls see policymakers accept its beliefs. Each economic school was founded by a dead white guy who wrote a book and garnered disciples who preach the faith and try to convert the "heathen." Whether it's believing that prayer and good works will be rewarded by a one-way ticket to heaven or avowing that the law of supply and demand will result in general wealth and prosperity, it's all a matter of faith. We will know the definitive answers only when it is too late to change the outcome.

At the risk of pushing the religious analogy a bit too far, we submit that inflation is best defined within an agnostic or polytheistic belief system. You have your inflation, I have my inflation, and both feel equally correct to each one of us. Without taking sides in that debate, we think it's clear that we all prefer to pay less for whatever we buy. Here is where we get polytheistic. If you live in South Florida, the price of snow blowers is not on your mind. Your personal inflation rate gives more weight to the cost of air conditioning. If you are a retiree in your 70s, rising college tuition costs have little direct impact on you (unless you happen to be helping your grandchildren with the cost of school). Rising prices for prescription drugs are much more important.

Yet all of us here in the United States are governed by the same people in Washington, and they define inflation in their own way, via the Consumer Price Index and various related benchmarks. Because the CPI tries to find a national "average" inflation rate, it is almost by definition inaccurate for any given person, family, business, city, or state. CPI is the least common denominator, a "one size fits all" coat that in reality fits no one very well.

Given the acknowledged limitations of the CPI, we nevertheless use it in myriad ways. It governs cost-of-living adjustments for Social Security beneficiaries, government employees, and many labor union members. CPI is baked into the general cake, even though we know it is an imperfect fit in almost every situation. As a result, some people get raises when their cost of living drops, while for others the cost of living rises faster than their income does.

Repression Hurts Retirees

If the government benefits from stealth taxes, then who is the loser? Economists have a saying, "There are no free lunches." In a world of financial repression, the biggest losers are savers and older people who rely on savings. Low rates punish savers, leaving them with less money to spend, and that financial hit hurts retirees' final consumer demand— or that is the view from the cheap seats where we sit. Inflation erodes their buying power over time. A 2 percent negative real rate means the buying power of a currency drops in half in 36 years. Does that seem like a long time? Try retiring at 60 at today's interest rates and watch as your buying power slowly erodes as you get older. It is down close to 25 percent in just 10 years. But your taxes and fixed expenses will have gone up!

Economists can argue that the trade-off is positive, but it seems to us that governments are defrauding a generation or two of hardworking savers. You did what you were supposed to do, and your reward is a 10-year bond at close to 2 to 3 percent or less, depending on the country. Since you paid off your mortgage a long time ago, the lower rates don't help you either! So you either cut back on your "lifestyle" or move out the risk curve. While better yields can be had with some serious research and homework, it is not easy. The Fed is not going to change its policy to help retirees and pension funds, so older people are left to fend for themselves.

The plight of retirees does not go unnoticed. At the latest Berkshire Hathaway's annual meeting in Nebraska, Warren Buffett said, "I feel sorry for people that have clung to fixed-dollar investments," he told investors. "Bernanke had tough choices to make, but he decided to step on the gas pedal in terms of monetary policy, and he brought down rates to virtually unheard of levels and kept them there. And he's still got his foot on the pedal, and that really does hurt savers. It has made it extremely difficult for all kinds of people who live on fixed-income investments."

Very low interest rates and financial repression have led to a situation where countless pension funds are massively underfunded. State and local pensions are among the worst because most of them are final salary. Estimates for the pension deficit on these plans are very high, probably more than $4 trillion. The deficits are so ludicrously high that it is a 100 percent certainty that many public sector workers will have their pensions reduced. Sadly, the recent vote by the citizens of San Jose, California, to cut their fire and police pension benefits dramatically (on the grounds that their city council had for years promised more than the tax base could afford) is going to become part of the new normal over the next few years. Seriously, the pensions of the state of Illinois are so badly underfunded that there is scant hope that retirees or even current workers will get what they were promised. And there are other states and government entities that are following in the footsteps of the Land of Lincoln. Detroit comes to mind.

For many of the 44 million Americans with pensions, employers have not set aside enough money to provide them a stable income through retirement. According to *The Economist*, at the end of 2012, after a serious stock market recovery, the deficit of U.S. corporate pension plans still amounted to a record $557 billion. The plans were only 74 percent funded. Even the huge stock market returns of the first quarter could not trim the deficit down below $372 billion. Those returns could disappear in another bear market just as rapidly as they materialized. Companies had to contribute $80 billion to their pension plans last year, double the amount of year before. The cost of rescuing these plans has saddled the federal Pension Benefit Guaranty Corporation with a record $26 billion deficit. They concluded, "The situation will likely worsen as more companies decide they can no longer afford their pension commitments and stick the government with the bill."

The problems of pension shortfalls are not just an American phenomenon. In the United Kingdom, corporate pension deficits are estimated to be about £80 billion. That is the frightening conclusion of new calculations by actuaries at Mercer, which demonstrate the difficulty of saving to fund old age.

Part of the problem is simply promising too much in the way of benefits, but an equally big part can be attributed to pension-fund consultants making assumptions based on the bull market of the 1980s and 1990s. And now, low interest rates make those assumptions look even worse—to the point where local and state governments cannot afford to keep the very generous promises they made. A crisis may not happen immediately, but hundreds of pensions funds will likely end up joining the queue for a taxpayer bailout.

It is not just pension funds that are hit. Insurance companies with annuities and death-benefit liabilities are also screwed (that technical economic term again). They will find it impossible to fund their annuities as the amount they earn in interest collapses.

Financial repression hurts banks, too. Low rates help governments, but they don't help banks. Rates are so low that banks have absolutely no incentive to lend. Three-month London Interbank Offered Rate (LIBOR), the rate at which banks say they can borrow in dollars from each other, was set at 0.273 percent as we write this paragraph. With rates like that, why lend at all?

If you are not wealthy and are trying to survive on your own savings, you'll have to save a lot more for the years ahead and work until you're much older. So even though central banks would like people to spend more money to kick-start the economy, lower rates punish savers, forcing them to dramatically increase their savings rate and reduce consumption. We live in an upside-down world.

Everything Is Overpriced

For investors, one of the biggest problems of financial repression is that not only are central banks distorting the yield on government bonds, they're also distorting all other asset prices. We now live in a new world where it is no longer necessary for the market to decide short rates or long rates.

For almost all investors, government bonds yields are like true north for a compass. All other risks are priced in relation to the risk-free rate. As Carmen Reinhart points out:

> Markets for government bonds are increasingly populated by nonmarket players, notably central banks of the United States, Europe and many of the largest emerging markets, calling

into question what the information content of bond prices are relatively to their underlying risk profile. This decoupling between interest rates and risk is a common feature of financially repressed systems.

If the risk-free rate no longer reflects risk properly, then almost all other asset classes that are priced in relation to the risk-free rate will also be mispriced.

The risk-free rate of return is the best rate that does not involve taking a risk. Both the return of the original capital and the payment of interest are completely certain. Normally, the rate is taken to be the return on government bonds over the period. In the United States, the bonds people look at are obviously U.S. government bonds; and in Europe, people look to German government bonds as being the most secure. Any risky investment should produce greater returns than the risk-free rate. The extra return reflects the extra risk involved.

Why does it matter if the risk-free rate is unnaturally low or suppressed by governments and central banks?

Normally, bond markets set the risk-free rate. Investors decide at what price they will lend money to the government for 2 years, 5 years, and even 30 years. All other lending in bond markets or banks loans takes its cue from the risk-free rate. For example, as we write this paragraph, the U.S. 10-year government bond is yielding 1.75 percent. If a company like Apple wants to borrow, it has to borrow at a spread to U.S. government bonds. When Apple borrowed to pay its dividend, it issued $5.5 billion of 2.4 percent, 10-year securities that have a spread of 75 basis points to government bonds.

Investors who buy bonds with very low yields will very quickly lose a lot of money as rates go up. The danger comes from reinvestment risk. You could easily sell the bond and go out and buy a higher-yielding one when rates go up. For investors who plan to hold the bonds to maturity, they won't lose any money. But if interest rates keep rising, investors are going to have to sit on very low-yielding bonds for an awful long time while inflation could accelerate.

(As an aside, if you think for a second about how central banks are unelected, independent, and often coordinate market prices of interest rates and currencies, you would call them a cartel. If they were manipulating the market price of copper, airline tickets, or semiconductors, the regulators would fine them. In fact, recently, a cartel of commercial banks colluded to rig the reference LIBOR interbank borrowing rate during the credit crisis (with the full knowledge, mind you, of certain central bank employees. As there was *no* trading in the interbank market, how could a true price exist? *Of course* they made it up!), and regulators are now going after bank employees who manipulated prices. Yet the regulators rig interest rates every day as part of their job! Think about that one for a while. But we digress . . . back to our risk-free discussion of return-free risk. . . .)

The distortion of the risk-free rate is forcing investors into chasing investments that will compensate them with a higher yield than the incredibly low rate available by buying government bonds. This is leading toward bubbles in emerging-market debt, emerging-market stocks, high-yield debt, real estate investment trusts (REITs), farmland, and defensive stocks that have high dividends. For example, high-yield, or junk-rated, debt is at the lowest level it has ever been. The level of yield on offer is so low that investors are barely even being compensated for the historical probability of default.

Nearly every traditional asset class is priced to achieve very poor long-term returns. It doesn't matter what you look at, whether it is stocks, corporate bonds, emerging-market bonds, or whatever. They're all overvalued, with high price-to-earnings multiples, low yields, and low margins of safety. As we write this, the yield on the United States 10-year note is a measly 2.75 percent, and 30-year yields are at still less than 3.75 percent. Corporate bonds are barely priced for their riskiness. The Dow Jones Corporate Bond Index is yielding just 3.5 percent. Central bankers have succeeded in driving investors into high-risk assets by depriving them of any real return on government bonds.

How have real investment returns played out in the past when real rates were so low? Our friend Niels Jensen of Absolute Return Partners pointed out a very helpful study that shows just how screwed investors are in a world of negative to low real rates. The very helpful *Credit Suisse Global Investment Returns Yearbook 2013* looks at returns over the past century. Intuitively, you would expect a strong positive relationship between real rates and subsequent real returns on bonds and equities. What is interesting is that the evidence backs up.

Let's look at what the study showed:

The authors of the study began by calculating real interest rates every year during the 1900–2012 period on each of the 20 countries in the study. Following that, real equity and real bond returns were calculated for the subsequent 5 years, leading to a total of 2,160 observations (20 countries times 108 overlapping 5-year periods between 1900 and 2012). Those observations were then ranked from lowest to highest real rates and 8 bands were established (lowest 5%, next 15%, etc.—see the x-axis in [Figure 4.5]).

The historical evidence shows that low real interest rates are correlated with low real returns, as you can see from Figure 4.5. **Unfortunately, real rates are negative right now, which means that in general you, as an investor, can expect very low to negative investment returns over the next few years**. The world would be a much happier place for investors without artificially distorted real interest rates.

If you think that the dangerous overvaluation in risk assets is a mistake, you'd be wrong. It is not a bug in the software of central banks. It is part of the program in a Code Red world. Central banks want people to take

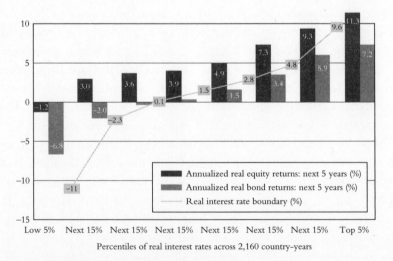

Figure 4.5   Real Returns vs. Interest Rates, 1900–2012
SOURCE: *Credit Suisse Global Investment Returns Yearbook 2013.*

their money out of safe investments and put them into risky investments. They call it the "portfolio balance channel," but you could call it "starve people for yield and they'll buy anything." In Bernanke's own words:

> We do think that these policies can bring interest rates down—not just Treasury rates, but a whole range of rates, including mortgage rates and rates for corporate bonds and other types of impor- tant interest rates. It also affects stock prices. It affects other asset prices—home prices, for example. So looking at all the different channels of effect, we think it does have impact on the economy.

Assets should be valued based on risk and possibilities of return, but in a world of Code Red policies and financial repression, people are forced to abandon treasuries and find investments elsewhere. In a Code Red world, the prices for assets bear little relation to risk and return.

In the 1970s financial repression led to inflation in consumer prices with all the devastating consequences. Recently financial repression has led to asset price inflation. We are all well aware of what happened when housing prices rose into bubble territory because of low interest rates and lax regulatory oversight of the lending channels. Somehow many investors think that the dramatic expansion of the money supply that is going into the stock and bond markets will end without a problem. Asset price inflation is often seen is good if you are holding the asset. We rationalize to ourselves that this time is different. It rarely ever is.

Investors have rarely faced a more difficult time to protect their savings. Thanks to central bankers, in a world of financial repression investors face a perfect storm of overvalued stocks and bonds that are guaranteed to provide poor returns.

Key Lessons from the Chapter

In this chapter we learned:

- One of the main reasons governments find it so easy to finance themselves is that central banks are printing money to buy most of the bonds.
- Financial repression results when governments and central banks artificially reduce the cost of borrowing for government debt while

they generate inflation at the same time. Negative real yields or interest rates benefit governments and punish bondholders and savers.

- Governments from developed markets benefit from financial repression, but emerging markets, which generally have higher inflation, benefit even more. Financial repression is a subtle, hidden tax on the population.

- Financial repression makes stocks and bonds more expensive, reduces the yield on financial assets, and ultimately lowers the future potential returns for investors. It is very difficult to invest profitably in a world where almost all returns are near zero or even negative.

- For the past several centuries, the expected return investors can make has been related to the level of real interest rates. When real interest rates were high, investors got high returns. When real rates were negative, investors could expect poor returns. Unfortunately, we're living in a negative real-rate environment.

- Pensioners are the most affected by financial repression. Pension plans across the United States and much of the developed world are underfunded and will not be able to pay out what people expect because future returns are so low due to financial repression.

- Keeping interest rates and government bond yields unnaturally low distorts markets. All investors refer to government bond yields as the risk-free rate. If the risk-free rate is mispriced, all other asset classes will be mispriced as well.

Chapter Five

Arsonists Running the Fire Brigade

The true measure of a career is to be able to be content, even proud, that you succeeded through your own endeavors without leaving a trail of casualties in your wake.

—*Alan Greenspan*

If economists could manage to get themselves thought of as humble, competent people on a level with dentists that would be splendid.

—*John Maynard Keynes*

And He spoke a parable to them: "Can the blind lead the blind? Will they not both fall into the ditch?"

—*Luke 6:39–40*

In the old days, central banks raised or lowered interest rates if they wanted to tighten or loosen monetary policy. In a Code Red world, everything is more difficult. Policies like zero interest rate policy (ZIRP), quantitative easing (QE), large-scale asset purchases (LSAPs), and currency wars are immensely more complicated. Knowing how much money to print and when to undo Code Red policies will require wisdom and foresight. Putting such policies into practice is easy, almost like squeezing toothpaste. But unwinding them will be like putting the toothpaste back in the tube.

While most central bankers who currently serve at the Fed, the Bank of England (BoE), or the Bank of Japan (BoJ) seem to think it will be easy to do their jobs in a Code Red world, many former central bankers disagree. Alan Blinder, a former vice chairman of the Federal Reserve, best described the immense challenges facing Federal Reserve Chairman Ben Bernanke:

> The Fed now finds itself on an alien planet, with a near-zero funds rate, a two-trillion-dollar balance sheet [Note to the reader: it has grown by over a trillion since!], a variety of dodgy assets, holes in the wall separating the Fed from the Treasury, Congress up in arms, and its regulatory role up in the air.
>
> Your mission, Mr. Bernanke, since you've chosen to accept it, is to steer the Federal Reserve back to planet Earth, using as principal aspects of your exit strategy some new instruments you have never tried before. As always, should you or any member of the Fed fail, the secretary and Congress will disavow any knowledge of your actions. This lecture will self-destruct in five seconds. Good luck, Ben.

The challenges central banks face are immense, and many of the strategies they are exploring have never been tried before. Managing the extraordinary burdens of monetary policy will require immense skill, courage, and foresight. Let's hope our central bankers are prepared.

With that thought in mind, let's see if our Colonel Jessups are up to the task of administering their unconventional methods. In this chapter and the next, we'll look at how they've done in recent years and how good their tools are for understanding where the economy is and where it is going. You'll find that truth is stranger than fiction when it comes to central bankers.

The Cult of Central Bankers

For the past two decades central bankers have been revered as a cross between the Oracle of Delphi and Elvis Presley. The names of central bankers have been household words in the United States, Europe, and

Japan. Much of this is owed to Alan Greenspan, an owlish man who used to play the saxophone, read and run around with Ayn Rand in his free time, and reassure people that all would be well right before big recessions. He was such a superstar that the Queen of England knighted him even though he is not British. The honor was conferred to recognize Greenspan's "contribution to global economic stability."

Investors hung on every word that Greenspan uttered, even though his statements were cryptic. Sometimes they were so impenetrable that you couldn't make heads or tails of what he was really trying to say. He once famously quipped: "If I seem unduly clear to you, you must have misunderstood what I said." The opaqueness and obscurity of his statements brought to mind the response of Wolfgang Pauli, the great Cambridge University physicist, when he was attempting to read a colleague's paper, "This isn't right. This isn't even wrong."

Greenspan was the Pied Piper of Hamelin, pretending central banks could solve every problem, fix every crisis, and make markets levitate. Journalists were like nervous schoolgirls when they interviewed him; congressmen fought to be the first to ask him questions at congressional hearings (nearly always parading their own ignorance of economics), lavishing praise on him for his wisdom. Senator Phil Gramm called him the greatest central banker of all time and suggested that even if he died they would simply prop him up in his seat and presumably let his aura reign supreme. The almost embarrassing worship reached its peak with the publication of Bob Woodward's *Maestro* in 2000.

Greenspan's time as chairman of the Fed was defined by his willingness to cut interest rates at the slightest weakness in the stock market and to leave rates too low for far too long. This one-way commitment to boost stock prices and investor sentiment became known as the "Greenspan put" by investors. Everyone thought the Fed would do anything to help financial markets. Arguably, his easy monetary policy created a culture that encouraged risk taking and promoted speculation. To Greenspan, stock market confidence and the economy's growth prospects were inseparable.

Under Greenspan, the default mode of the central bank was to pump more money into the system and cut rates. He argued that:

Policy practitioners operating under a risk-management paradigm may, at times, be led to undertake actions intended to provide insurance against especially adverse outcomes. The 1998 liquidity crisis and the crises associated with the stock market crash of 1987 and the terrorism of September 2001 prompted the type of massive ease that has been the historic mandate of a central bank.

After the dot-com bust, Greenspan took the Fed Funds rate to 1 percent in June 2003 and left it there for over a year, even though the economy was roaring back by then. And when the Fed did start raising rates, it raised them in baby steps and far too slowly. The ultra-low rates helped feed the housing bubble that then blew up. Not to mention there was no—none, nada—regulation or attempt to control the obviously fraudulent practices in the mortgage market.

For Greenspan the answer to any problem was always more liquidity, more liquidity. If Greenspan were a character on *Saturday Night Live*, he would be the music producer played by Christopher Walken, demanding, "More cowbell! More cowbell!" And all the other members of the Fed, including Bernanke and Yellen, played right along.

Under Greenspan, the Federal Reserve became a massive cult of personality. Early on, many members of the bank dissented during committee meetings, particularly around the recession of 1990–1991. Interest rate decisions were divisive, and many disagreed about the health of the economy. However, the dissent rapidly disappeared in the 1990s as the economy grew and the stock market started rising. As the stock bubble got bigger, the Greenspan bubble inflated as well. Whenever Greenspan appeared before Congress, ignorant legislators who wouldn't understand what an interest rate was if it hit them on the head bent over backwards to praise the Maestro. Almost no one dissented from Greenspan's views. From 2000 until 2006, when Ben Bernanke was appointed chairman of the Fed, there was, on average, one dissent per year. Sadly, the cult of Greenspan and the slavish groupthink at the Fed was particularly evident when dissent was needed most, in the run-up to the Great Financial Crisis of 2008.

When Greenspan was about to retire in January 2006, he held his last meeting as chairman. He was leaving behind him a time bomb of poorly regulated banks, excessively loose monetary policy, and the crazy idea that you can't spot bubbles beforehand and they're best left alone even if you can spot them. When he retired, the housing bubble was already bursting. It would take another year before most of the subprime mortgage lenders would go bust.

The adoration of Greenspan is almost embarrassing to read. Roger Ferguson, then Fed vice chairman and now head of the Teachers Insurance and Annuity Association–College Retirement Equities Fund (TIAA–CREF) financial services group, called Greenspan a "monetary policy Yoda." Yes, you read that correctly. Tim Geithner, who was completely clueless about the potential for problems in the very banks he was regulating as head of the Federal Reserve Bank of New York, was even more effusive. You could almost think he had a teenage crush. You can't make this stuff up. Here is Geithner speaking:

> I'd like the record to show that I think you're pretty terrific. [Laughter] And thinking in terms of probabilities, I think the risk that we decide in the future that you're even better than we think is higher than the alternative. [Laughter]

In case you're wondering what happened to Geithner, he was appointed to be secretary of the Treasury for his starring role in the Great Financial Crisis.

While some of Greenspan's brownnosers have moved on, Janet Yellen, the head of the San Francisco Federal Reserve, was promoted to be vice chairman of the Federal Reserve. She is widely expected to be the next head of the Federal Reserve. At a January 2006 meeting of the Federal Reserve, Yellen extolled Greenspan:

> Needless to say, it's fitting for Chairman Greenspan to leave office with the economy in such solid shape. And if I might torture a simile, I would say, Mr. Chairman, that the situation you're handing off to your successor is a lot like a tennis racquet with a gigantic sweet spot.

We do apologize if any of these quotes have caused you to spew your coffee or choke on your breakfast.

The Federal Open Market Committee (FOMC) meeting minutes before the crisis are notable for their absence of concern over housing and the economy. In fact, if you record the incidence of laughter at the

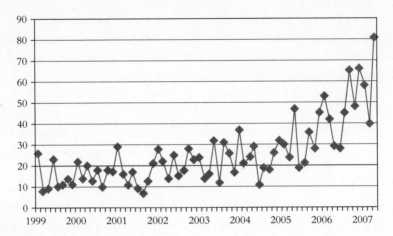

Figure 5.1 The Number of Laughs at the Fed Correlated Directly with the
Housing Bubble
SOURCE: www.acting-man.com.

Fed, you can see from Figure 5.1 that the bigger the housing bubble
got, the more the Committee laughed. We're tempted to say they were
fiddling while Rome burned, but it would be more appropriate to say
they were giggling while subprime burned.

It is important to make a point here. There were many voices
pointing out the distortions in the housing market and the subprime
securitization markets. These were well-known and well-explored phenomena. The purpose of a central bank is to take away the punch bowl
when the party gets started. The excuse that "we can't recognize a bubble in advance" and all we can do is clean up the mess after it breaks
rings hollow. Significant academic research exists to help determine the
process of the creation of a bubble in the markets.

The simple fact is that asset price inflation in the stock markets
and the housing markets were seen as good things. Everyone likes what
they own to go up, and so, just as in the 1920s, the party continued. In
the 1970s, when the Federal Reserve kept rates too low, we had consumer price inflation and we know how that ended. In the 2000s the
Federal Reserve kept rates too low and we had asset price inflation and
now we know how that ended. To think that a committee can somehow steer an economy to a nirvana-like ending by keeping monetary
policy too easy should be thoroughly discredited. Sadly, it has not been.

While there is an increasingly large chorus in the United States calling into question current Federal Reserve policy, the overwhelming majority of participants still believe that focusing on asset prices is an appropriate benchmark for determining the success or failure Federal Reserve policy.

Paul Volcker was willing to allow both the stock market to fall and unemployment to rise as he pursued the number one objective of what all central banks should have at the center of their focus: price stability.

Promoting Failure

We'll admit that we're having too much fun criticizing central bankers, the Colonel Jessups of the Code Red world. But please don't just take our word for it when we tell you that they're clueless. Let's look at what others have written.

In 2009, Congress created the Financial Crisis Inquiry Commission to uncover the causes and consequences of the financial catastrophe that almost brought down the world financial system. They roundly condemned the Federal Reserve:

> We conclude this crisis was avoidable. The crisis was the result of human action and inaction. . . . The prime example is the Federal Reserve's pivotal failure to stem the flow of toxic mortgages, which it could have done by setting prudent mortgage lending standards. The Federal Reserve was the one entity empowered to do so and it did not. . . . We conclude widespread failures in financial regulation and supervision proved devastating to the stability of the nation's financial markets.

Not surprisingly, public confidence in the Fed has plummeted.

The Federal Reserve performed disastrously before the Great Financial Crisis, but almost all central banks were asleep at the wheel. The record of central banks around the world leading up to the Great Financial Crisis was an unmitigated disaster. All countries that had housing bubbles and large bank failures failed to spot them beforehand. In the case of England, where almost all major banks went bust (some rather spectacularly!) and required either nationalization or fire sales to foreign banks, the Bank of England never saw the crisis coming. Let's look at what *The Economist* has to say about central bank failures:

> In 1996 the Bank of England pioneered financial-stability reports (FSRs); over the next decade around 50 central banks and the IMF followed suit. But according to research cited by Howard Davies and David Green in "Banking on the Future: The Fall and Rise of Central Banking," published last year, in 2006 virtually all the reports, including Britain's, assessed financial systems as healthy. In the basic function of identifying emerging threats, "many central banks have been performing poorly," they wrote.

Housing bubbles swelled and burst everywhere: Spain, Ireland, Latvia, Cyprus, and the United Kingdom. Countries that had to recapitalize or nationalize their banks were broadsided by a disaster they did not anticipate, prepare for, or take action to prevent. In the case of Spain, even after the crisis unfolded, the Bank of Spain acted like a pimp for its own banks. It insisted nothing was wrong and proceeded to help its banks sell loads of crap to unsuspecting Spaniards in order to recapitalize the banks. (We apologize for our language, but there is no other word besides *crap* that properly characterizes selling worthless securities to poor pensioners—well, there are, but they are even less suitable for public consumption.)

In fairness, central bankers did save the world after the Lehman Brothers bankruptcy. The money printing that the Federal Reserve oversaw after the failure of Lehman Brothers was entirely appropriate to avoid another Great Depression. But giving them credit for that is like praising an arsonist for putting out the fire he started.

The failure of central banks makes it all the more remarkable that they were given even more responsibility in the wake of crisis. Since 2007 central banks have expanded their remits, either at their own initiative or at governments' behest. They have exceeded the limits of conventional monetary policy by buying massive amounts of long-dated government bonds, mortgage-backed securities, and other assets. They have also taken on more responsibility for the supervision of banks and the stability of financial systems.

The Banking Act of 1933, more popularly known as the Glass-Steagall Act, forced a separation of commercial and investment banks by preventing commercial banks from underwriting securities. Investment banks were prohibited from taking deposits. Until it was repealed in 1999, the Glass-Steagall Act worked brilliantly, helping to prevent a major financial crisis. It was replaced by the Graham-Leach-Bliley Act, which ended regulations that prevented the merger of banks, stock brokerage companies, and insurance companies. The American public's interests were thrown to the wolves of Wall Street, and the Fed and the Clinton administration gave the middle finger to financial stability.

After the Great Financial Crisis, Congress could have simply reinstated Glass-Steagall. The act was only 37 pages long, but it had worked incredibly well. Instead, after an orgy of bank lobbying and congressional kowtowing to the bankers who had brought the world to the brink of a global depression, Congress passed the Dodd-Frank Act. It is over 2,300 pages long; no one is sure what is in it or what it means; and it has added a dizzyingly complex tangle of regulations and bureaucracy to what should have been a simple, straightforward reform of the financial sector. You can compare the length of Dodd Frank against other major pieces of legislation in Figure 5.2. (The act is so long and complicated that it was nicknamed the "Lawyers' and Consultants' Full Employment Act of 2010.") You will hardly be reassured to learn that the Federal Reserve's powers were expanded through Dodd-Frank.

Please note that it was the same banks and investment firms that lobbied to repeal Glass-Steagall in 1999 that so aggressively and successfully lobbied for the Dodd-Frank Act. While there are some features contained in the plan that are good the basic problems still remain. Industry insiders were able to assure that business as usual could continue. And to judge from their profits it has done so remarkably well.

The Fed didn't need more powers. In the years leading up to the Great Financial Crisis, the Fed already had almost all the tools it needed to prevent the subprime debacle. It simply failed to use them. You could call that lapse nonfeasance, dereliction of duty, going AWOL, or anything other than doing their duty. If you don't believe you are capable of recognizing a bubble in advance, then all

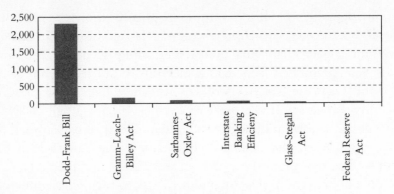

Figure 5.2   Major Financial Legislation: Number of Pages

the additional regulations in the world won't make any difference in preventing a bubble. Dodd-Frank merely gave them more regulations not to enforce. It is the mindset that needs changing, not simply the regulations.

According to the Financial Crisis Inquiry Commission, the Federal Reserve failed to use the tools at its disposal to regulate mortgages or bank holding companies or to prevent the abusive lending practices that contributed to the crisis. The central bank didn't "recognize the cataclysmic danger posed by the housing bubble to the financial system and refused to take timely action to constrain its growth," the report said. It also "failed to meet its statutory obligation to establish and maintain prudent mortgage lending standards and to protect against predatory lending."

The most sordid part of the Great Financial Crisis was not the extreme failure by central banks to regulate. The most egregious violation of the public interest came in the form of the massive subsidies and aid the central banks gave to the banking system when the crisis was under way. The great journalist and essayist Walter Bagehot argued in the mid-nineteenth century that during a financial crisis central banks should lend freely but at interest rates high enough to deter borrowers not genuinely in need, and only against good collateral. During the crisis, the Fed and other central banks lent trillions of dollars at zero cost against the shoddiest of collateral. And the Fed went out of its way to provide gifts to Wall Street banks via the back door.

For example, when AIG went bust, Timothy Geithner decided that the U.S. taxpayer should pay out credit default swaps to AIG's counterparties at full price. Goldman Sachs was given a parting gift of $10 billion. Geithner did not even negotiate a haircut. The money went to dozens of banks, many which were not even American. It is no wonder Geithner became well known as "Wall Street's lapdog."

Our good friend Dylan Grice wrote a fascinating piece on what happens when you have too many rules and too little common sense. In a Dutch town called Drachten, local government decided to take out all traffic lights and signs. They hoped people would pay more attention to the road rather than fixate on rules and regulations. They were right. In Drachten there used to be a road death every three years, but there have been none since traffic light removal started in 1999. There have been a few small collisions, but these are almost to be encouraged. A traffic planner explained, "We want small accidents in order to prevent serious ones in which people get hurt." Let's see what Dylan has to say about the lessons for capital markets:

> You might be thinking that traffic lights don't have anything to do with the markets we all work in. But I think they do. Instead of traffic lights and road signs, think rating agencies; think Basel risk weights for Core 1 and Core 2 bank capital; think Solvency 2; or think of the ultimate market regulators of our currencies—the central banks—and the Greenspan/ Bernanke "put" which was once imagined to exist. Haven't these regulators provided the same illusion of safety to financial market participants as traffic safety tools do for drivers? And hasn't this illusion of safety been even more lethal?

Wouldn't it be nice if central bankers thought more like Drachten town planners? But central bankers and parliaments prefer extensive rules to a common-sense approach.

Unlike the planners of Drachten, the Federal Reserve and central banks around the world issue extensive sets of regulation, fail to enforce them, encourage everyone to speed, and then when crashes happen they protect as many banks as possible from the consequences of their own actions.

The Federal Reserve is in desperate need of reform. This doesn't mean that politicians should be deciding interest rates or that banking supervision should be taken away from central banks. But central bankers should be answerable to the public for how they do their jobs. Accountability has been completely missing throughout the entire crisis. Almost all central banks failed to do even the basics of their job. The regulations they created, especially in Europe, made it possible for banks to take massive risk and make huge profits that ultimately had to be bailed out by taxpayers.

They believe the banks and other institutions they were regulating when they showed the models which they created which demonstrated conclusively there was no risk. Everyone, bankers and regulators, believed we were in a new era where the old rules of common sense didn't apply. Central bankers didn't need more rules or regulations. They failed miserably at even carrying out the simple job they had. The regulatory functions of central banks should be treated like those of any other regulatory agency. It is critical that we hold central bankers accountable for their management of the banking system.

No Apologies, Only Promotions

One of the most disastrous battles of World War I was the British Gallipoli campaign in Turkey in 1915. It was utterly devastating, leaving more than 50,000 British wounded and almost 100,000 dead. Winston Churchill, first lord of the Admiralty, was one of the architects of the campaign. In the wake of the outcome, he resigned his post to become a soldier in the war. Churchill was a humble man who felt he was at fault. He was honorable. But if Churchill had been a central banker, he would never have had to accept responsibility or resign. He would have kept his job and been given even more far-reaching powers and a big pay raise to boot.

For the past few years, central bankers have been living large. The same people who brought us the Great Financial Crisis are now bringing us a world of Code Red policies and financial repression. The arsonists are running the fire brigade.

Where is the central banker who has apologized for contributing to the crisis or for being asleep at the wheel? Given how disastrous their performance has been, it is extraordinary that the same cast of characters is still running the show. Central bankers are lucky that they still have jobs. As far as we are aware, no central banker was fired for incompetence or mismanagement. Many have retired and are now enjoying generous pensions and highly paid consulting careers advising investment funds as to what their former colleagues might do next.

Central bankers have had plenty of time to discuss the financial crisis since 2008, but they have provided only scholarly disquisitions as to what went wrong in the banking crisis, without accepting any responsibility at all. At no time have any central bankers admitted that they might have ignored the warning signs of excessive debt, kept interest rates too low for too long, ignored bubbles in housing markets, failed to regulate banks correctly, or proved themselves even mildly incompetent.

Not only were central bankers not fired, many were promoted instead and given pay raises. Timothy Geithner, who headed the Federal Reserve Bank of New York, not only failed to regulate a host of banks that needed massive government bailouts but was an active apologist for Wall Street banks. For his efforts he was promoted to secretary of the Treasury under President Obama. In Europe, Spanish central bankers stand out as perhaps the most incompetent ever, having overseen dozens of banks that created the biggest housing bubble in European history and having failed to recognize problems not only before but after they happened. Bankers like Jose Viñals, Jose Caruana, and others were given plum jobs at the International Monetary Fund (IMF) and the ECB after being asleep at the wheel in Spain.

Perhaps the most egregious example of musical chairs and pay raises was the appointment of Mark Carney to be governor of the Bank of England. Carney was previously the head of the Bank of Canada, where he oversaw one of the bigger housing bubbles in recent memory. While Canadians pride themselves on being infinitely more prudent than their crazy neighbors to the south, Canada has to this day a bigger housing bubble, based on a wide variety of measures, than the United States had. You can see this in Figure 5.3. That bubble simply hasn't burst yet. Fortunately for Carney, he's getting a pay raise, moving on to the Bank of England, and leaving a bag filled with old garbage on his successor's doorstep.

The massively overvalued Canadian housing market may have popped by the time you read this, but Carney will be doing quite

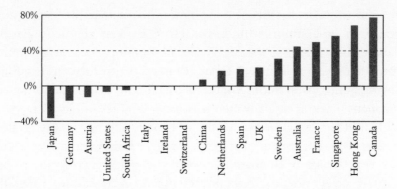

Figure 5.3 Forever Blowing Bubbles—Canada's Growing Housing Bubble
SOURCE: *The Economist*.

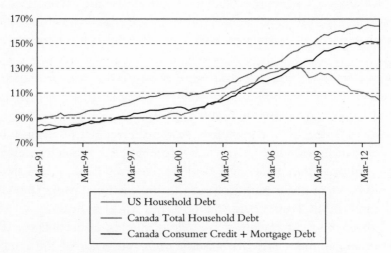

Figure 5.4 Canadian Debt vs. U.S. Debt
SOURCE: *Variant Perception*, Bloomberg.

well. The United Kingdom is facing government cutbacks, while
Carney managed to negotiate for himself a salary of $750,000 a year,
a $215,000 annual pension benefit, and a $385,000 a year rent subsidy.
The ex–Goldman Sachs banker's total pay will be about $1,355,000.
That is six times what the British prime minister gets paid. Damn, it
feels good to be a central banker!

Granting extra powers to central banks without a change in the philosophy behind their management is like encouraging an irresponsible teenager. Imagine your teenage son borrowed the family car and crashed it, and instead of punishing him you bought him a new Ferrari to test drive. Conventional monetary policies are like a sturdy old family station wagon, but Code Red policies are like a modified Ferrari 288 GTO capable of hitting 275 miles per hour. Given how spectacularly central banks failed during the Great Financial Crisis, it blows the mind that they've been handed the keys to a faster set of wheels.

One last thought: You might get from reading this that we are against rules and regulations. Far from it. We just like very simple, workable rules. Reinstate Glass-Steagall. Limit the ability of banks to create leverage, and require even more capital as they get larger. Banks that are systemically too big to fail are too big, period. Take away the incentive to grow beyond what is prudent for the deposit insurance scheme of a nation to maintain. Allowing bankers to take the profits and then hand taxpayers the losses in a crisis is not good policy, even if it is bolstered by 1,000 pages of regulations written by lawyers and bank lobbyists who then proceed to "massage" them in order to do what they want to anyway.

But, alas, such hopes may remain dreams deferred until there is yet another crisis and taxpayers are asked to absorb even greater losses (but we can always hope!). So, in the meantime, as prudent investors and managers, we must be aware of the realities we face. The saying in Africa is that it is not the lion you can see that is the danger; instead, it is the one hidden in the grass that leaps out at you as you try to escape the one you see. Later, we will talk about a few strategies that can help you handle the risks that crouch hidden in the grass.

Key Lessons from the Chapter

In this chapter we learned:

- The world is placing an enormous amount of trust in central bankers to get monetary policy right and do the right thing at the right time.
- Before the Great Financial Crisis, central bankers were held up as gurus and oracles by the press. In retrospect, that adoration was entirely misplaced.

- Central bankers almost everywhere failed to see the Great Financial Crisis coming, and many actively contributed to the crisis. Most notable among these was Chairman Greenspan, who provided too much liquidity to markets at the hint of any setback, yet didn't have a clue about bubbles.
- Central bankers have a dismal record at managing monetary policy even in the good times. It is hard to imagine they will do better in the difficult times just ahead, managing unconventional policy tools.
- Today, people trust central bankers less, but bizarrely, governments have given central bankers more power. More regulation is useless if the regulators fail to do their job.
- In a Code Red world, central bankers have more power than they have ever had. Unfortunately, the same cast of characters that helped cause the Great Financial Crisis is still running the show.

Chapter Six

Economists Are Clueless

Economists set themselves too easy, too useless a task if in tempestuous seasons they can only tell us that when the storm is past the ocean is flat again.

—John Maynard Keynes,
A Tract on Monetary Reform

There can be few fields of human endeavor in which history counts for so little as in the world of finance. Past experience, to the extent that it is part of memory at all, is dismissed as the primitive refuge of those who do not have insight to appreciate the incredible wonders of the present.

—John Kenneth Galbraith

Hitler must have been rather loosely educated, not having learned the lesson of Napoleon's autumn advance on Moscow.

—Sir Winston Churchill

In November 2008, as stock markets crashed around the world, the Queen of England visited the London School of Economics to open the New Academic Building. While she was there, she listened in on academic lectures. The Queen, who studiously avoids controversy and almost never lets people know what she's thinking, finally asked a simple question about the financial crisis, "How come nobody could foresee it?" No one could answer her.

If you suspected that mainstream economists are useless at the job of seeing a crisis in advance, you would be right. Dozens of studies show that economists are completely incapable of forecasting recessions. But forget forecasting. What's worse is that they fail miserably even at understanding where the economy is today. In one of the broadest studies of whether economists could predict recessions and financial crises, Prakash Loungani of the International Monetary Fund (IMF) wrote very starkly, "The record of failure to predict recessions is virtually unblemished." This was true not only for official organizations like the IMF, the World Bank, or government agencies but for private forecasters as well. They're all terrible. Loungani concluded that the "inability to predict recessions is a ubiquitous feature of growth forecasts." Most economists were not even able to recognize recessions once they had already started.

In plain English, economists don't have a clue about the future.

If you think the Fed or government agencies know what is going on with the economy, you're mistaken. Government economists are about as useful as a turd flavored lollipop. Their mistakes and failures are so spectacular you couldn't make them up if you tried. Yet now, in a Code Red world, we trust the same bankers to know where the economy is, where it is going, and how to manage monetary policy.

Central banks say that they will know when the time is right to end Code Red policies and when to shrink the bloated monetary base. But *how* will they know, given their record at forecasting? The Federal Reserve not only failed to predict the recessions of 1990, 2001, and 2007, it didn't even recognize them after they had *already begun*. Financial crises frequently happen because central banks cut interest rates too late and hike rates too soon.

Trusting central bankers now is a big bet that (1) they'll know what to do and (2) they'll know the right time to do it. Sadly, they generally don't have a clue about what is going on.

Unfortunately, the problem is not that economists are simply mediocre at what they do. The problem is that they're *really, really bad*. And they're so bad that their ineptitude cannot even be a matter of chance. As the statistician Nate Silver pointed out in his book *The Signal and the Noise*:

Indeed, economists have for a long time been much too confident in their ability to predict the direction of the economy. If economists' forecasts were as accurate as they claimed, we'd expect the actual value for GDP to fall within their prediction interval nine times out of ten, or all but about twice in eighteen years.

In fact, the actual value for GDP fell outside the economists' prediction interval six times in eighteen years, or fully one-third of the time. Another study, which ran these numbers back to the beginning of the Survey of Professional Forecasters in 1968, found even worse results: the actual figure for GDP fell outside the prediction interval almost *half* the time. There is almost no chance that economists have simply been unlucky; they fundamentally overstate the reliability of their predictions.

So it gets worse. Economists are not only generally wrong, they're extremely confident in their bad forecasts.

If economists were merely wrong at betting on horse races, their failure would be harmlessly amusing. But central bankers have the power to create money, change interest rates, and affect our lives in every way—and they don't have a clue.

Despite their cluelessness, there's no overestimating the hubris of central bankers. On *60 Minutes* in December 2010, Scott Pelley interviewed Chairman Ben Bernanke and asked him whether he would be able to do the right thing at the right time. The exchange was startling:

Pelley: Can you act quickly enough to prevent inflation from getting out of control?

Bernanke: We could raise interest rates in 15 minutes if we have to. So, there really is no problem with raising rates, tightening monetary policy, slowing the economy, reducing inflation, at the appropriate time. Now, that time is not now.

Pelley: You have what degree of confidence in your ability to control this?

Bernanke: One hundred percent.

There you have it. Bernanke was not 95 percent confident, he was not 99 percent confident—no, he had *zero* doubts about his ability to know what is going on in the economy and what to do about it. We would love to have that kind of certainty about anything in life.

We're not picking just on Bernanke; we're picking on all central bankers who think they're infallible. The Bank of England (BoE) has had by far the largest quantitative easing (QE) program relative to the size of its economy (though the Bank of Japan [BoJ] is about to show it a thing or two). It has also had the worst forecasting track record of any bank, and the worst record on inflation. Sir Mervyn King, the head of the BoE, was asked if it would be difficult to withdraw QE. He very confidently replied, "I have absolutely no doubt that when the time comes for us to reduce the size of our balance sheet that we'll find that a whole lot easier than we did when expanding it." (Are central bankers just naturally more arrogant than regular human beings, or are they smoking some powerful stuff at their meetings?)

Let's see whether this sort of absolute certainty is at all warranted.

In his book *Future Babble*, Dan Gardner wrote that economists are treated with the reverence the ancient Greeks accorded the Oracle of Delphi. But unlike the vague pronouncements from Delphi, economists' predictions can be checked against the future, and as Gardner says, "Anyone who does that will quickly conclude that economists make lousy soothsayers."

(As an aside, we suspect that economists may be the modern-day functional equivalent of tribal shamans. Instead of peering at the intestines of sheep to forecast the future, we look at data through the lenses of models we create, built with all our inherent biases, and then confidently predict the future or try to guide government policy in one direction or another, generally along paths that fit the predisposition of our immediate tribe. The most brazen of us move in and out of favor depending on whether we are telling our fellow tribe members and leaders and potential leaders what they want to hear. It may be that economics is more like religion and less like science than most of us want to admit.)

The nearsightedness of economists is nothing new. In 1994, Paul Ormerod wrote a book called *The Death of Economics*. He pointed to economists' failure to forecast the Japanese recession after their bubble burst in 1989 or to foresee the collapse of the European Exchange Rate Mechanism in 1992. Ormerod was scathing in his assessment of economists: "The ability of orthodox economics to understand the workings of the economy at the overall level is manifestly weak (some would say it was entirely non-existent)."

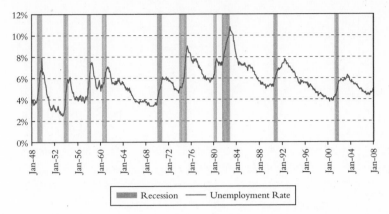

Figure 6.1 Recessions Lead to Falls in GDP and Spikes in the
Unemployment Rate
SOURCE: *Variant Perception*, Bloomberg.

When people think of economic forecasts, they almost always
think of recessions, while economists think of forecasting growth
rates or interest rates. But the average person in the street only wants
to know, "Will we be in a recession soon?"—and if the economy is
already in a recession, he or she wants to know, "When will it end?"
The reason most working Americans care is that they know recessions
mean job cuts and firings You can see in Figure 6.1 that whenever
recessions happen, there is a large surge in initial unemployment claims
as companies fire workers.

Unfortunately, economists are of no use to the man or woman in the
street. If you look at the history of the last three recessions in the United
States, you will see that the inability of economists and central bankers
to understand the state of the economy was so bad that you might be
tempted to say they couldn't find their derrieres with both hands.

Let's remind ourselves what a recession is and how economists
decide that one has started. A recession is a downturn in economic
activity. Normally, a recession means unemployment goes up, gross
domestic product (GDP) contracts, stock prices fall, and the economy
weakens. The lofty body that decides when a recession has started or
ended is the Business Cycle Dating Committee of the National Bureau
of Economic Research (NBER). It is packed with eminent economists
and other extremely smart people. Unfortunately, their pronouncements are completely unusable in real time. Their dating of recessions

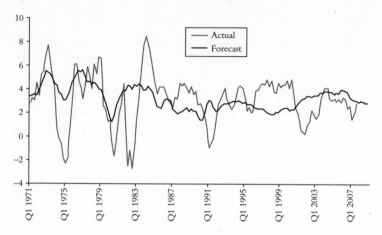

Figure 6.2 Economists Have Never Predicted a Recession Correctly
SOURCE: Societe Generale Equity Research.

is authoritative and more or less accurate, but this exercise in hindsight comes together long after a recession has started or ended.

To give you an idea just how late recessions are officially called, let's look at the past three. The NBER dated the 1990–1991 recession as beginning in August 1990 and ending in March 1991. It announced these facts in April 1991, by which time the recession was already over and the economy was growing again. The NBER was no faster catching up with the recession that followed the dot-com bust. It wasn't until June 2003 that the NBER pinpointed the 2001 recession—a full 28 months after the recession ended. The NBER didn't date the recession that started in December 2007 until exactly one year later. By that time, Lehman had gone bust, and the world was engulfed in the biggest financial cataclysm since the Great Depression.

The Federal Reserve and private economists also missed the onset of the last three recessions—even after they had started. Let's look quickly at each one.

Starting with the 1990–1991 recession, let's see what the head of the Federal Reserve—the man who is charged with running American monetary policy—was saying at the time. That recession started in August 1990, but one month before it began, Alan Greenspan said, "In the very near term there's little evidence that I can see to suggest the economy is tilting over [into recession]." The following month—the month the recession actually started—he continued on the same theme: ". . . those who argue that we are already in a recession I think are reasonably certain to be wrong." He was just as clueless two months later in October 1990, when he persisted, ". . . the economy has not yet slipped into recession." It was only near the end of the recession that Greenspan came around to accepting and acknowledging that it had begun.

The Federal Reserve did no better in the dot-com bust. Let's look at the facts. The recession started in March 2001. The tech-heavy Nasdaq Index had already fallen 50 percent in a full-scale bust. Even so, Chairman Greenspan declared before the Economic Club of New York on May 24, 2001, "Moreover, with all our concerns about the next several quarters, there is still, in my judgment, ample evidence that we are experiencing only a pause in the investment in a broad set of innovations that has elevated the underlying growth rate in productivity to a level significantly above that of the two decades preceding 1995."

Charles Morris, a retired banker and financial writer, looked at a decade's worth of forecasts by the geniuses at the White House's Council of Economic Advisers. In 2000, the council raised their growth estimates just in time for the dot-com bust and the recession of 2001–2002. In a survey conducted in March 2001, 95 percent of American economists said there would not be a recession. The recession had already started that March, and the signs of contraction were evident. Industrial production had already been contracting for five months.

You would have thought that their failure to forecast two recessions in a row might have sharpened the wits of the Federal Reserve, the Council of Economic Advisers, and private economists. Maybe they would have tried to improve their methods or figured out why they had failed so miserably. You would be wrong. Because along came the Great Recession, and—once again—they completely missed the boat.

Let's look at what the Fed was doing as the world was about to go up in flames in 2008. Recently, complete minutes of the Fed's October 2007 meeting were released. Keep in mind that the recession started two months later, in December 2007. The minutes make for depressing reading. The word *recession* does not appear once in the entire transcript.

It gets worse. The month the recession started, the Federal Reserve was all optimistic laughter. Dr. David Stockton, the Federal Reserve chief economist, presented his view to Chairman Bernanke and the meeting of the Federal Open Market Committee on December 11, 2007.

When you read the following quote and choke on your breakfast or lunch, remember that at the time the Fed was already providing ample liquidity to the shadow banking system after dozens of subprime lenders had gone bust in the spring, the British bank Northern Rock had been nationalized and spooked the European banking system, dozens of money market funds had been shut due to toxic assets, credit spreads were widening, stock prices had started to fall, and almost all the classic signs of a recession were evident. These included an inverted yield curve, which had received the casual attention of New York Fed economists even as it screamed recession. (John had pointed to it numerous times in *Thoughts from the Frontline*.)

Read these words of the Fed's chief economist and weep. You can't make this stuff up.

> Overall, our forecast could admittedly be read as still painting a pretty benign picture: Despite all the financial turmoil, the economy avoids recession and, even with steeply higher prices for food and energy and a lower exchange value of the dollar, we achieve some modest edging-off of inflation. So I tried not to take it personally when I received a notice the other day that the Board had approved more frequent drug-testing for certain members of the senior staff, myself included. [Laughter] I can assure you, however, that the staff is not going to fall back on the increasingly popular celebrity excuse that we were under the influence of mind-altering chemicals and thus should not be held responsible for this forecast. No, we came up with this projection unimpaired and on nothing stronger than many late nights of diet Pepsi and vending-machine Twinkies.

We do not want to pick on Dr. Stockton unnecessarily, as all other government economists were equally awful. The President's Council of Economic Advisers' 2008 forecast saw positive growth for the first half of the year and foresaw a strong recovery in the second half.

Unfortunately, private-sector economists didn't do much better. With very few exceptions, they failed to foresee the financial and economic meltdown of 2008. Economists polled in the Survey of Professional Forecasters also failed to see a recession developing. They forecasted a slightly below-average rate of 2.4 percent for 2008, and they thought there was almost no chance of a recession as severe as the one that actually unfolded. In December 2007 a *Business Week* survey showed that every single one of 54 economists predicted the U.S. economy would avoid a recession in 2008. The experts were unanimous that unemployment wouldn't be a problem, leading to the consensus conclusion that 2008 would be a good year.

As Nate Silver has pointed out, the worst thing about the bad predictions isn't that they were awful; it's that the economists in question were so confident in them:

> This was a very bad forecast: GDP actually *shrank* by 3.3% once the financial crisis hit. What may be worse is that the economists were extremely confident in their bad prediction. They assigned only a 3% chance to the economy's shrinking by any margin over the whole of 2008. And they gave it only about a 1-in-500 chance of shrinking by 2 percent, as it did.

It is one thing to be wrong. It is quite another to be consistently and confidently and egregiously wrong.

As the global financial meltdown unfolded, Chairman Bernanke, too, continued to believe that the United States would avoid a recession. Mind you, the recession had started in December 2007, yet in January 2008 Bernanke told the press, "The Federal Reserve is not currently forecasting a recession." Even after banks like Bear Stearns needed to be rescued, Bernanke continued seeing rainbows and candy-colored elves ahead for the U.S. economy. He declared on June 9, 2008, "The risk that the economy has entered a substantial downturn appears to have diminished over the past month or so." At that stage, the economy had already been in a recession for the past six months!

Why do people listen to economists anymore? Scott Armstrong, an expert on forecasting at the Wharton School of the University of Pennsylvania, has developed a "seer-sucker" theory: "No matter how much evidence exists that seers do not exist, suckers will pay for the existence of seers." Even if experts fail repeatedly in their predictions, most people prefer to have seers, prophets, and gurus with titles after their names tell them something—anything at all—about the future.

So, we have cataloged the incredible failures of economists to predict the future or even to understand the present. Now, with their record in mind, think of the vast powers Fed economists have to print money and move interest rates. When you contemplate the consummate skill that would actually be required to manage Code Red policies, you realize they're really just flying blind. If that doesn't scare the living daylights out of you, you haven't understood this chapter so far.

Assume a Perfect World

The great Harvard statistician George Box once said, "All models are false but some are useful."

Your authors are not against models. We use them constantly in our day (and night) jobs. But as Clint Eastwood's character Dirty Harry said, "A man's got to know his limitations." We would paraphrase that to read, "An economist has to know the limitations of his models."

One of our favorite central bankers (yes, we really are true fans of several), Richard Fisher of the Dallas Fed, offered the following story in a recent speech. He was leading up to making a forecast, but only after he explained "Arrow's Caveat," which derives from the experience of Ken Arrow, one of the greatest economists of the last century.

> During World War II, future Nobel laureate Ken Arrow served as a weather officer in the Army Air Corps. He and his team were charged with producing month-ahead weather forecasts. Being a disciplined analyst, Arrow reviewed the record of his predictions and, sure enough, confirmed statistically that the corps' forecasts were no more accurate than random rolls of dice. He asked to be relieved of this futile duty. Arrow's recollection of the response from on high was priceless: "The commanding general is well aware that the forecasts are no good. However, he needs them for planning purposes."

As an investor and in your business, you are confronted with economic models every day and asked to make decisions based on what you are shown. You want something to help guide you so, you turn to models. Let's take a few pages to look at how economic models are constructed. (In the last part of the book, we offer a way to reduce reliance on the predictive role of models.)

A good way to lead off the discussion is to start with the oldest joke about economists:

> An engineer, a chemist, and an economist are stranded on a deserted island. They are starving, when miraculously they find a box filled with canned food. What to do? They consider the problem, bringing their collective lifetimes of study and discipline to the task.
>
> Being the practical, straightforward sort, the engineer suggests that they simply find a rock and hit the cans until they break open. "No, no!" cry the chemist and economist, "we would spill too much food and the birds would get it!"
>
> After a bit of thought, the chemist recommends that they start a fire and heat the cans. The pressure in the cans will force them open and the food will conveniently already be heated. But the engineer and economist object, pointing out correctly that the cans would likely explode and splatter the food all over the beach.
>
> The economist, after carefully studying the cans and reading the labels, starts scrawling a series of equations in the sand, which eventually cover the entire beach. After much pondering, he excitedly announces, "I've got it! I've got it!," as he points to the final equation. They ask him to explain, with their visions of finally getting a meal inspiring them to regard the economist with a new sense of respect.
>
> The economist clears his throat and begins, "First, assume a can opener . . ."

We are not sure how old that joke is, but it dates to about the time when economists discovered mathematics and models, which is to say, about the time when economists developed physics envy and decided they would like to be regarded as scientists rather than philosophers.

Like our castaways with their abundance of canned food but no can opener, economists, whether they are forecasting the growth of an economy or the budget of a government, are faced with the problem of predicting the fiscal future of very large, very real economic systems, but without a crystal ball. And as we saw earlier, economists are not particularly good at telling us what happened in the year that just passed, let alone in the year to come. (And we often see national budgets that presume to extend out for 10 years or more.)

To discuss the limitations of models and why they are often so wrong, we are going to analyze recent U.S. government projections of the budget, something that should be far simpler and more straightforward than forecasting the trajectory of an economy. But, as we will see, the results are the same.

The basic challenge is pretty simple. There is a need to forecast revenues and expenses. We get that. You can't just vote to tax and spend without having some idea about what you are voting on will cost. So government officials ask economists to make projections.

Expenses are the more straightforward of the two. Most government expenses are line items in a budget. "We project we will spend $5 billion a year fixing roads and bridges, $1 billion on our national parks, $925 billion on defense, etc." Social Security, too, is straightforward. Health care involves a lot of guesstimates, and unemployment costs go up and down with the economy.

Revenues are a bit trickier. Income tax revenues obviously go up and down with incomes, as do corporate taxes and Social Security and Medicare taxes. If there is a recession, revenues will fall. If you get an economic boom, then revenues could turn out better than projected. In the middle of the past decade, John predicted a Muddle Through Economy, which to him meant 2 percent GDP growth, down from the average of 3 percent we had experienced for decades. Two percent turns out to have been slightly optimistic, although it once sounded so bearish. We would be very happy if we could manage 2 percent average growth for the current decade. There are several respected forecasters, including Jeremy Grantham and Robert Gordon, who think 1 percent (or less!) is more likely.

In 2012 we were at a real inflation-adjusted growth rate of 1.7 percent. The first quarter of 2013 saw a 1.8 percent annual growth rate. Nominal growth of 3.5 percent for 2012 was the lowest since the end of WWII. So what do our intrepid budget forecasters predict for the next 10 years? Not content to project that current trends will persist, they have whipped on their rose-colored glasses to deliver us bright promises of spectacular growth.

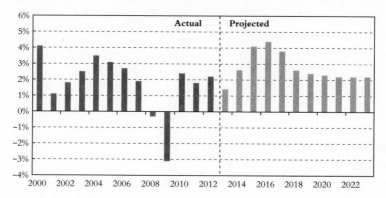

Figure 6.3   CBO GDP Growth Assumptions
SOURCE: Congressional Budget Office.

David Malpass wrote in the *Wall Street Journal* that Obama's 2013 budget projections make a prediction of 3.6 percent growth by 2016, with tax revenues up by 50 percent. But the Obama administration may seem to be conservative by comparison if we look at the projections of the Congressional Budget Office (CBO).

Figure 6.3 is from work done by Veronique de Rugy. It shows that the CBO projects that growth in 2013 will slow to 1.4 percent and then *triple* to 4.2 percent over the next three years! For the years 2015 to 2017, economists at the CBO project the U.S. GDP to grow 4 percent annually on average. And that is real growth they're foreseeing, not nominal growth. Note that we have to go back to the 1960s to find a period where GDP grew by 4 percent for three years running!

We read that and went straight to the latest CBO report to check. But there on page 40 and following were the actual numbers. Who could have guessed the mind-bending power of those vending-machine Twinkies?

Figure 6.4 is from page 41 of that 77-page report, which contains extensive details as to how they arrive at their various expense and revenue projections. I should note that they are consistent in that they do not project low interest rates during their predicted economic boom of the next several years. The Obama administration, however, assumes in their budget proposal that interest rates will be only 1.2 percent in 2016, to accompany their 3.6 percent growth rate (with inflation of

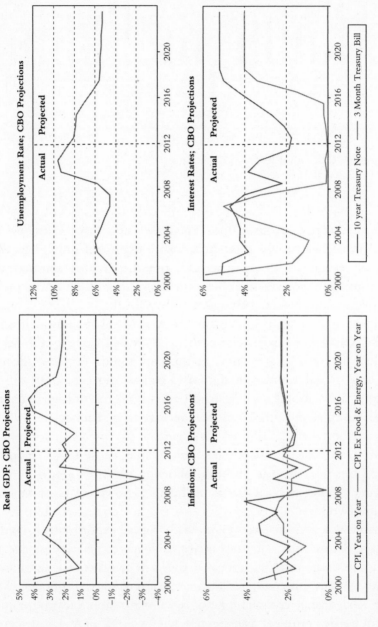

Figure 6.4 Actual Values and CBO Projections

only 2.2 percent). Now *that* would be a very accommodative Federal Reserve. (We wonder if President Obama will share that projection with his future appointment to replace Ben Bernanke and, if so, what the reaction of that nominee might be? *That* would make for interesting conversation!)

Either way, interest costs are projected to rise dramatically as the decade progresses, more than doubling in real terms. In nominal terms, interest-rate costs are expected to increase almost *fourfold*, from a current $224 billion to a projected $857 billion! That means interest rate costs are projected to grow to *roughly* 16 percent of the federal budget within this decade (back-of-the-napkin estimate).

The increase in debt (in dollar terms), along with an anticipated substantial rise in interest rates as the economy strengthens, is expected to sharply boost interest payments on the debt. The CBO projects that, under current law, the government's yearly net interest spending will double as a share of GDP—from 1.5 percent in 2014 to 3.3 percent in 2023, a percentage that has been exceeded only once in the past 50 years, according to the CBO.

We should note that both the CBO's and the Obama administration's assumptions are much more optimistic than those of Federal Reserve economists (to the extent that they make projections). And the track record of the Fed is that, on average, they have projected 2.1 percent more GDP growth than has actually occurred, just one year out.

Philippa Dunne and Doug Henwood of *The Liscio Report* supplied that surprising figure, and continued on with this comment:

> What does this mean for the future? Since the timing of the withdrawal of ease is highly dependent on these major economic indicators, we should take the Fed's forecasts of their future course skeptically. Given the demonstrated difficulties they have forecasting a year or less ahead, forecasts two years or more in the future seem especially questionable. (Corroborating a remark from a CBO official we relayed back in 2007 that forecasting out even two years is a waste of time.) Since so many forecasts tend to be extrapolations of the present and recent past, the timing of QE withdrawal is likely to be more dependent on the real-time trajectory of major economic indicators than on imagined futures.

Objects in the Rearview Mirror Are
Larger than They Appear

Optimistic GDP projections mean that whatever revenue projections accompany them are also likely to be overly optimistic. Given the federal government's lack of control over expenses and its track record in forecasting expenses, it is likely that expenses will be underestimated, making actual deficits larger than they expect. One example: we have already seen Obamacare costs rise by over 40 percent from the projections just two years ago.

But don't think that is true just for programs backed by liberals. Defense cost overruns are legendary. And farm bills always cost more than projected and benefit ever fewer farmers. Figure 6.5 from Veronique de Rugy gives us the dismal news about recent farm bills. Of course, the same guys who got it wrong before are once again telling us that the costs will be as projected, based on their models.

Now let's get to the meat of the problem. Look at Figure 6.6. Notice the shaded gray areas. Those are recessions. Now notice that there is not one decade without a recession, and most have two. Obama, the Senate, and the House all assume that we have vanquished

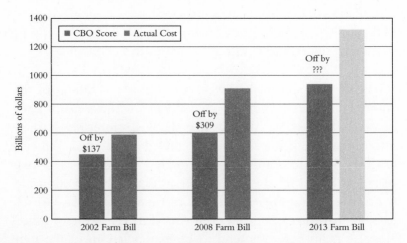

Figure 6.5   Actual vs. Scored Cost of Farm Bills
SOURCE: Congressional Budget Office data via Taxpayers for Common Sense, www.taxpayers.net.
Produced by Veronique de Rugy, Mercatus Center at George Mason University.

the recession virus and will not experience that economic malady again in our near future.

Can we get any of our readers to make a wager with us that the United States will somehow get through the rest of this decade without a recession? Anyone? We thought not.

But that is exactly the wager that Congress and Obama are making with your tax dollars or the Fed is making with its projections. Their budgets show expenses rising for the next 10 years. And if we get a recession they will want to run even larger deficits. Their argument will be that we can't possibly cut the fiscal deficit during a recession—that would make things even worse! Austerity doesn't work; we all know that.

What happens if we do get a recession? Revenues go down, of course. Unemployment goes up, as do associated costs like unemployment checks.

Note the graph in Figure 6.6. CBO forecasters assume that GDP will recover back to its former trend line instead of simply growing from a lower base, and that is where they get their obscenely rosy back-to-back-to-back 4 percent increases.

And that is the problem. We keep using the word *assume*. And then we create models based on our generally rosy assumptions.

What happens if we land in a recession instead? Not only do we not get back to that trend, but we drift farther from it! Will the CBO

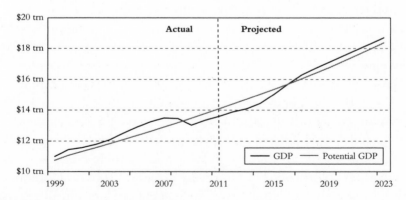

Figure 6.6   CBO GDP Gap Assumptions
SOURCE: Congressional Budget Office, *The Budget and Economic Outlook, FY 2013 to 2023*. OMB Historical Tables.

then project 5 percent GDP growth for three years running to get us back to the original trend? That would be no more or less absurd than what they are doing now.

The reality is that no politician or government agency can forecast a recession (unless, as in 2012, they are arguing against a sequestration that is projected to actually cut spending). None of us really know when the next recession will happen. Theoretically, we could go another 10 years without one. It is also possible that the government will reveal that there really are aliens in Area 51. We leave it to you to decide which is more likely.

While acknowledging that forecasting a recession is impossible and politically a nonstarter, it would be nice if forecasters and politicians were to admit the possibility of lower-than-estimated revenues and willingly contemplate what might happen if a recession did transpire. As the United States approaches a truly debilitating debt level, we want to ask them, "Will you please tell us what the plan is if we experience recession rather than expansion?"

We can hear the answer now: "I don't want to speculate about possible recessions. That is pointless." But our rejoinder would be, "You are perfectly willing to speculate that we will have no recession and that we will grow at a rate not seen in over 40 years, not even during the Reagan and Clinton boom years. How speculative is that?" (Where is Nixon when we need him? Or was the growth during his reign a legacy from Kennedy and Johnson? Or was it just American productivity?)

Budget forecasts are generally useless. A politician wants to enact a certain deficit-reduction policy. He wants to make assumptions that work to his benefit. So he calls in his friendly local economist, who obligingly responds, "You need 4 percent growth to make this work? No problem. Here's the data and math to back up those assumptions."

The CBO is supposed to be politically neutral. And it is: those 4 percent projections it came up with are good for *both* parties. If it were to project a 2 percent real GDP growth for the next eight years, the agency would be disbanded. And gods forbid it pull a Jeremy Grantham or (Northwestern University professor) Robert Gordon and project 1 percent. Or a Bill Gross, at 1.5 percent. Spin up the models with those low growth expectations, and the CBO's projected budget deficits get blown sky-high, projected new expenditures seem just a tad extreme, and those tax cuts they're talking about will be much more difficult to budget.

Government economists would like to assume a perfect world—a world unperturbed by recessions and blessed instead with unprecedented and endless growth, a world of unruffled peace where deficits and unemployment fall hand in hand over time, where interests rates bend to economists' desires, and tax revenues obligingly rise year by year even though government spending takes a huge chunk out of the economy, and on and on.

It's not easy being an economist. It is absolutely necessary that we make forecasts as part of a responsible approach to government spending, but we need to be more skeptical of those forecasts and use some common sense in our budgets in order to allow for a rainy day here and there.

Liberal-socialist Sweden allows its pensions to rise and fall with GDP to keep from blowing out their budget process. They made that hard choice in the midst of a credit crisis. Perhaps we, too, in the rest of the developed world should make a hard choice now, in order to make sure that we don't precipitate a major crisis of our own.

Waiting for our unrealistically rosy forecasts to be proven wrong before we adopt yet another "solution" (based on what will almost inevitably turn out to be yet another temporary fix of yet another faulty forecast) just doesn't work. It is no way to run a railroad unless you want your train running off a cliff.

The Definition of Insanity

Given the dismal failure of the Federal Reserve to anticipate the course of the economy, you might think they would begin to wonder about their own models. Nothing could be further from the truth.

Economic models are playing an ever more important part in the Federal Reserve's policy making. For example, the Fed announced in December 2012 that it would keep short-term interest rates near zero until the unemployment rate falls to 6.5 percent and inflation is tame. In order to predict the effects of their monetary policy, the Fed relies on complex financial models.

The economists at the Fed have given their financial models names like Ferbus, Edo, and Sigma. These computer models are incredibly complicated and incorporate hundreds of variables. Ask Fed economists about them, and they'll tell you they're using Bayesian vector autoregressive systems and dynamic stochastic general equilibrium models in high-dimensional systems. Never mind all that. Judging by past successes, the models can't fight their way out of a wet paper bag, much less tell us what we need to know in order to formulate intelligent policy.

If you're wondering what tools the Fed might have at its disposal to enable it to foresee where employment and inflation will go in the future, when to tighten monetary policy, and when and how to exit Code Red policies, look no further than these fancy models. As Jon Hilsenrath of the *Wall Street Journal* explains, "The fingerprints of Ferbus and its friends are all over the Fed's latest interest-rate decisions. In two important speeches this year, Fed Vice Chairwoman Janet Yellen described in detail how she and Fed staff used the models to gauge how long interest rates could remain low without generating too much inflation." Are you feeling reassured?

One of the biggest problems is that the models aren't very interested in history or empiricism. They aren't interested in how the economy *actually* works. They're dependent instead on theories about how the economy is *supposed* to work, which require big assumptions. This reminds us of yet another economist joke. Do you know what an economist does when he falls down a well? First, he assumes a ladder.

Given how poorly their models performed in the last recession, you might think the Fed would chuck them out and find new ones, but you would be wrong. In a speech at Princeton University, where he was a professor for two decades, Bernanke defended the Fed's failed models. He said, "Although economists have much to learn from this crisis . . . calls for a radical reworking of the field go too far."

Albert Einstein once said the definition of insanity is trying the same thing over and over again and expecting different results. We might thus have to conclude that our central banks are insane.

Using Leading Indicators

Why are economists so bad at forecasting upturns and downturns in the economy? They're all extremely smart, have PhDs from prestigious universities, and are generally decent, honest people trying to do their job well. Something more systematic and profound must be behind their complete failure to understand the direction of economic growth.

One of the main reasons that economists have no clue about the direction of the economy is that turning points are hard to predict, and so forecasters generally just extrapolate current trends. They tend to rely heavily on the persistence of trends in spending, output, and the price level. If you want to see how economists think, just look at Figure 6.7. For example, in the January 2006 Fed meeting, Donald Kohn gave us a priceless insight into how the Fed thinks about the economy. Defending his optimism, Kohn enlightened his colleagues: "My forecasts for 2006 are very close to those I submitted last January and June. That's partly a product of innate stubbornness."

Despite the difficulty in identifying turning points in the economic cycle, it is possible to forecast the direction of growth. Economists miss turning points for two main reasons: (1) they focus on the wrong

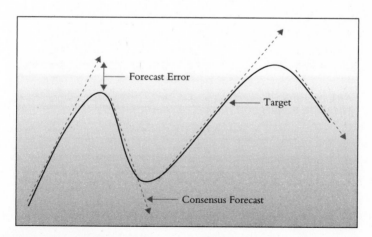

Figure 6.7   Turning Points Are Hard to Predict
SOURCE: *Variant Perception*, Bloomberg.

things, and (2) they rely on incomplete data that is later revised. The good news is that it is possible to overcome both problems.

Many economists and politicians look at economic data as a big jumble of numbers that get reported each month. Sometimes that jumble proves too much, and it all seems to be noise. However, there is always order in the data.

Broadly speaking, economic data fall into three categories: leading, coincident, and lagging (see Figure 6.8). The best way to understand the economy is to think of it as a car going down the road. Lagging indicators tell you where the car has been. Looking at them is like looking in the rearview mirror. Coincident indicators tell you about the present. Looking at them is like looking out your side windows. They tell you where you are right now. But not all economic data are created equal: the most useful indicators are leading indicators. These show you the often twisty, sometimes pothole-riddled road ahead. Unfortunately, most central bankers spend all their time looking in the rearview mirror and pay scant attention to the road ahead. (Just imagine trying to drive a car that way. Where do you think you would end up?)

Let's think intuitively about how the economy works. The Federal Reserve targets inflation and jobs. But both of these indicators, as

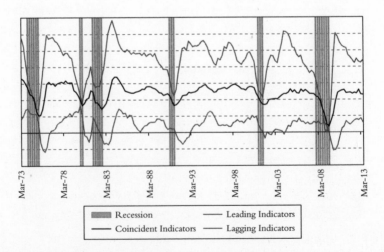

Figure 6.8   Leading, Coincident, and Lagging Indicators
Source: *Variant Perception*, Bloomberg.

measured, can tell you only about the past, not the future. If you run a factory, you don't fire workers just because you have one or two months of bad sales; you wait until you're very sure that the economy is not doing well before you take that measure. Otherwise, you might have to rehire the same workers again. It costs money, takes time, and creates ill will to fire and rehire people. Likewise, if you look at inflation, supermarket managers do not raise prices just because sales are good one month. They wait until they are very sure that demand is strong and sustained before they decide to pass on higher prices. Repricing products is a chore, and if you raise prices prematurely, you might have to lower them again quickly, which is time-consuming and expensive.

Now that we've done our little thought experiment, you will not be surprised to learn that unemployment and inflation are two of the most lagging economic indicators around. They tell you about where the economy was, not where it is going. In fact, they are usually contrary indicators. By focusing intently on two of the most lagging indicators, central banks attempt to drive by looking in the rearview mirror. Believe it or not, the unemployment rate is usually at its lowest level when a recession is starting. And inflation usually peaks in a recession and troughs in expansion.

Some things, however, do provide a good advance view of economic activity with a very long lead. Building permits are the longest, most reliable leading indicator of economic activity. Think about it logically: if you get a permit to build a house, then within a few weeks you hire builders, who turn up, work on the house anywhere from a few months to a couple of years until the house is finished; and then you have to buy furniture, appliances, and other home goods. Building has a huge positive knock-on effect on many other parts of the economy. Knowing whether building permits are rising or falling gives you a pretty good advance read on where the economy is going. Changes in building permits have led every economic cycle over the past 70 years. You can see this relationship clearly in Figure 6.9. So how is it that the Federal Reserve failed to foresee the serious knock-on effects that the bursting of the housing bubble would inevitably have on the rest of the economy? The lapse boggles the mind.

While central banks focus on fancy models that don't work, leading economic indicators like building permits, growth in the money supply,

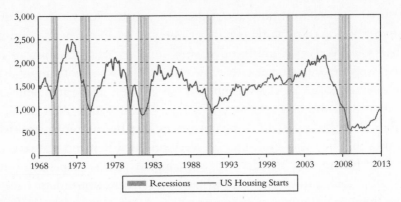

Figure 6.9 Housing Starts vs. Recessions (vertical bars indicate recessions) (value in thousands)
SOURCE: *Variant Perception*, Bloomberg.

average hours worked, and the yield curve all tell us things about the future. (Fed researchers have written extensively on the yield curve, only to ignore it or to then dismiss their own work.) These leading economic indicators are the most useful, and they are generally ignored. Investors who focus on them will find themselves ahead of the game.

The sad thing is that almost all the work done to understand leading, coincident, and lagging data has been around for decades. Indeed, it was in 1938 that NBER researchers Arthur Bums and Wesley Mitchell initially proposed and developed their system of coincident, leading, and lagging indicators that to this day is still published by the U.S. Department of Commerce to this day.

Anyone can find the leading economic indicators on the Web (the Federal Reserve Bank of St. Louis even hosts them!), and the Federal Reserve has access to them but seems to pay almost no attention. Before every single recession, leading economic indicators were negative and had turned down sharply. Yet every time, the Federal Reserve staff failed to see the recession looming ahead.

Making Decisions in Real Time

The dirty little secret as to why economists are so bad at forecasting the future is that they systematically rely on data useless for that purpose. They rely on old or "vintage" data. If you have the wrong data, you can't make decisions in real time.

Almost all economic data series are revised. The revisions happen 3, 6, or even 12 months after the data is initially published; and some data series are changed years later. For some series the updates are very small, but for others the changes are huge. The biggest changes are for employment and GDP. The worst news is that the revisions tend to be the largest at turning points. If you're a central banker or an investor who is relying on accurate data to make decisions, you're screwed if you rely on official estimates. We find the obsession with the release of the unemployment data on the first Friday of each month to be humorous in a macabre sort of way. People who trade on such data, which is subject to huge revisions, deserve any losses they incur.

For a perfect example of just how far off initial estimates for growth have been, let's look at the last recession. When Lehman Brothers went bust and the U.S. economy experienced a sharp contraction, the initial estimate of GDP growth for the last quarter of 2008 indicated that it had fallen 3.8 percent (annualized). But when Fed economists revised the GDP figure, it turned out to have fallen a whopping 9 percent (on an annualized basis—see Figure 6.10). In other words, the data the Federal Reserve relies on are not only inaccurate at turning points, but they are wildly inaccurate.

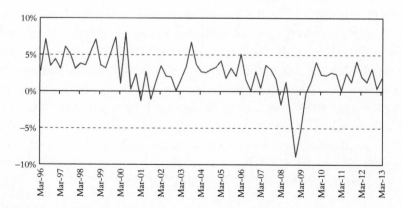

Figure 6.10 U.S. Real GDP Growth
SOURCE: *Variant Perception*, Bloomberg.

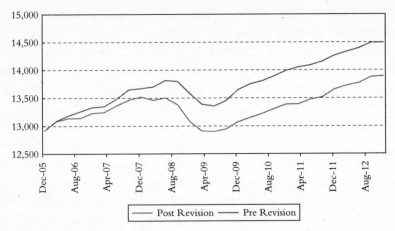

Figure 6.11   GDP Estimates before and after Revisions ($ in billions)
SOURCE: *Variant Perception*, Bloomberg.

Over the past 40 years, initial estimates of quarterly GDP were eventually revised an average of 1.7 percent. That's an enormous revision. You can see just how big the revisions are in Figure 6.11. In practice, that means it's likely that the economy could have been in a *recession* even as the initial GDP data was reporting *growth*. As an investor, you would have traded on the economic data very differently if you had known the final number.

Let's look at how data revisions work in practice.

Do you remember the slogan of President Clinton's successful 1992 campaign, "It's the economy, stupid"? It is one of the most memorable phrases trotted out in any campaign, and it really resonated with voters. During the Gulf War in 1990–1991, George H. W. Bush was wildly popular, with over 90 percent approval ratings; but less than a year later, the electorate voted him out of office. The recession that happened on Bush's watch most likely cost him reelection. ("Read my lips" didn't help either!)

In the popular imagination, the United States was mired in a deep recession during the 1992 election. As Professor James Hamilton wrote in a paper titled "Calling Recessions in Real Time":

In the October 13, 1992 debates, then vice-presidential-candidate
Al Gore referred to the "worst economic performance since

the Great Depression." Although the recession of 1990–91 is now seen as one of the shortest and mildest of the postwar recessions, it was not until December 22, 1992—after the presidential elections—that the NBER announced that the recession had actually ended in March of 1991. If it had been the case that the recession that began in August 1990 was still ongoing as of October 1992, Gore's statement would have factual support in the sense that the ongoing recession would have been the longest on record since 1933.

Even President Bush was worried about the economy and begged the Fed to lower interest rates. But just as the recession had started before anyone realized, it was in fact over before any economists knew it.

This is a classic vintage data problem. The information that economists had at hand in July 1991 was simply wrong. Economic growth appeared weak in 1990, and it looked as if the downturn had not begun until the fourth quarter of that year and had lasted only two quarters.

But a year later the government produced revised data that showed a different picture. The updated numbers indicated that the recession had begun in the third quarter of 1990 and had continued through the first quarter of 1991. That is a very different picture of economic activity. You can see the huge changes to the data from Figures 6.12 and 6.13.

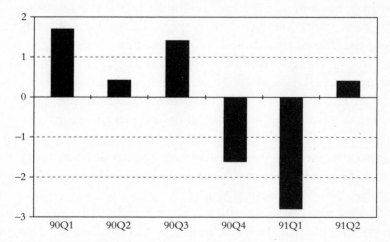

Figure 6.12   Initial Estimates of 1990–1991 GDP Growth
SOURCE: *Variant Perception*, Bloomberg.

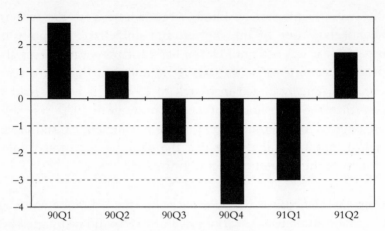

Figure 6.13 Revised Estimates of 1990–1991 GDP Growth
SOURCE: *Variant Perception*, Bloomberg.

Not only did the downturn happen earlier than economists thought, the upturn came earlier as well. By October 1992, when President Bush ran for reelection against Bill Clinton, the economy was 18 months into a recovery. But as *Investor's Business Daily* noted at the time, 90 percent of newspaper stories on the economy were negative. The popular press produced a steady stream of doomsday economic coverage, including a stark black September 1992 *Time* magazine cover that asked, "The Economy: Is there light at the end of the tunnel?" *Time* could not have got the timing more wrong. As it turned out, 1992 was a great year for the U.S. economy, and GDP actually grew 4.2 percent in the fourth quarter that year. For the whole year, GDP growth was strong, at 3.4 percent. Yet the Fed and most economists missed the growth as it was happening.

If doctors were as slow to diagnose diseases as economists are to diagnose recessions, they would be able to tell you that you were sick only when you were already dead.

We can hear many of you asking the right questions: If almost all economic data gets revised later, how can you know in real time what is actually happening in the economy? How can you avoid the vintage data problem? The key to making decisions in real time as an economist, investor, or policy maker is to use unrevised data and prices that are not subject to change. For example, everything from mortgage bonds to corporate bonds to stock prices contains reliable clues about the future. You can find their prices and yields in the newspaper every day. The prices are never revised three months or a year or even two years later. With prices, what you see is what you get.

Have you ever watched a movie where the hero travels *back* in time to find out what will happen in the *future?* We thought not. We can't either. With the economy, you don't need a time machine. By far the best real-time predictor of economic activity is the yield curve. The yield curve is the spread between bond yields for shorter-dated and longer-dated government bonds. For example, traders generally look at the 2-year note versus the 10-year note or the 3-month Treasury bill versus the 10-year note. In normal times, the yields for longer-dated bonds are always higher than for shorter-dated bonds. However, before recessions, the yield curve inverts, and shorter-dated bonds have higher yields than longer-dated ones. Believe it or not, a yield-curve inversion has preceded each recession since the mid-1960s (with the exception of one inversion that preceded a significant slowdown).

Although the original work on the yield curve was done by Professor Campbell Harvey of Duke, a couple of Bernanke's colleagues at the Fed, Frederic Mishkin and Arturo Estrella, produced one of the best studies of the yield curve. The Federal Reserve Bank of New York published their research. They didn't mince words:

> The yield curve—specifically, the spread between the interest rates on the ten-year Treasury note and the three-month Treasury bill—is a valuable forecasting tool. It is simple to use and significantly outperforms other financial and macroeconomic indicators in predicting recessions two to six quarters ahead.
>
> The yield curve spread averaged −2.18 percentage points in the first quarter of 1981, implying a probability of recession of 86.5 percent four quarters later. As predicted, the first quarter of 1982 was in fact designated a recession quarter by the National Bureau of Economic Research.
>
> . . . [T]he fact that the yield curve strongly outperforms other variables at longer horizons makes its use as a forecasting tool even more compelling.

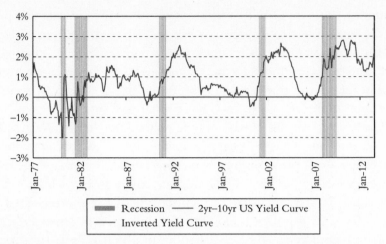

Figure 6.14   The Yield Curve Has Signaled Every Single Recession
SOURCE: *Variant Perception*, Bloomberg.

So while most economists couldn't identify a recession if it fell on their heads, the yield curve would have given you 6 to 18 months' lead on a recession. You can see from Figure 6.14 that an inversion of the yield curve predicted every recession in the past forty years.

Sadly, the Fed has ignored its own research on the yield curve. The yield curve inverted in August 2006. That was a full 16 months before the recession. That should have been a huge warning sign to economists. It wasn't. Then, in late 2006 and early 2007, the yield curve inverted much more strongly. If you had simply ignored Greenspan, Bernanke, and almost all professional economists and looked only at the yield curve, you would have seen the recession coming in 2007. [John saw that signal and began to predict a recession based on the yield curve and other recession indicators. He was severely taken to task on TV and in print for being a bear. There were no retractions when his call turned out to be right.]

What is extraordinary is that recessionary signals were everywhere. In late 2007 and early 2008 almost all yield curves were inverted. Rarely had yield curves in so many countries been inverted at the same time. This should have been a very loud warning bell that the world was going to see a pronounced global recession. All you had to do was buy *The Economist* and look at the back page, which we've reproduced in Table 6.1. However, many central banks completely

Table 6.1 Inverted Yield Curves around the World

	Trade Balance* Latest 12 Months, $bn	Current-Account Balance		Currency Units, per $		Budget Balance % of GDP 2007†	Interest Rates, %	
		Latest 12 Months, $bn	% of GDP 2007†	Dec 18th	Year Ago		3-Month Latest	10-Year Gov't Bonds, Latest
United States	−806.4 Oct	−752.4 Q3	−5.5	—	—	−1.2	4.16	4.12
Japan	+107.6 Oct	+211.3 Oct	+4.7	113	118	−2.6	0.73	1.51
China	+259.8 Nov	+249.9 2006	+11.4	7.39	7.82	0.2	4.35	4.87
Britain	−165.8 Oct	−86.6 Q2	−3.3	0.50	0.51	−3.1	6.41	4.74
Canada	+49.0 Oct	+16.3 Q3	+1.5	1.01	1.16	1.0	3.86	4.02
Euro area	+51.7 Oct	+34.2 Sep	+0.1	0.69	0.76	−0.9	4.88	4.32
Austria	+0.9 Sep	+12.3 Q2	+2.8	0.69	0.76	−0.6	4.88	4.40
Belgium	+19.2 Oct	+13.0 Jun	+2.5	0.69	0.76	−0.4	4.94	4.42
France	−47.4 Oct	−28.3 Oct	−1.2	0.69	0.76	−2.4	4.88	4.39
Germany	+263.1 Oct	+207.8 Oct	+5.8	0.69	0.76	−0.3	4.88	4.31
Greece	−52.1 Sep	−43.2 Oct	−13.6	0.69	0.76	−2.7	4.88	4.59
Italy	−12.0 Oct	−47.7 Sep	−2.5	0.69	0.76	−2.4	4.88	4.59
Netherlands	+54.4 Oct	+57.2 Q3	+7.6	0.69	0.76	−0.3	4.88	4.38
Spain	−126.0 Sep	−126.1 Aug	−9.3	0.69	0.76	1.8	4.88	4.41
Czech Republic	+3.7 Oct	−5.4 Oct	−3.8	18.2	21.0	−3.9	4.09	4.72
Denmark	+4.2 Oct	+4.3 Oct	+1.5	5.18	5.66	3.8	5.00	4.40
Hungary	−0.8 Oct	−6.8 Q2	−5.8	177	193	−6.0	7.50	7.05
Norway	+56.3 Nov	+59.9 Q3	+14.6	5.59	6.19	18.9	5.89	4.69
Poland	−11.7 Oct	−16.2 Oct	−4.1	2.51	2.90	−1.8	5.69	5.95
Russia	+124.0 Oct	+73.5 Q3	+6.1	24.7	26.3	3.0	10.00	6.31

(continued)

163

Table 6.1 Inverted Yield Curves around the World (*continued*)

	Trade Balance* Latest 12 Months, $bn	Current-Account Balance Latest 12 Months, $bn	% of GDP 2007†	Currency Units, per $ Dec 18th	Year Ago	Budget Balance % of GDP 2007†	Interest Rates, % 3-Month Latest	10-Year Gov't Bonds, Latest
Sweden	+18.5 Oct	+29.4 Q3	+7.0	6.56	6.86	2.9	4.02	4.35
Switzerland	+11.2 Oct	+64.9 Q2	+16.2	1.15	1.22	0.3	2.78	2.99
Turkey	−59.6 Oct	−35.2 Oct	−7.4	1.19	1.43	−2.5	17.13	6.05‡
Australia	−15.9 Oct	−49.9 Q3	−5.8	1.16	1.28	1.6	7.35	6.28
Hong Kong	−21.9 Oct	+24.9 Q2	+9.6	7.80	7.78	2.0	3.73	3.26
India	−66.0 Oct	−9.7 Q2	−1.1	39.5	44.8	−3.4	7.42	8.15
Indonesia	+41.2 Oct	+11.0 Q2	+2.4	9,395	9,140	−1.4	8.04	6.61‡
Malaysia	+29.3 Oct	+27.6 Q2	+13.5	3.35	3.58	−3.2	3.62	4.77‡
Pakistan	−15.2 Nov	−7.3 Q3	−4.7	60.7	60.9	−4.6	9.84	8.19‡
Singapore	+35.8 Nov	+46.3 Q3	+24.5	1.46	1.54	0.3	2.56	2.76
South Korea	+17.4 Nov	+9.7 Oct	+1.0	939	932	0.7	5.71	5.79
Taiwan	+17.6 Nov	+28.4 Q3	+6.3	32.6	32.7	−2.1	2.70	2.61
Thailand	+10.5 Oct	+12.9 Oct	+4.6	33.7	35.9	−1.9	3.90	4.72
Argentina	+10.7 Oct	+7.4 Q2	+2.7	3.14	3.06	1.2	14.50	na
Brazil	+41.4 Nov	+7.4 Oct	+0.7	1.81	2.15	−1.8	11.18	6.16‡
Chile	+24.8 Nov	+6.7 Q3	+4.4	499	527	8.8	6.36	4.78‡
Colombia	−1.8 Sep	−4.8 Q2	−3.8	2,011	2,254	−0.2	8.90	5.88‡
Mexico	−12.1 Oct	−7.5 Q3	−0.5	10.9	10.8	nil	7.44	8.08
Venezuela	+23.4 Q3	+20.2 Q3	+9.2	5,675	3,283§	−1.4	11.35	6.55‡
Egypt	−15.8 Q2	+2.7 Q2	+1.8	5.53	5.71	−7.5	6.98	5.50‡
Israel	−9.7 Nov	+5.9 Q3	+3.8	3.95	4.19	−0.1	4.64	5.71

Saudi Arabia	+146.6 2006			+25.5	3.76	3.75	21.8	4.01	na
South Africa	−11.3 Oct	98.9 2006	−19.9 Q3	−6.8	6.92	7.02	1.0	11.30	8.50
MORE COUNTRIES Data for the countries below are not provided in printed editions of *The Economist*									
Estonia	−4.1 Sep	−3.2 Oct		−14.8	10.9	11.9	3.0	7.30	na
Finland	+12.7 Oct	+14.2 Oct		+6.2	0.69	0.76	4.4	4.65	4.38
Iceland	−1.6 Nov	−3.0 Q3		−16.9	63.0	69.1	5.3	14.15	na
Ireland	+36.9 Sep	−10.5 Q2		−5.2	0.69	0.76	1.2	4.88	4.48
Latvia	−7.2 Oct	−6.4 Sep		−22.2	0.48	0.53	0.4	9.46	na
Lithuania	−6.7 Oct	−4.6 Oct		−14.5	2.40	2.62	−0.5	7.22	na
Luxembourg	−5.9 Sep	+4.6 Q2		na	0.69	0.76	1.0	4.88	na
New Zealand	−4.2 Oct	−9.2 Q2		−8.1	1.33	1.44	4.6	7.30	6.37
Peru	+8.6 Oct	+2.2 Q3		+1.9	2.98	3.20	0.7	5.00	na
Philippines	−4.3 Sep	+6.4 Jun		+6.7	42.0	49.4	−0.8	6.56	na
Portugal	−24.1 Sep	−18.4 Sep		−8.5	0.69	0.76	−3.0	4.88	4.50
Slovakia	−0.9 Oct	−4.0 nil		−4.7	23.3	26.5	−2.9	4.14	4.62
Slovenia	−2.8 Oct	−1.6 Sep		−3.3	0.69	0.76	−0.5	na	na

*Merchandise trade only. †*The Economist* poll or Economist Intelligence Unit forecast. ‡Dollar-denominated bonds. §Unofficial exchange rate.

SOURCE: *The Economist*, December 22, 2007.

ignored the message from the yield curve and continued hiking interest rates. For example, in June of 2008 the European Central Bank
hiked interest rates six months after the United States entered a recession and once the recession in Europe had already started!

Given how useful the yield curve is as a predictor of economic
activity, you're probably wondering what it is telling us today about
future growth. We're glad you asked that question. It is one we ask ourselves a lot.

The yield curve has become a lot less useful, sadly. Earlier in the
book, we discussed financial repression and how central banks are artificially driving down the yield on government bonds. Central banks
are not only distorting the level of government yields, they're distorting
the shape of the yield curve.

Let's look at what the yield curve is telling us today. Figure 6.15
shows the shape of the yield curve against the industrial production of
the big G7 countries. As you can see, the yield curve leads economic
ups and downs by a little over a year. Currently, the yield curve has
flattened, which means that industrial activity should be turning down
in 2014. We know that the yield curve is the best predictor of industrial activity, yet the Fed wants to flatten the curve rather than steepen

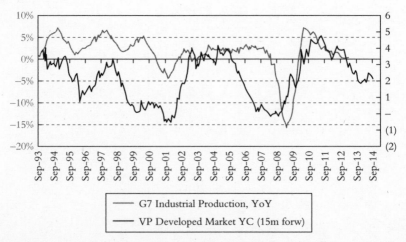

Figure 6.15   The Yield Curve Predicts Global Industrial Activity
Source: *Variant Perception*, Bloomberg.

it. They would rather financially repress savers than create a healthy economy. We live in an upside-down world.

The distortions created by central banks' manipulations don't end with the yield curve. The Fed and other central banks are also distorting inputs into the economy and leading indicators. There are almost no indicators that haven't been affected by the Fed: stock prices, commodity prices, credit spreads, yield curve. Leading indicators are extremely useful at indicating where the economy is going, but given the distortions created by central banks, the next time a recession comes around we all might be flying blind.

Too Loose for Too Long

The legendary hockey player Wayne Gretzky once said that good players skate toward the puck, but great players skate where the puck is going to be. In the world of monetary policy, you could say the same thing. Great policy has nothing to do with where the economy is today, but instead with where it will be tomorrow.

Monetary policy operates with a lag. It does not impact the economy immediately, but rather along timelines characterized by what the great economist Milton Friedman called "long and variable lags." Changes in interest rates have very little influence on growth or inflation for 6 to 12 months, and sometimes even longer. Hiking interest rates does not have its full effect on reducing inflation for well over a year. So in order for the Fed to prevent an increase in inflation, it has to shoot early. If it waits until it actually sees inflation, it will be acting a year too late. As former Fed vice chairman Alan Blinder observed, the Bunker Hill strategy does not work for monetary policy: if you wait to see the whites of their eyes, you're dead.

Let's look at the Fed's record with rate hiking in two recent recessions.

Remember how most economists thought the United States wasn't in a recession in 1990? When they finally woke up to the recession, they were still looking backwards and thought the United States was stuck in a downturn in 1992. By that time, though, the United States was growing strongly. By 1994 the United States economy was booming and enjoying its highest growth rate since 1984. The Fed was far behind the curve. It finally started hiking interest rates, incrementally raising them by 3 percent over the next 12 months. By the time the Fed finally acted, however, the rate hikes could not have any immediate impact on the inflation the country was seeing in 1994. In fact, the hikes would not dampen inflation until 1995 and 1996.

Whenever the Fed hikes rates, bad things happen somewhere. It's that simple. In 1994 the quick rise in rates killed a lot of leveraged investors in the bond market. Orange County had interest rate derivatives that blew up in its face. It was the largest municipal bankruptcy in history. Emerging-market stocks and bonds were hammered, and Mexico was even forced to devalue its currency in a major financial market crisis. If (when) the Fed hikes rates today, we'll see lots of bankruptcies like Orange County's and blow-ups like the Mexican Tequila Crisis. The very low rates globally in a Code Red world mean that now there are probably hundreds or thousands of investors like Orange County. You can bet on that. And that is why the market gets so nervous about suggestions that the Fed might start tapering its quantitative easing. If QE is finally ended, can rising rates be far behind?

Let's fast-forward to the economic recovery after the dot-com bust of 2000.

After the Nasdaq crashed and the U.S. economy entered a recession, the Fed cut the Federal Funds rate from 6.5 percent in late 2000 to 1.0 percent by mid-2003. Greenspan and Bernanke were afraid of deflation, even though leading economic indicators suggestive of growth or inflation completely contradicted their view. Even as the economy started to boom and accelerate, the Fed kept interest rates low. It was so far behind the curve that by the time it started hiking very slowly, the U.S. housing bubble was inflating. Unfortunately, we all know how that ended.

The Return of the 1970s

We have every reason to believe that central bankers everywhere will be looking in the rearview mirror this time, too, as they struggle to steer their Code Red policies. In Chapter 2, we looked at how economists in the 1970s believed in the idea that higher inflation would lead to a lower unemployment rate. So far, we have no proof that QE helps employment, but Bernanke and other governors of the Fed have stated that the reason they will keep on printing money to buy government bonds is that the labor market is weak. Notice that they're not doing it to fight deflation. They're targeting employment, and they think that slightly higher inflation is the best way to get higher employment. We've gone back to the 1970s and the Phillips curve. The Fed has promised it will keep easing until unemployment hits 6.5 percent, even though there is no direct connection between QE and the unemployment rate. That's a recipe for letting inflation creep up over time.

(And don't even get us started on how unemployment is calculated and reported. It makes the calculation of inflation seem straightforward!)

Central bankers have also warned repeatedly that they will act later rather than sooner to rein in their unconventional policies. In testimony before the Joint Economic Committee of Congress, Bernanke let investors know that the Fed would err on the side of staying looser longer. He said, "A premature tightening of monetary policy could lead interest rates to rise temporarily but would also carry a substantial risk of slowing or ending the economic recovery and causing inflation to fall further."

For the moment, moderate inflation is giving central banks and deflation-obsessed economists like Paul Krugman a false sense of security. Inflation is low at present because it is a very lagging indicator. As we have seen, businesses do not raise prices immediately when the economy starts to grow. They wait until they are certain demand is strong. Likewise, businesses do not immediately start cutting costs just because their sales have slowed down a little. If they did, they might find it hard to raise prices in the future. This is why, over the past century, inflation has almost always been at its highest in the middle of recessions and at its lowest point as expansions were starting again. Inflation tells you very little about the future and a lot about the past. A weak global economy over the past year and a half has kept inflation subdued. When inflation starts ticking upward, central bankers will be looking in the rearview mirror and sitting on trillions of dollars of monetary base.

If central banks could not manage conventional monetary policy well in the "good old days," why do we think they can manage unconventional monetary policy today?

A comedian once said that a second marriage is the triumph of hope over experience. You could say that trusting central banks to get things right is exactly the same thing.

Key Lessons from the Chapter

In this chapter we learned:

- Central banks are counting on being able to do all the right things at the right times to exit their Code Red policies. Unfortunately, central banks have a dismal track record at understanding where the economy is heading.
- Economists are useless at forecasting recessions. They've missed almost every single recession around the world over the past few decades.
- Central bankers are clueless about where the economy is and where it is going. Almost all economists have dismal forecasting records and have failed to identify every previous recession in real time.
- The main reason that economists systematically miss recessions is that they focus on the wrong things. They look at lagging economic indicators.
- Economic data are heavily revised months and years after they are released. This is called the vintage data problem. You can't understand what is happening in real time if you pay attention to most economic data. In order to know what is happening, economists should focus on prices that are not revised.
- Leading economic indicators tell you about the future; coincident indicators tell you about the present; and lagging indicators tell you about the past. Sadly, most economists focus on lagging economic indicators. That is like driving by looking in the rearview mirror.
- The Fed is still depending on models that completely failed to foresee the previous recession.
- Central banks are distorting the yield curve, stock prices, credit spreads, and other prices that might give useful signals about the future.

Chapter Seven

Escape Velocity

The importance of money flows from it being a link between the present and the future.

—*John Maynard Keynes*

The use of quantity of money as a target has not been a success. I'm not sure that I would as of today push it as hard as I once did.

—*Milton Friedman,*
Financial Times, June 7, 2003

Recently, the evangelist/broadcaster Harold Camping predicted that Jesus Christ would return to Earth on May 21, 2011. His followers took to the streets to hand out pamphlets warning, "The end of the world is almost here." Even one of your humble writers was accosted on the streets of New York with literature warning of the impending Judgment Day. Fortunately for us, the world did not end. Unfortunately for Harold Camping, his credibility was shot to pieces. You might have assumed that his followers felt let down and decided to change their minds when May 21, 2011, came and went. But you would be wrong. People have a tremendous capacity for self-delusion. Camping changed the date, and almost all followers continued to believe, at least until that prophecy proved wrong, too. (That was his third strike at calling the end of the world, though, and it seems to have sent him back to the dugout. Which serves us a caution: if you are going to predict "Apocalypse soon!," don't set a date that will fall in your own lifetime.)

In the world of economic policies, you can see something very similar happening. You have two sides that are mortal enemies, both predicting dire outcomes. So far, the apocalypse has not happened. Yet neither side will give in or even accept that it is wrong when reality belies entrenched expectations.

Inflationistas believe that extremely high inflation lies just around the corner. When central banks embarked on quantitative easing (QE), many of them predicted rising inflation and even hyperinflation. They think the world is trapped in a rerun of the Weimar Republic, a time when money was printed so prolifically that people needed to carry it around in wheelbarrows.

The inflationistas recommended investors buy gold as a hedge against currency debasement. They predicted that if the money supply doubled and central banks financed government spending, we'd see soaring inflation and the price of gold would skyrocket. As we write this chapter, though, most measures of inflation in the United States, Europe, and many emerging markets are rising only very moderately, and gold has fallen over 30 percent. But the failure of their predictions to materialize has not dampened inflationista spirits in the slightest. Like cultists, they merely postponed the date when they expect inflation to grip the world and argued that devious central bankers have suppressed the price of gold.

On the other side you have the deflationistas. They believe the world is trapped in a rerun of the 1930s and that the best solution is for governments to spend money freely, for central banks to print money to finance the spending, and for countries to weaken their currencies. They want grand, ambitious spending and a central bank that will be bold and even slightly reckless—*responsibly irresponsible*, to use their term. If we don't follow their policies, they maintain, we could plunge into another Great Depression at worst or enter a long, drawn-out slump, as Japan has done.

Even though most countries around the world are in fact following the deflationista playbook, the deflationistas (mostly neo-Keynesians) argue that we have hardly seen enough government spending, central bank financing, or currency devaluation. The failure of Code Red policies to generate any meaningful economic growth has not dented their spirits. In their minds, spending and money creation have not been nearly sufficient. To them, the current state of the world's economies constitutes proof that their prescriptions require higher dosages.

Inflationistas and deflationistas are much like the cultish followers of Harold Camping, and no amount of evidence will convince proponents of either side that they are wrong. As almost always, the truth lies somewhere in the middle. Large increases in the money supply can and do lead to high inflation. And the deflationists are right that sometimes you do need Code Red policies. But everything has a time and a place.

In this chapter, we'll show you what is really happening in the economy and why we have not had either much inflation or much growth, despite the best efforts of central bankers. The economy is not unlike a complicated car. We'll look under the hood and see how the engine, transmission, and running gear work together. We'll also look at where the global economy is today and what current realities should tell central bankers.

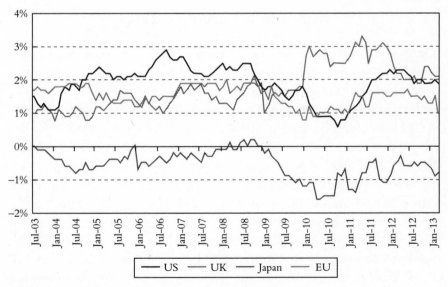

Figure 7.1 Inflation Is Moderate in Most Countries

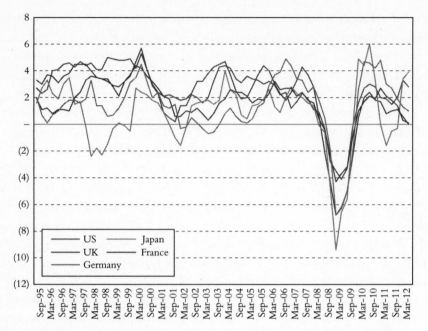

Figure 7.2 Low Growth in the United States, United Kingdom, and Japan; Contraction in EU
SOURCE: *Variant Perception*, Bloomberg.

Stuck in a Liquidity Trap

Like a car, an economy has lots of moving parts, everyone thinks they know how to drive it when they're in the backseat, and it crashes too often. But on a more serious note, the analogy of a car works especially well when you think of where large parts of the global economy are.

Today, central banks can make money cheap and plentiful, but the money that is created isn't moving around the economy or stimulating demand. They can step on the accelerator and flood the engine with gas, but the transmission is broken, and the wheels don't turn. Without a transmission mechanism, monetary policy has no effect. This has not always been the case, but it is today. After some credit crises, central banks can cut the nominal interest rate all the way to zero and still be unable to stimulate their economies sufficiently. Some economists call that a *liquidity trap* (although that usage of the term differs somewhat from Lord Keynes's original meaning).

The Great Financial Crisis plunged us into a liquidity trap, a situation in which many people figure that they might just as well sit on cash. Many parts of the world found themselves in a liquidity trap during the Great Depression, and Japan has been stuck in a liquidity trap for most of the time since its bubble burst in 1989.

Economists who have studied liquidity traps know that some of the usual rules of economics don't apply when an economy is stuck in one. Large budget deficits don't drive up interest rates; printing money isn't inflationary; and cutting government spending has an exaggerated impact on the economy.

In fact, if you look at recessions that have happened after debt crises, growth was almost always very slow. For example, a study by Oscar Jorda, Moritz Schularick, and Alan Taylor found that recessions that occurred after years of rapid credit growth were almost always worse than garden-variety recessions. One of the key findings from their study is that it is very difficult to restore growth after a debt bubble.

Central banks want to create modest inflation and thereby reduce the real value of debt, but they're having trouble doing it. Creating inflation isn't quite as simple as printing money or keeping interest rates very low. Most Western central banks have built up a very large store of credibility over the past few decades. The high inflation of the 1970s is a very distant memory to most investors nowadays. And almost no one seriously believes in hyperinflation. The United Kingdom has never experienced hyperinflation, and you'd have to go back to the 1770s to find hyperinflation in the United States—when the Continental Congress printed money to pay for the Revolutionary War and so started a period of extremely high inflation. (That's why the framers of the Constitution introduced Article 1, Section 10: "No state shall . . . coin money; emit bills of credit; make any thing but gold and silver coin a tender in payment of debts. . . .") Japan and Germany have not had hyperinflation for over 60 years.

Today's central bankers want inflation only in the short run, not in the long run. As Janet Yellen recognized, central banks with established reputations have a credibility problem when it comes to committing to future inflation. If people believe deep down that central banks will try to kill inflation if it ever gets out of hand, then it becomes very hard for those central banks to generate inflation today. And the answer from many economists is that central bankers should be even bolder and crazier, sort of like everyone's mad uncle—or, more politely, to be "responsibly irresponsible," as Paul McCulley has quipped.

In a liquidity trap, the rules of economics change. Things that worked in the past don't work in the present. The models of economies that we mentioned above become even less reliable. In fact, they sometimes suggest actions that are in fact actually quite destructive. So why aren't the models working?

Sometimes the best way to understand a complex subject is to draw an analogy. So with an apology to all the true mathematicians among our readers, today we will look at what we can call the *Economic Singularity*.

The Economic Singularity

Singularity was originally a mathematical term for a point at which an equation has no solution. In physics, it was proven that a large enough collapsing star would eventually become a black hole, so dense that its own gravity would cause a singularity in the fabric of spacetime, a point where many standard physics equations suddenly have no solution.

Beyond the "event horizon" of the black hole, the models no longer work. In general relativity, an event horizon is the boundary in spacetime beyond which events cannot affect an outside observer. In a black hole, it is "the point of no return," that is, the point at which the gravitational pull becomes so great that nothing can escape.

This theme is an old friend to readers of science fiction. Everyone knows that you can't get too close to a black hole or you will get sucked in; but if you can get just close enough, you can use the powerful and deadly gravity to slingshot you across the vast reaches of spacetime.

One way that a black hole can (theoretically) be created is for a star to collapse in upon itself. The larger the mass of the star, the greater the gravity of the black hole and the more surrounding space stuff that will get sucked down its gravity well. The center of our galaxy is thought to be a black hole with the mass of 4.3 million suns.

We can draw a rough parallel between a black hole and our current global economic situation. (For physicists this will be a very rough parallel indeed, but work with us, please.) An economic bubble of any type, *but especially a debt bubble*, can be thought of as an incipient black hole. When the bubble collapses in upon itself, it creates its own black hole with an event horizon beyond which all traditional economic modeling breaks down. Any economic theory that does not attempt to transcend the event horizon associated with excessive debt will be incapable of offering a viable solution to an economic crisis. Even worse, it is likely that any proposed solution will make the crisis more severe.

The Minsky Moment

Debt (leverage) can be a very good thing when used properly. For instance, if debt is used to purchase an income-producing asset, whether a new machine tool for a factory or a bridge to increase commerce, then debt can be net-productive.

Hyman Minsky, one of the greatest economists of the past century, saw debt in three forms: hedge, speculative, and Ponzi. Roughly speaking, to Minsky, hedge financing was when the profits from purchased assets were used to pay back the loan, speculative finance occurred when profits from the asset simply maintained the debt service and the loan had to be rolled over, and Ponzi finance required the selling of the asset at an ever higher price in order to make a profit.

Minsky maintained that if hedge financing dominated, then the economy might well be an equilibrium-seeking, well-contained system. However, the greater the weight of speculative and Ponzi finance, the greater the likelihood that the economy would be what he called a deviation-amplifying system. Thus, Minsky's Financial Instability Hypothesis suggests that over periods of prolonged prosperity, capitalist economies tend to move from a financial structure dominated by (stable) hedge finance to a structure that increasingly emphasizes (unstable) speculative and Ponzi finance.

Minsky proposed theories linking financial market fragility, in the normal life cycle of an economy, with speculative investment bubbles that are seemingly part of financial markets. He claimed that in prosperous times, when corporate cash flow rises beyond what is needed to pay off debt, a speculative euphoria develops; and soon thereafter debts exceed what borrowers can pay off from their incoming revenues, which in turn produces a financial crisis. As the climax of such a speculative borrowing bubble nears, banks and other lenders tighten credit availability, even to companies that can afford loans, and the economy then contracts.

"A fundamental characteristic of our economy," Minsky wrote in 1974, "is that the financial system swings between robustness and fragility and these swings are an integral part of the process that generates business cycles."

In our previous book, *Endgame*, we explored the idea of a debt supercycle, the culmination of decades of borrowing that finally ends in a dramatic bust. Unfortunately, much of the developed world is at the end of the 60-year-long debt supercycle. It creates our economic singularity. A business-cycle recession is a fundamentally different thing than the end of a debt supercycle, such as much of Europe is tangling with, Japan will soon face, and the United States can only avoid with concerted action in the next few years.

A business-cycle recession can respond to monetary and fiscal policy in a more or less normal fashion, but if you are at the event horizon of a collapsing debt black hole, monetary and fiscal policy will no longer work the way they have in the past, or in a manner that the models would predict.

There are two contradictory forces battling in a debt black hole: expanding debt and collapsing growth. Raising taxes or cutting spending to reduce debt will have an almost immediate impact on economic growth.

But there is a limit to how much money a government can borrow. That limit clearly can vary significantly from country to country, but to suggest there is no limit puts you clearly in the camp of the delusional.

The Event Horizon

In our analogy, the event horizon is relatively easy to pinpoint. It is what Rogoff and Reinhart call the "Bang!" moment, when a country loses the confidence of the bond market. For Russia it came at 57 percent of debt-to-GDP (gross domestic product) in 1998. Japan is at 240 percent of debt-to-GDP and rising, even as its population falls—the Bang! moment approaches. Obviously, Greece had its moment several years ago. Spain lost effective access to the bond market last year, minus European Central Bank (ECB) intervention, as did Italy, with other countries to follow.

As an aside, it makes no difference how the debt was accumulated. The black holes of debt in Greece and Argentina had completely different origins from those of Spain or Sweden or Canada (the latter two in the early 1990s). The Spanish problem did not originate because of too much government spending; it developed because of a housing bubble of epic proportions. Seventeen percent of the working population was employed in the housing industry when it collapsed. Is it any wonder that unemployment is now 25 percent? If unemployment is 25 percent, that both raises the cost of government services and reduces revenues by proportionate amounts.

The policy problem is: how do you counteract the negative pull of a black hole of debt before it's too late? How do you muster the "escape velocity" to get back to a growing economy and a falling deficit—or, dare we say, even a surplus to pay down the old debt? How do you reconcile the competing forces of insufficient growth and too much debt?

The problem is not merely one of insufficient spending; the key problem is insufficient income. By definition, income has to come before spending. You can take money from one source and give it to another, but that is not organic growth. We typically think of organic growth as having to do with only individual companies, but the organic growth of a country can come from natural circumstances like energy resources or an equable climate or land conducive to agricultural production, or it can come from developing an educated populace. There are many sources of potential organic growth: energy, tourism, technology, manufacturing, agriculture, trade, banking, and so on.

While deficit spending can help bridge a national economy through a recession, normal business growth must eventually take over if the country is to prosper. Keynesian theory prescribed deficit spending during times of business recessions and the accumulation of surpluses during good times, in order to be able to pay down debts that would inevitably accrue down the road. The problem is that the model developed by Keynesian theory begins to break down as we near the event horizon of a black hole of debt.

Deficit spending is a wonderful prescription for Spain, but it begs the question of who will pay off the deficit once Spain has lost the confidence of the bond market. Is it the responsibility of the rest of Europe to pay for Spain or Greece? Or Italy or France, or whatever country chooses not to deal with its own internal issues?

Deficit spending can be a useful tool in countries with a central bank, such as the United States. But at what point does borrowing from the future (and our children) come to be seen as a failure to deal with our own lack of political will in regards to our spending and taxation policies? There is a difference, as I think Hyman Minsky would point out, between borrowing money for infrastructure spending that will benefit our children and borrowing money to spend on ourselves today, with no future benefit.

The deficit has to be controlled, of course. To continue on the current path will only feed our Black Hole of Debt even more "mass," making it that much harder to escape from. But to try and power away (cutting the deficit radically) all at once will blow the engines of the economy. Suddenly reducing the deficit by 8 percent of GDP, either by cutting spending or raising taxes, is a prescription for an almost immediate depression. It's just basic math.

As we outline in *Endgame* (shameless plug), each country has to find its own path. But it's clear that Spain, like Greece, is simply going to have to default on part of its debt. So will Ireland and Portugal. Japan will resort to printing money in amounts that will boggle the imagination and terrify the world, as they finally come to grips with the fact that they must deal with their deficit spending.

The Glide Path

Indulge us for a moment as we think about our own country. The United States still has the chance to pursue what we call the "glide path" option. We can reduce the deficit slowly, say by 1 percent a year, while aggressively pursuing organic growth policies such as unleashing the energy and biotechnology sectors, providing certainty to small businesses about government health care policies, reducing the regulatory burden on small businesses and encouraging new business start-ups, creating a competitive corporate tax environment (a much lower corporate tax with no deductions for anything, including oil-depletion allowances), implementing a pro-growth tax policy, and so on.

We can balance the budget within five to seven years. If the bond market perceived that the United States was clearly committed to a balanced budget, rates would remain low, the dollar would be stronger (especially as we become energy independent), and we would steam away from the black hole. If something like Simpson-Bowles could be accomplished, with an even more radically restructured tax policy, it would be enormously bullish for the United States in particular and for the world in general. Health care is clearly the challenge, but a compromise can be crafted, as has been demonstrated by the several bipartisan a that have been sponsored by conservative Republicans and liberal Democrats. The key word is *compromise*.

The crucial outcome is whether we can achieve the compromise that will be needed to get us on a glide path to a balanced budget.

If a compromise is not crafted in the next few years, it will be even more difficult in 2016, which is an election year. That may be too late, as the bond market may be watching Europe and Japan imploding and wonder why the United States is any different. Remember, the event horizon is determined by the confidence of the bond market in the willingness and ability of a country to pay its debts with a currency that has a value that can be maintained. Trillion-dollar deficits will call into question the value of the dollar. That will mean higher interest rates, which will mean a much bigger, more deadly black hole.

We should note that something similar to the glide path was tried during the Clinton administration. Spending growth was controlled, and the economy was allowed to grow its way out of debt. While the U.S. economy is fundamentally weaker today than it was then, it should still be possible for the U.S. free-market economy to once again become an engine of growth.

We think the analogy of an Economic Singularity is a good one. The Black Hole of Debt simply overwhelms the ability of current economic theories to craft solutions based on past performance. Each country will have to find its own unique way to achieve escape velocity from its own particular black hole. That can be through a combination of reducing the debt (the size of the black hole) and growth. Even countries that do not have such a problem will have to deal with the black holes in their vicinity. As an example, Finland is part of the Eurozone and finds itself gravitationally affected by the black holes of debt created by its fellow Eurozone members. And China has recently seen its exports to Europe drop by almost 12 percent. I would imagine that has been more or less the experience of most countries that export to Europe.

In science fiction novels, a spaceship's straying too close to a black hole typically results in no spaceship. There are also hundreds of examples of what happens to nations that drift too close to the Black Hole of Debt. None of the instances are pretty; they all end in tears. For countries that have been trapped in the gravity well of debt, there is only the pain that comes with restructuring. It is all too sad.

The usual response by central banks when confronted with a debt crisis is to provide liquidity and create more money. But as we'll discover in the next section, not all money is created equal; and central banks don't really control the broad money supply at all.

Where's the High Inflation?

When the Fed and the Bank of England embarked on their Code Red policies and started buying government bonds through QE programs, the inflationistas thought we'd get hyperinflation very quickly. Well, three years have passed, and we have no hyperinflation. So what's up? Why are Japan, the United Kingdom, the United States, and Europe not like Zimbabwe, Argentina, or Weimar Germany?

Let's start from the beginning and see what money is and how it is created. That will explain a lot.

When people think of money, they generally think of the dollar bills, euros, or pounds in their pocket. That is money in circulation, and it's a very particular kind of money. But money has many different forms, and each kind of money has different properties.

The best way to think of money is to imagine it that it is like water. (In fact, the water analogy works well, and economists talk about liquidity when they talk about money supply and growth.) Water can be a solid when it is ice, a liquid when it is plain old water, or a gas when it evaporates away. All of these forms are H_2O, but they have very different properties.

When central banks create money, they generally buy government bonds in the open market from banks. The central banks keep the bonds on their balance sheets, and the banks keep the money. The money that is created is generally called the monetary base. It is like ice. It has the *potential* to be liquid and to travel around the economy, but until that money is converted into loans in the banking system and the cash actually ends up in people's pockets, the money doesn't move—it is "frozen." The monetary base is *potential* money. Many economists refer to the monetary base as high-powered money because it can be multiplied into a lot more money by banks.

The monetary base becomes liquid money that can move around the economy through the process of bank lending. Commercial banks can take their monetary reserves and lend them out. Central banks determine how much commercial banks can lend out. In the United States, for example, the Fed demands that all banks keep 10 percent of their assets on reserve with the Fed overnight. This practice allows the bank to have cash to cover withdrawals. Banks generally loan out the other 90 percent of the money. For example, money might go to a shoe factory as a loan. The shoe factory would then deposit the money in another bank. And that bank would sit on 10 percent and lend out the other 90 percent. This cycle would recur again and again and again. The money would keep being lent out through the banking system—dozens and dozens of times. No single bank is creating money, but the banking system as a whole has multiplied the money. The result is that banks can multiply money by up to 10 times in the United States. That is how the money multiplier works.

(*Slightly technical note:* A 10 percent required reserve ratio creates a money multiplier of 10: 1 divided by 10 percent = 10. A 5 percent required reserve ratio would create a money multiplier of 20: 1 divided by 5 percent = 20. So the money multiplier is the reciprocal of the required reserve ratio.)

What does this have to do with the Fed and hyperinflation? We're glad you asked. Remember that the monetary base is *potential* money. It becomes liquid and enters the economy only when banks multiply it by lending it.

Since the Great Financial Crisis, businesses and households haven't really wanted to borrow a lot more. They already have too much debt. And banks are sitting on heaps of bad loans, so they're in no rush to make new ones, as the regulators tell them that they need to reserve more capital for future losses (talk about mixed messages). One side doesn't want to borrow and the other doesn't want to lend. The Fed increases the monetary base, but banks have no interest in lending and deposit all their reserves at the Federal Reserve overnight. In the end, the money goes nowhere in the economy.

Central banks around the world have created an enormous, bloated monetary base; but they've failed miserably at creating a broader money, or M2, as economists call it. Let's see what our friend Lacy Hunt at Hoisington Investment Management has to say about how money growth and the money multiplier have changed over the past couple of years:

> At the end of 2007, the money multiplier was 9.0. That meant that the monetary base of $825 billion . . . was multiplied nine times to create the level of M2 that stood at $7.4 trillion. At the end of March 2013, the monetary base had exploded to $2.9 trillion, but the money multiplier had collapsed to only 3.6, creating an M2 balance of $10.4 trillion. The central bank has very little control over the movement of the money mul-

tiplier; the actions of the banks and their customers primarily control this variable.

This lack of control was evident in the first quarter of 2013 when the monetary base *rose* by $264 billion and M2 *fell* because the money multiplier declined from 3.9 to 3.6. Therefore, the Fed's balance sheet expansion was thwarted. [Emphasis added.]

As the evidence clearly shows, central banks cannot create money without the help of the banking system and borrowers.

The great physicist Stephen Hawking wrote in *A Brief History of Time and Space*, "Someone told me that each equation I included in the book would halve the sales." At the risk of completely ruining the sales of *Code Red*, we'll discuss an equation. Stay with us because this equation is important, and it will explain why we don't have runaway inflation or hyperinflation despite all the "money printing" that is going on.

A great American economist of the 1920–1930s, Irving Fisher, quantified this link between money and economic growth with a straightforward formula:

$$Money \times Velocity = Price \times Real\ GDP$$

Generally, this equation tells you that if you increase money or velocity, you can increase nominal GDP. Rookie economists like to change one variable and assume that the other parts of the equation stay constant. For example, inflationistas assume that doubling the monetary base will simply double the price level, but that result requires velocity to stay constant. That almost never happens, as we've seen by looking at previous liquidity traps. Deflationistas believe that increasing the money supply will generate more economic output, but this outcome requires holding velocity and price relatively constant, and that doesn't always happen, either.

Ultimately, the Fed doesn't control the broad money supply. Why, you ask? Simply because Fed cannot control the *velocity*, the speed at which banks lend out the money and the speed at which it then turns over in the general economy. They can take a horse to water, but they can't make it drink.

The story of money is much easier to tell visually, so let's look at a few charts that can explain what is happening in the U.S. economy and the money supply. The charts look pretty much the same for the United Kingdom, European Union, Japan, and Switzerland. If you look at Figure 7.3, you can see that the Federal Reserve's balance sheet has grown very, very quickly over the past few years. It looks like an Internet stock in the late 1990s.

In normal times, whenever the Federal Reserve's balance sheet grows, banks take the newly created money and lend it out. As you can see in Figure 7.4, commercial and industrial loans rise and fall depending on how the economy is doing. Banks make lots of loans in good times and fewer loans in bad times.

In the past few years, however, despite the massive increase in the Federal Reserve's balance sheet, lending has not remotely kept pace with the underlying growth in the monetary base. All the money that the Fed has created sits on bank balance sheets as reserves. The vast majority of these funds represent *excess* reserves, that is, reserves exceeding the 10 percent reserve requirement. Historically, banks never

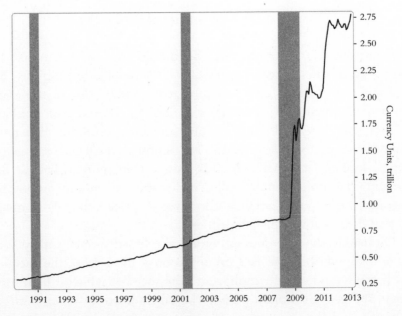

Figure 7.3   Rapidly Rising Money Supply

kept excess reserves because they earn no interest on them. If they could lend the money out elsewhere, why leave it at the central bank? However, in the United States, the Emergency Economic Stabilization Act of 2008 allowed the Federal Reserve to pay interest on excess reserves. Not surprisingly, the amount of excess reserves in American banks increased dramatically, as you can see from Figure 7.5. *So the Fed created money, and very little happened with it. It did not circulate as an infusion of liquidity, the fuel that enables an economy to accelerate. Instead, it sat around frozen in excess reserves.*

We should note that the term *excess reserves* is a misleading concept, a mere regulatory fiction. U.S. regulators decided that banks should keep a reserve of 10 percent. European regulators have different rules for loans invested in sovereign debt. A central bank can change the definition of *excess* at any time. But a banker can also decide to not lend as much as the regulator allows. What may be an "excess reserve" for the regulator may be for the banker money prudently managed in difficult times.

Perhaps it might be easier to think of the reserve requirement as a speed limit. In good weather and driving conditions, you can go this fast and no faster. But in bad weather, with the roads covered in ice and a blizzard in the forecast, slower driving is prudent.

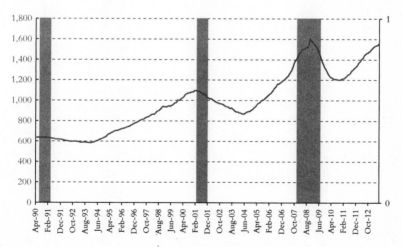

Figure 7.4   In Normal Times, Money Growth Turns into Loans
SOURCE: *Variant Perception*, Bloomberg.

With that understanding, we can see what's really going on: the disconcerting divergence between the ballooning monetary base and the modest increase in actual lending has widened because the velocity at which money circulates—the speed at which banks, businesses and consumers drive around the economy—has slowed. Consumers and businesses are borrowing less, and banks are lending less. You can see from Figure 7.5 how velocity typically rises in good times and falls in bad times. The dark bars are recessions, and the white spaces are expansions. Whenever a recession happens, velocity slows down. You could think of a liquidity trap as an extended recession that suppresses velocity.

When velocity falls and banks don't lend, it is difficult to get money into consumers' hands in order to stimulate the economy. When the banking multiplier doesn't work, that is when you need the *fiscal* (government spending) multiplier to kick in. In his now-famous speech on November 21, 2002, entitled "Deflation: Making Sure 'It' Doesn't Happen Here," Bernanke noted that creating inflation is much

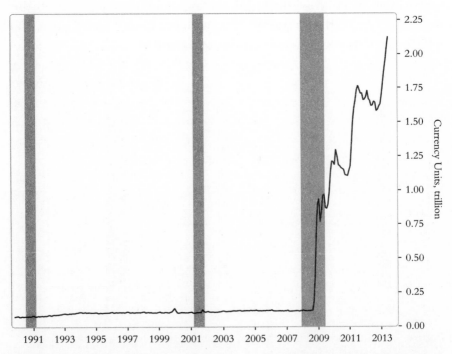

Figure 7.5   In Bad Times, Excess Money Growth Turns into Excess Reserves

easier if a central bank simply bypasses the banking system and works closely with the government:

> In practice, the effectiveness of anti–deflation policy could be significantly enhanced by cooperation between the monetary and fiscal authorities. A broad-based tax cut, for example, accommodated by a program of open–market purchases to alleviate any tendency for interest rates to increase, would almost certainly be an effective stimulant to consumption and hence to prices. . . . A money-financed tax cut is essentially equivalent to Milton Friedman's famous "helicopter drop" of money.

Creating money and handing it straight to the government that could then write a check to every taxpayer is one way to get around the falling velocity problem. That is not something that the United States or any other country is doing. Instead, taxes are going up almost everywhere.

Before the Great Financial Crisis, the only country that had experimented with quantitative easing was Japan, from 2003 to 2006. While the size of the Bank of Japan's balance sheet doubled, the broad money supply barely grew, and loans in fact declined throughout that period. *While the monetary base grew quickly, the velocity of money fell even faster.* The Bank of Japan's experiment failed to generate any meaningful growth, inflation, or lending. (It did manage to devalue the Japanese currency and fuel all sorts of bubbles around the world, funded in Japanese yen. Other countries borrowed from the Japanese in the "yen carry trade," but very little lending happened in Japan.)

One of the key reasons that velocity fell in Japan, just as it is falling today, is that interest rates were so low that banks had no incentive to lend money out. Also, with very low returns on investment in Japan, people did not want to borrow, either.

Central banks want to increase lending and increase the velocity of money, but they're doing all the wrong things to achieve their goals. The approach is nonsensical, driven more by the interests of the powerful financial sector than by reality or logic. Interest rates are one of the key drivers of money velocity. When interest rates are rising, velocity tends to be high; and when interest rates are low, velocity tends to fall. With low rates, people who have already borrowed money are

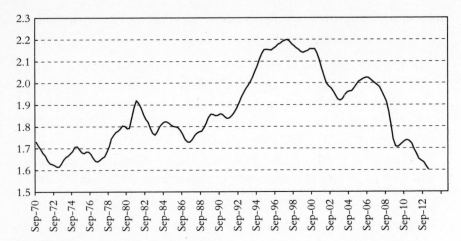

Figure 7.6 The Reason Increases in the Monetary Base Don't Translate to Higher Broad Money Is Low Velocity
SOURCE: Federal Reserve Bank of St. Louis.

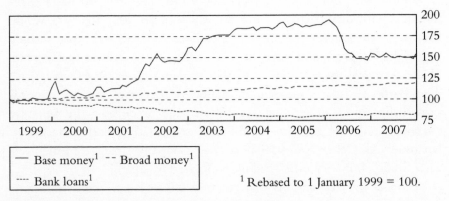

Figure 7.7 QE Failed to Increase Lending in Japan
SOURCE: Bank of Japan.

bailed out. But with very low rates, lenders have absolutely no incentive to lend. As you can see from Figures 7.8 and 7.9, lower rates and a larger money supply tend to depress monetary velocity. By keeping the world trapped near zero, central banks are depressing velocity. *Paradoxically, the best policy to forestall falling velocity and the hoarding of cash would be to raise interest rates.*

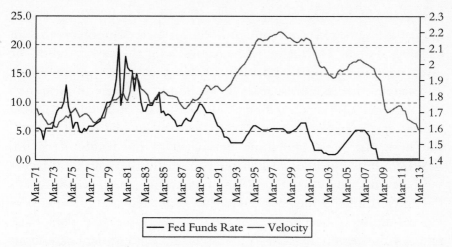

Figure 7.8   Interest Rates and Velocity Move in the Same Direction
SOURCE: *Variant Perception*, Bloomberg.

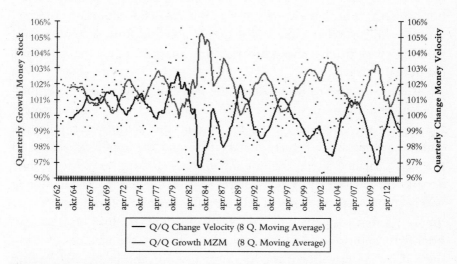

Figure 7.9   Changes in Money Stock and Money Velocity Move in
Opposite Directions
SOURCE: *Variant Perception*, Bloomberg.

In fact, velocity is falling for many reasons. One reason is the
actions of the central banks themselves. In the chapter on financial repression, we looked at the shortage of government bonds and

how that was forcing people to take all sorts of risks. When a central bank buys up all government bonds, it creates problems for the banking system. Normally, when banks, money market funds, or investment funds need cash, they pledge their government bonds as collateral in the repo market. Their bonds are as good as money, and they get cash against them. This is all part of a multi-trillion-dollar repo market that many call the "shadow banking system." But now that more and more bonds are in the hands of central banks, there is not enough collateral to grease the wheels of banking or even shadow banking. Manmohan Singh, an economist with the International Monetary Fund, has estimated that the narrowing definition of acceptable collateral in the interbank market has reduced the repledging rate of collateral by the big banks to about 2.4 times, from 3.0 before the crisis. This doesn't sound like much, but it involves a drop of up to $5 trillion in the cash generated by the banks. That's more than the cash injected by the central banks' bond-buying programs since 2008. Who (beyond economic theoreticians with no experience in the actual ebb and flow of trading and banking) would have thought distorting markets could be good for the actual markets?

If velocity were to keep falling, the Fed could create an almost infinite amount of money, and inflation would not rise. Unfortunately, the higher the monetary base, the higher the *potential* for inflation. The huge increase in the monetary base and the rapid expansion of the Fed's balance sheet are not inflationary as long as velocity stays very low. However, if velocity starts to rise, all that potential money will become *broad* money that will circulate. Inflation could start to rise quickly if that happens. The Fed keeps pouring gasoline on wet logs, hoping to light a fire. As long as the logs are wet, the chances of starting a blaze are low. But if the logs ever dry out, the Fed could end up with an almighty blaze. That is what the inflationistas are rightly worried about.

What might cause velocity to rise and inflation to pick up? For the money multiplier to go back to a more normal level, one of two things could happen. Either the economy could recover and the demand for money would go back to precrisis levels, or people's expectations about inflation would change, which would cause them to want to spend money instead of sit on large amounts of cash.

Velocity is not stable and can rise or fall. It is what statisticians call *mean reverting*. Prior to the crisis, it was very high and now it has fallen—the lowest it has been in many decades and getting closer to the all-time lows—but it is not destined to stay low forever. The velocity of money is what economists call a *mean-reverting statistic*. That means it doesn't continue in one direction forever. The lower velocity simply means that we are closer to the point at which it begins to accelerate to a faster pace. Trust us, everyone will be surprised when that moment happens. When it rises, it will most likely pose a grave challenge to central bankers and investors.

Escaping the Liquidity Trap

How does a country escape a liquidity trap? This is a key question that politicians and central bankers have been struggling to find the answer to. As long as an economy has too much debt, a country can be stuck in a liquidity trap; so the real question is: what is the right way to reduce the debt?

One of the clearest pieces we have read on escaping a debt crisis and liquidity trap comes from one of the world's greatest fund managers, Ray Dalio at Bridgewater. In a study entitled "An In-Depth Look at Deleveragings," Dalio examined countries that have tried to reduce their debt.[1] Whenever countries are drowning in too much debt, they have to deleverage. Countries can manage the process well; and through a combination of defaults, debt forgiveness, inflation, and growth, they can produce a relatively smooth deleveraging (debt reduction). Some countries, however, have not managed debt reductions effectively and have caused extremely high levels of unemployment, social upheaval, and even outright wars. As Dalio explained, "The differences between how deleveragings are resolved depend on the amounts and paces of (1) debt reduction, (2) austerity, (3) transferring wealth from the haves to the have-nots, and (4) debt monetization. . . . [B]eautiful ones balance these well and ugly ones don't."

Normally, in a deleveraging, the initial phase is a sharp economic contraction as businesses and households confront problems paying their debts and stock market and real estate prices fall. Early in this phase, the only debt reduction comes through outright defaults, a painful process that leads to more banking crises and less lending. During this period, the fall in private-sector credit growth and the tightness of liquidity lead to declines in demand for goods, services, and financial assets. Once the worst of the crisis is over, the amount of debt relative to incomes starts to improve, while economic activity strengthens and financial asset prices rise. This happens because there is enough "printing of money/debt monetization" to bring the nominal growth rate above the nominal interest rate, making it easier for debtors to pay off their debts. At the time, countries usually experience a currency devaluation to offset the deflationary forces.

If you look around the world, you can find many examples of deleveragings that worked and others that didn't turn out very well. Bridgewater breaks the outcomes down into three groups:

1. "Ugly deflationary deleveragings" (which occurred before enough money was "printed" and deflationary contractions existed and when nominal interest rates were above nominal growth rates).
2. "Beautiful deleveragings" (those in which enough "printing" occurred to balance the deflationary forces of debt reduction and austerity in a manner in which there is positive growth, a falling debt/income ratio and nominal GDP growth above nominal interest rates).
3. "Ugly inflationary deleveragings" (in which the "printing" is large relative to the deflationary forces and nominal growth through monetary inflation and interest rates are in a self-reinforcing upward spiral).

How does Dalio rate the deleveragings that are now happening around the world? Dalio thinks the United States is experiencing "the most beautiful deleveraging yet seen." The government debt level has gone up, but households have steadily reduced their debt levels, and modest growth has returned. Europe's, by contrast, is an ugly deleveraging where debt-to-income levels for governments and households alike have risen over the past few years, and growth remains elusive. Japan's is much like Europe's: government debt ratios have continued to climb as the economy has stagnated and even contracted.

When an economy goes through a beautiful deleveraging, it comes out the other side ready to grow again. Former Secretary of the Treasury Larry Summers has argued that the U.S. economy needs to achieve "escape velocity" to clear the crisis. He believes the Great Financial Crisis has not impaired America's long-term growth outlook.

We would generally agree, but with the caveat that the transition phases are not smooth. In order for the economy to escape from the downturn effectively, like a three-stage space rocket, three transitional mechanisms have to trigger at the right points: (1) government spending stops the downturn from becoming worse, (2) companies rebalance inventories, and (3) consumers gain confidence and begin spending again.

Let's look at the evidence: the government has spent an enormous amount of money; companies have pared their inventories down to record low levels; and if you look at retail sales, car sales, and home sales, consumers are slowly starting to spend again. The U.S. economy still faces large challenges—bringing down unemployment, for instance—but to us it looks as if the U.S. economy has gone through a beautiful deleveraging and achieved escape velocity. Now, if only Europe and Japan could do the same.

Overstaying One's Welcome

Dr. Johnson said that guests are like fish: they start to stink after the third day. No one likes guests that overstay their welcome, and the question we have to ask is: when should central banks say goodbye to Code Red policies?

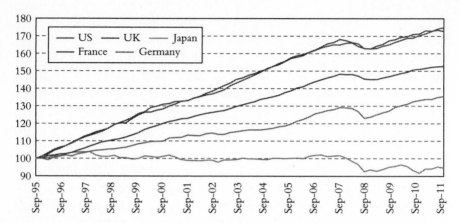

Figure 7.10   Clearly, the United States Has Recovered but Europe Has Not
SOURCE: *Variant Perception*, Bloomberg.

The massive expansion of the Fed's balance sheet that Fed Chairman Bernanke undertook after the failure of Lehman Brothers was completely appropriate in order to avoid another Great Depression. As the great monetarist economist Milton Friedman once observed, the Federal Reserve definitely caused the Great Depression by contracting the amount of money in circulation by one third from 1929 to 1933. Under Bernanke, the Fed created credit that offset, though only partially, the contraction in bank lending in the Great Financial Crisis; although, despite the rapid growth in the Fed's balance sheet starting in late 2008, total banking-system lending has been growing far below its historical rate. On balance, however much we may rue the necessity for intervention, Bernanke deserves respect for taking bold and difficult steps during an emergency and immediately afterwards.

But now that the crisis has passed, Code Red policies have moved in like guests that have overstayed their welcome. We can praise what Bernanke did during the crisis, but today we have legitimate grounds to criticize central bankers. In the United States, nominal GDP growth has been far above the central bank interest rate for the past few years; inflation has been moderate, with no signs of deflation anywhere;

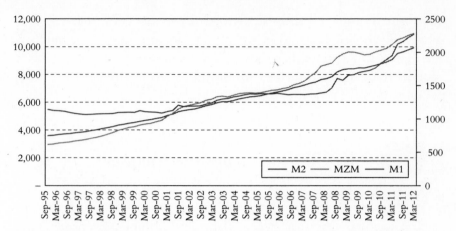

Figure 7.11 All Measures of Money Are Growing Strongly, but not Weimar or Zimbabwe Style
Source: *Variant Perception*, Bloomberg.

commercial and industrial lending in the United States has picked up; auto sales are back to normal historical rates; housing markets have come back to prebubble (and sustainable) levels; stock markets are at five-year highs in most of the world; and credit spreads are now so low that investors are getting almost no return for their risks. All measures of money growth are positive with M1, M2 and MZM rising at a healthy clip. The Fed should pat itself on the back for engineering a beautiful deleveraging and achieving escape velocity for the U.S. economy; that done, it should call an end to Code Red. Unfortunately, rather than declaring victory and going home, the Fed appears to have little intention of abandoning its unconventional policies. Bernanke and other Fed governors seem to subscribe to the Mae West school of central banking: "Too much of a good thing is wonderful."

Code Red policies were once a temporary emergency measure deployed to revive the economy, but now they have become an open-ended life-support system for zombie companies, banks, and governments, allowing them to borrow cheaply. But all the while, Code Red simultaneously squeezes savers, disincentivizes lending, and goads investors to chase returns in risky assets. Money printing on the scale we've seen has gone far beyond a necessary remedy. It has been transformed from a legitimate temporary emergency measure into a lifestyle choice. During an operation, doctors need to administer anesthetics to a patient, but today Code Red policies are the medical equivalent of regularly delivering morphine to a patient—years after the operation is over.

Key Lessons from the Chapter

In this chapter we learned:

- Inflationistas fear that hyperinflation is around the corner. They think that increases to the money supply are always inflationary. Deflationistas believe the world is trapped in a rerun of the 1930s and that the best solution is for governments to spend money freely and for central banks to print money to finance that spending.
- In normal times, inflationistas are right, but in a liquidity trap after a debt crisis, many normal economic rules do not apply. Driving down interest rates can fail to stimulate the economy, and governments can borrow cheaply despite high deficits.
- Central banks are creating *potential* money, not money that any of us can immediately spend. Money is like water, taking different forms: sometimes it's like ice, at other times liquid like water, and at others like a gas that evaporates. The kind of money that central banks are creating is monetary base, and that is like ice. It will not move until commercial banks lend it out and it can slosh around in the economy.
- The velocity of money is the measure of how quickly money moves around the economy. Since central banks have created lots of money, velocity has plunged and offset almost all of the increase in the monetary base.
- In a liquidity trap, businesses and households don't want to borrow, and banks don't want to lend. The monetary base can grow, but velocity will fall. So it becomes very hard for the central bank to influence the broader money supply.

- Monetary velocity is highly correlated to the level of central bank interest rates. Low interest rates depress velocity. In a Code Red world, central banks have kept interest rates at zero, and velocity has plunged. Paradoxically, central banks should raise rates if they want velocity to rise and money to flow through the economy.
- It was right for central banks to embark on Code Red policies during the Great Financial Crisis and immediately afterwards, but today most of the policies have outlived their usefulness. Inflation is moderate, and there are no signs of deflation outside of Japan and a few countries in the European periphery.

Chapter Eight

What Will Happen When It All Goes Wrong

Experience shows that what happens is always the thing against which one has not made provision in advance.

—John Maynard Keynes

We could raise interest rates in 15 minutes if we have to. So, there really is no problem with raising rates, tightening monetary policy, slowing the economy, reducing inflation, at the appropriate time.

—Ben Bernanke on 60 Minutes,
December 5, 2010

I beseech you, in the bowels of Christ; think it possible you may be mistaken.

—Oliver Cromwell

Central banks around the world have created an enormous amount of high-powered monetary reserves since 2008, which is to say they've created the seeds of money, but it would take private-sector loan demand to plant those seeds and commercial bank lending to germinate and water them before the new reserves could grow into real money in the hands of the nonbanking public. As we discussed in *Endgame*, deleveraging pressures across the developed world continue to suppress aggregate demand and drive money velocity to its lowest levels in over 50 years; but what happens when private-sector deleveraging ends?

The level of central bank reserves is so high that there is the potential to create very high inflation if the monetary multiplier—the technical term for the rate at which banks lend out their reserves—returns to levels we saw before the financial crisis and if the central banks do nothing to address the inflation risk. For example, the U.S. money supply could surge to more than $33 trillion if the money multiplier returns to pre–quantitative easing (QE) 2008 levels. But that would not happen overnight. At some point, central banks would be forced to act by "mopping up" reserves.

The big problem is that, because rates are so low and the size of the monetary base is so out of whack relative to the past, the potential adjustment due to inflationary pressures on even modestly higher short-term interest rates is equally extreme.

Currently, banks are very happy sitting on trillions of dollars of excess reserves and not lending them out. But if interest rates were to go up and velocity increase, that could change relatively quickly. People would want to put money to work at higher rates. The problem for the economy is that very small increases in interest rates from near-zero levels will trigger massive changes in the amount of money people want to hold and in the velocity of money movement. In order to counteract the sudden move by banks to lend the trillions of dollars they are sitting on and by businesses and individuals to spend that money, the Fed would have to shrink its balance sheet very quickly.

In order to avoid a very large surge in inflation, central banks are going to have to figure out not only *when* to end their Code Red policies but *how*. Unfortunately, that is much easier to do in theory than in practice.

As we noted earlier, Fed Chairman Ben Bernanke said in his *60 Minutes* interview that he was "100 percent" confident the Fed could keep inflation below 2 percent and reverse its Code Red policies at the right time. Not only was he extremely confident, he also thought policy makers "could raise interest rates in 15 minutes" if needed.

In theory, Bernanke was right. But as Yogi Berra once observed, "In theory there is no difference between theory and practice. In practice there is." There are almost no strictly technical problems involved in reversing the Code Red policies, but that doesn't necessarily mean things will go smoothly.

In previous chapters we've shown you that central bankers have a terrible record when it comes to foreseeing financial crises or even turns in the business cycle. There is a small chance that central banks will manage to end or reverse Code Red policies without a major policy error, but history suggests that the odds are not good. It is the hope of both your humble analysts that central bankers figure it out and our concerns become unjustified. But hope is not a strategy, especially when that hope has little basis in history.

In a moment of intellectual humility, long before he started implementing Code Red policies, Chairman Bernanke admitted as much during a December 2004 speech before the National Economists Club. He pointed out that it is tempting to think that the Federal Reserve is the driver of the U.S. economy and can steer it well—but, he said, steering the U.S. economy is not so easy:

> First, policy makers working to keep the economy from going off the road must deal with informational constraints that are far more severe than those faced by real-world drivers. Despite the best efforts of the statistical agencies and other data collectors, economic data provide incomplete coverage of economic activity, are subject to substantial sampling error, and become available only with a lag. Determining even the economy's current "speed," consequently, is not easy, as can be seen by the fact that economists' estimates of the nation's gross domestic product (GDP) for the current quarter may vary widely. Forecasting the economy's performance a few quarters ahead is even more difficult, reflecting not only problems of economic measurement and the effects of unanticipated shocks but also the complex and constantly changing nature of the economy itself. Policy makers are unable to predict with great confidence even how (or how quickly) their own actions are likely to affect the economy. *In short, if making monetary policy is like driving a car,*

then the car is one that has an unreliable speedometer, a foggy wind-shield, and a tendency to respond unpredictably and with a delay to the accelerator or the brake. [Emphasis added]

Keep those words from Bernanke in mind when he assures you that he knows exactly when and how to withdraw Code Red policies.

In one sense, we can be critical of Bernanke when he said he is 100 percent confident that he can deal with inflation. The chairman of the most powerful central bank in the world simply cannot be seen to have doubts in the midst of a crisis. We've had the privilege of talking with more than a few central bank governors over the years. In person and in private they almost all express the real concerns about the difficulties of setting economic monetary policy.

In fact, when you read the speeches of many of the members of the Federal Open Market Committee (FOMC), you will find they have serious doubts about the current direction of economic policy. You have only to read the minutes of the meetings to understand that even though there is a tone of collegiality in the room, there are some serious disagreements. But the one thing they understand is they cannot shout "fire" in a full theater. The chairman (or potentially chair-woman) of the major central banks have to exude confidence. It is a requirement of the job. Just understand that when you watch their press conferences.

How Are Your Navigation Skills?

"The Federal Reserve will need to carefully navigate through the completion of quantitative easing," the Organization for Economic Cooperation and Development wrote in its May 2013 global economic forecast. "A premature exit could jeopardize the fragile recovery, but waiting too long could result in a disorderly exit from the program, with sizable financial losses."

Unfortunately, the Fed's track record strongly suggests that the Fed is almost guaranteed to get its timing wrong for exiting Code Red policies. And whenever the Fed starts its tightening cycles, you always get blow-ups of thinly capitalized speculators and banks because cheap funding disappears. Once the tightening cycle has started for good, it usually triggers a large explosion. You don't have to look very far back to see all the sectors that blew up when the Fed tightened rates. Think of commercial property in 1989, the stock market in 2000, or housing and banks in 2008.

This time around, we have lived through more than four years of central bank rates near zero. This is a far longer period of accommodative policy than we saw in 1992–1993 and 2002–2004 together, and there is no apparent end in sight. That's why tightening monetary policy is going to be extremely painful. The greater the policy accommodation, the greater the difficulties withdrawing it will cause. Expect blowups and bankruptcies when the Fed starts to tighten. As Warren Buffett said, the ending of QE will be "the shot heard round the world."

Once again we will see the playing out of Minsky's stability-leads-to-instability thesis—the Minsky Moment. Central banks, fearful of small instabilities, have fought long and hard for seeming stability, but meanwhile an even greater potential for instability is building.

It turns out that preventing small forest fires actually makes a large forest fire more likely and more costly when it does break out. This is Nassim Taleb's antifragility hypothesis writ large. Just as human bones get stronger when subjected to stresses, and rumors or riots intensify when someone tries to repress them, many things in life derive resilience from adapting to stress, disorder, volatility, and turmoil. Taleb characterizes as "antifragile" that category of things that not only gain from chaos but need it in order to survive, strengthen, and flourish. And the financial markets number among those "living things" that need to experience regular minor stresses in order to develop the capacity to withstand larger problems. Just as you can't train to run a race or play football by sitting on the couch, you can't develop the mechanisms to balance the flow of capital and markets by trying to strictly control what needs to be as free as possible.

A Red Balloon Full of Nitroglycerin

One of the best writers on the problems with the Fed's bloated balance sheet has been John Hussman. He notes that for the past 80 years there has been an extremely stable relationship between the monetary base and the growth of the economy. Between 1929 and 2008, the ratio of

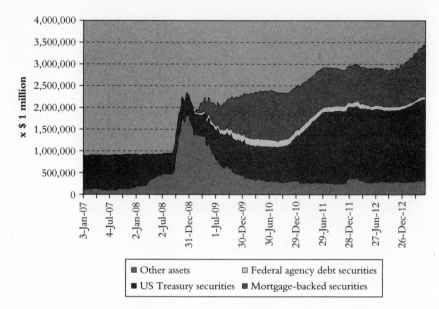

Figure 8.1   Size and Composition of the Fed's Bloated Balance Sheet
SOURCE: http://commons.wikimedia.org/wiki/File:US_Federal_Reserve_balance_sheet_total.png

the monetary base to nominal gross domestic product (GDP) has been between 5 percent and 12 percent. There have been two exceptions to this tight relationship. The most recent was in the 1980s when Fed Chairman Paul Volcker killed inflation by shrinking the monetary base to less than 5 cents per dollar of nominal GDP, ending a 15-year period of escalating inflation. The earlier exception came in World War II, when the U.S. government ran massive deficits and the Fed more than doubled the monetary base. As a result, the quantity of base money rose as high as 17 cents per dollar of GDP in the early 1940s, just as the massive deleveraging of the 1930s drew to a close and the U.S. debt-to-GDP ratio approached its low point.

Let's look at what happened the last time the monetary base was as high as it is today. John Hussman enlightens us:

How did the Fed get the ratio of monetary base to GDP back to pre-war levels of less than 10 cents per dollar of GDP (a level that has historically been consistent with Treasury bill yields still only about 2%)? Did the Fed reverse course, as Bernanke promises can be done "in 15 minutes" to avoid inflation?

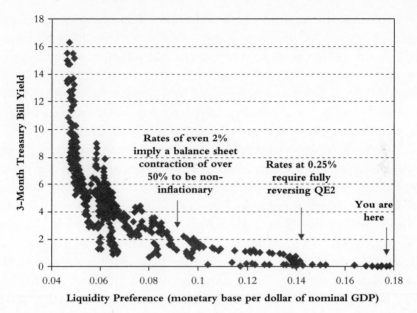

Figure 8.2   Uncharted Territory for Yields and Liquidity Preference
SOURCE: Hussman Funds.

No, it did not. Instead, the consumer price index shot up by 90% between 1940 and 1951, with the majority of that inflation in the back-half of the 1940s.

You will not be surprised to hear that economic deleveraging, followed by wartime money growth, eventually gave way to improving money velocity and high inflation. We should keep this pattern in mind as we watch the Fed prepare to extricate the economy from Code Red.

Not only is there a stable relationship between the monetary base and GDP, but there is a close relationship between short-term interest rates and the amount of non-interest-bearing money that people are willing to hold. Basically, the lower interest rates are, the more cash people are willing to carry around per dollar of nominal GDP. As interest rates move higher, people naturally respond to the opportunity to earn interest by reducing the amount of cash they hold.

Inflation and prices can become very unstable when an enormous amount of money has sat around in the form of excess reserves, earning very low interest. Small increases in interest rates from near-zero levels will spur a demand for liquidity and investment, and velocity will pick up quickly. If the monetary base doesn't shrink proportionately, you'll end up with high inflation. That inflation will not appear overnight, but you will see it after 6 to 18 months. The Fed's bloated balance sheet is like a red balloon full of nitroglycerin. As long as the economy remains in a liquidity trap, with low velocity, everything is okay. But any increase in velocity could prove deadly.

Any increase in interest rates, even a 0.25 percent boost, would require a rapid contraction in the Fed's balance sheet, or else strong inflationary pressures will quickly develop. For example, Hussman calculates that " larger increase in Treasury bill yields to 4% would imply a GDP deflator of about 2.35, which is more than double the current price level." The implication is that any normalization of interest rates would need to be accompanied by a massive contraction of the Fed's balance sheet in order to avoid inflation. Otherwise, the collapse in liquidity preference could trigger a collapse in the purchasing power of cash.

The Mechanics of Exit

Almost every army in the world has contingency plans for what to do in case it needs to invade its neighbors. Believe it or not, even countries like the United States and Canada, whose relations are very friendly, have prepared contingency plans in case they need to invade each other. In the 1930s, both countries drew up such strategies. Canada's plan was code-named Defence Scheme 1, and America's was called War Plan Red. Fortunately, the plans have never been needed.

Central banks around the world may have a real monetary war on their hands when they decide to undo their Code Red policies. The problem for the Colonel Jessups of the monetary policy world is that they've never, ever had to undo these kinds of experimental monetary policies before. They're in uncharted territory when it comes to withdrawing trillions of dollars from the global monetary system. Even worse, all of the major central banks may feel pressure to retighten at the same time. Given the mobility of capital and the interconnectedness of markets, what happens when one central bank tries to trim its sails may make the path forward for other developed and emerging economies far more difficult.

"Colonel" Bernanke has given many speeches over the past four years on how the Federal Reserve would exit its unconventional policies, so there is not a lot of guesswork as to how the Fed thinks the exit will happen.

Greater minds than ours have looked at the mechanics of unwinding Code Red policies. In theory, the key principles of unwinding Code Red policies (QE, zero interest rate policy [ZIRP], large-scale asset purchases [LSAPs]) are pretty much the same for the Fed as they are for the Bank of Japan, the Bank of England, or even the European Central Bank.

By far the best paper to read on the mechanics of exiting Code Red comes from Alan Blinder, a former Federal Reserve member and an old colleague of Bernanke's at Princeton University. Blinder wrote a paper titled "Quantitative Easing: Entrance and Exit Strategies." Based on speeches by Ben Bernanke, it outlined the key steps the Fed would have to take to shrink its balance sheet:

1. *Stop buying bonds.* It may seem blindingly obvious, but as long as central bankers keep buying bonds, it will be hard, if not impossible, to undo their Code Red policies. Markets are like junkies, and stock markets have become addicted to the heroin central banks have been pushing. (Things will start to go bump in the night.)

2. *Sell bonds in the open market.* Central banks will have to start selling the bonds they have on their balance sheets. This is not going to make governments at all happy. Bond yields and borrowing costs for governments have been very low because of Code Red. Central bank bond selling will mean horrific losses for anyone who owns treasuries and much higher bond rates.

3. *Passively redeem agency debt and mortgage-backed securities (MBSs) as they mature.* In plain English, this means that the Fed would sit on its MBSs and not sell them on the open market. Instead, it would wait for the mortgages to be repaid, allowing the MBSs to mature. As they matured, the Fed would then withdraw the cash from the monetary base.

4. *Increase the interest paid on excess reserves.* If banks decided to lend out the massive reserves parked at central banks, broad money

would explode. By paying interest on the excess reserves, central banks would try to keep the money parked at the Fed so that it didn't contribute to runaway inflation.

5. *Offer term deposits to depository institutions.* These deposits could not be counted as reserves. This policy would be a new development. The Fed has never before issued term deposits. At present, banks buy treasuries and T-bills to manage their cash. The Fed is hoping it can start offering deposits to lock up cash for a long time so that it won't be lent out and start circulating.

You will be reassured to know that the Fed has a plan. But as Mike Tyson once so eloquently put it, "Everyone has a plan till they get punched in the mouth." What Tyson was describing, on the level of the individual, was the "fog of war" that the great military theorist Carl von Clausewitz wrote about. Everything changes and plans go out the window once the fighting starts.

It is difficult to imagine that the financial markets won't throw up some unexpected surprises, and things will likely not play out the way central banks intend. Perhaps more important, it is difficult to imagine that governments will allow central banks to walk away from financing them.

QE = Hotel California

In theory, the Fed could reverse its Code Red policies in a second. However, the problems with undoing Code Red policies are all political and practical, not technical. In this section, we'll look at why it will be much harder to unwind the policies than central banks think.

The first problem is that if central banks were to stop buying government bonds or to sell the bonds they already own, government borrowing costs could skyrocket. Central banks are providing subsidies to elected governments to the tune of hundreds of billions of dollars by keeping borrowing costs down. If borrowing costs rise, the largely hidden subsidy will immediately be visible to everyone. The enormity of financial repression will be apparent if the Fed and other central banks end Code Red policies. It is highly likely, for this reason alone, that central banks will want to persist with their unconventional policies.

One of the best papers by far on the political problems associated with reversing Code Red policies is Willem Buiter's "Reversing Unconventional Monetary Policy: Technical and Political Considerations." It is extremely honest, direct, and informative. Buiter concludes that governments will not want to let central banks end Code Red policies, and central banks will have to bend over backwards and comply. Amazingly, Buiter is a former central banker himself and was on the Bank of England's Monetary Policy Committee. His words are very strong and worth heeding:

> Reversing the unconventional policies is likely to bring out into the open the extraordinary quasi-fiscal role played by some central banks during this crisis (most notably by the Fed), their usurpation of budgetary powers assigned to the legislative branch of government by constitutions, laws or deeply embedded conventions, and the extraordinary (and unnecessary) financial largesse bestowed by some central banks on a small number of financial institutions and a limited number of stakeholders in these institutions. This "quiet coup" by a body of unelected technocrats has political and constitutional consequences that have to be considered fully when a comprehensive evaluation of this episode is attempted.

Let's do a back-of-the-napkin calculation to estimate the costs of normalizing interest rates in the United States. The average interest rate paid by the U.S. Treasury on its marketable debt in June 2007 was 4.958 percent. By June 2013 it was down to 1.992 percent, a drop of almost 3 percent. On a debt of $17 trillion (an amount which will be a reality shortly after this book is published), that is a difference of $510 billion a year in interest payments. While Congress might be able to come up with a few tens of billions here or there, where will they come up with hundreds of billions of cuts from programs that one party or the other deems absolutely necessary? And such projections are *not* in the CBO forecasts.[1]

The U.S. Treasury has been increasing the average duration of U.S. debt, recently to 5.5 years. Even so, in a world of rising rates, as the old debt must be refinanced, it will have to be refinanced at higher rates. A 1 percent increase is a given, 2 percent is certainly not extreme, and

3 percent would take us back to where we were precrisis. This one factor could double the deficit over the coming years and complicate further what is already a very politically difficult conversation. And for politicians—too few of whom understand economics and markets— blaming the Fed for higher rates will be easy.

Should we cut entitlements or interest rates? Create havoc at the ballot box or in the markets? We must choose wisely. The pressure is going to be enormous.

Even former central bankers like Frederic Mishkin, who was a Fed governor with Bernanke, have been warning about the problem of allowing the central bank to become a puppet of the government. With three colleagues, Mishkin wrote a paper in which he warned, "The bottom line is that no matter how strong the commitment of a central bank to an inflation target, fiscal dominance can override it."

Fiscal dominance is a fancy term economists use to describe the situation when a central bank is forced to buy government debt so that the government can keep spending freely. If the central bank doesn't keep buying government bonds, interest rates could rise, making it difficult for the government to finance itself. When you think of fiscal dominance, think of the Bank of Japan bending to Shinzo Abe's will, or on a grander scale think of the Reserve Bank of Zimbabwe doing Robert Mugabe's bidding.

If the Federal Reserve becomes a large net seller of government bonds, either the private sector or foreign central banks will have to buy a lot more bonds. It is highly unlikely that either will want to change their portfolios without receiving much higher yields on government bonds. Bonds will have to sell off significantly and become cheap to induce the private sector to want to hold trillions of dollars of government bonds.

If interest rates rise at a rate it deems too fast, the Federal Reserve will start to loosen monetary policy very quickly. In the old days, central banks took very little interest rate risk and held mainly government bills. Bills are short-term instruments that pose almost no interest rate risk. Bills don't change price much with changes in interest rates. Furthermore, if a central bank that holds government bills wants to shrink its balance sheet, it simply has to wait a few weeks until the short-term bills mature, and it gets cash. Currently, the Fed has absolutely no bills on its balance sheet. This is simply extraordinary. It is the mother of all painting yourself into a corner problems. Shrinking the Fed's balance sheet is significantly more difficult without bills.

At the beginning of 2008, the Fed had a small, clean, low-duration balance sheet on the asset side. Today, the asset side of its balance sheet is much larger, duration has doubled, and the assets are of much lower quality. (In normal times, central banks buy only government debt of relatively short duration. Buying longer-term debt injects liquidity for longer periods of time, so staying short maintains flexibility.) Nowadays, the Fed is stuffed to the gills with longer-dated bonds that are highly sensitive to rising interest rates. If interest rates start to go up, the value of the bonds will go down very quickly. The longer their duration, the greater the mark-to-market move of the bonds the Fed will be holding when interest rates change. With yields at historical lows, finding ready buyers for long-term bonds will be difficult in a world of rising interest rates.

And just to provide an extra degree of difficulty, 40 percent of the Fed's balance sheet is in mortgage-backed securities. If they started to sell those interest rates on new mortgages would rise and provide a significant headwind of the housing market. How popular would that be? That almost forces the Fed to concentrate its "mopping up actions" on government bonds.

How much could the Fed lose? Bloomberg News and MSCI estimate that if the bonds on the Fed's balance sheet lose value, there could be more than a half trillion dollars in losses. They applied scenarios devised by the Fed itself for stress-testing the nation's 19 largest banks. MSCI sees the market value of Fed holdings shrinking by $547 billion over three years under an adverse scenario. Many forecasters put the losses the Fed could accumulate much higher still.

As we write this, a 2 percent increase in interest rates on a 30-year bond with a 4 percent coupon would see the bond price drop by about 28 percent. The same 2 percent increase would cause a 20-year bond's price to fall by about 23 percent and a 10-year bond's price by 15 percent. Under such a scenario, investors who have been buying U.S. government bonds could take big losses on their mark-to-market portfolios.

Some might ask, where's the problem? If an institution has the time, it can simply hold the bonds and get its money. There are institutions that can wait, but pension funds are generally required to have a certain amount of current assets to offset future liabilities. If the *current* value of their assets drops substantially, they must raise more capital to come into compliance. That capital comes from corporate shareholders, taxpayers (in the case of government pension funds), and current retirees who might risk lower pension payments.

Unfortunately, the very large losses will make the Fed and other central banks technically insolvent. If they were regular banks, they'd go broke, but central banks only go bust on paper. The Fed and most other central banks are like giant hedge funds on steroids.

The Fed has borrowed more than $3.24 trillion and has only $55 billion of equity. Thus, the Fed is levered about 59-to-1. That is an insane amount of leverage for a bank or fund. To put this in perspective, the Fed's balance sheet is already far more overleveraged than the balance sheets of Lehman Brothers, Bear Stearns, CIT, FreddieMac, or FannieMae were before those institutions failed. But no need to worry—it's all just on paper.

Every year, the Fed pays out its net income as dividends to its sole shareholder, the U.S. Treasury. This practice helps flatter the U.S. deficit figures and represents the value of seigniorage, or money printing. Because the Fed never retains earnings, it has no built-up equity—no reserves—and is thus incredibly leveraged.

Given the very large losses that the Fed will sustain, it should have stopped paying out its earnings to the government and instead retained its earnings in order to cover future losses from changes in interest rates. If the Fed had done that for the past few years, it would already be sitting on top of over $250 billion of reserves. As the Fed keeps rates low for the next year or two, this number would rise, and it would likely have almost enough capital to cover the extremely large losses that are coming down the pipeline.

Of course, that would mean even less income to the U.S. Treasury and higher fiscal deficits.

We can pretty much guarantee that the Fed will be technically insolvent as it starts to wind down its Code Red policies, and this situation will have major implications for its policy independence from the

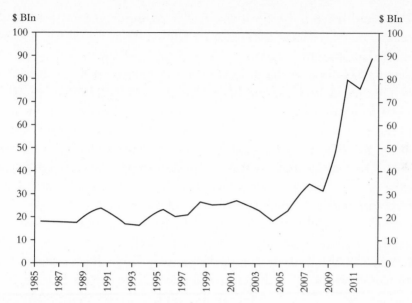

Figure 8.3   The Fed Sends Checks to the Treasury
SOURCES: FRB, Haver Analytics, DB Global Market Research.

U.S. government. The Fed's suspending remittances and carrying unrealized losses would be a shocking development. We would start to see headlines stating that the central bank had gone bust. Clearly, the Fed would keep operating, but a capital shortfall could lead to suspending the remittances it has been sending to the government every year and/or would require the Fed to start borrowing from Treasury. Now, if the Fed is borrowing money from the government and not the other way around, how long do you think the Fed could keep its independence? Not long. And the thought of the Fed's doing whatever the government wants it to should frighten you.

At the same time that the Fed will need to borrow money from the government, it also may need to pay out very large checks to Wall Street banks. In order to neutralize the very large excess reserves banks are holding, the Fed will be forced to pay interest on those reserves. The higher the rate it pays, the bigger the gift to the banking sector.

The problem is that interest paid to banks is a gift, and banks can then lend out that money at many multiples. In the United States the money multiplier is 10. So if the Fed is paying 3 percent interest on reserves, and the excess reserves are a trillion, then it will pay $30 billion. If that amount is lent out at a multiplier of 10, then the Fed will create $300 billion in the process of trying to neutralize a trillion dollars. The Fed will in the end have neutralized only $700 billion. If the Fed were paying 5 percent, banks could create $500 billion in loans; and the Fed would only be able to neutralize $500 billion. At 10 percent on $1 trillion, the banking system could create $1 trillion in loans, and the Fed would not neutralize any money. Paying high interest on excess reserves means the Fed will run just to stand still. And it will borrow money from the taxpayer in order to pay banks.

For decades Western central banks have not changed the required reserve ratio, the amount of money banks have to keep as reserves overnight at the Fed. As central banks exit Code Red policies, they will likely have to hike the ratio and then further adjust it to regulate monetary policy. The required reserve ratio is a very blunt instrument with an impact that is extremely large. We doubt they'll be able to do it smoothly.

Let's recap quickly. If the Fed exits Code Red policies, it will likely become technically insolvent, will have to borrow money from the Treasury (on paper at least), and will then have to make large payments to Wall Street banks that will turn around and lend out the money again, multiplying it 10 times. What could go wrong?

When Deleveraging Gives Way to Credit Expansion, Watch Out for Inflation

As we discussed in *Endgame*, credit deleveraging across the developed world will eventually give way to credit expansion, opening the door for a recovery in money velocity and trend economic growth. At that point, the mountain of money reserves created through Code Red policies may start to flow through to the public and fuel high inflation in some parts of the world. In order to maintain price stability, central banks will need to accurately anticipate this secular shift from credit deleveraging to credit expansion and immediately begin to exit their Code Red monetary policies. Timing is critical on this front. If they react too quickly, their haste could result in a deflationary bust. If they react too late, their slow response could result in very high inflation. Navigating this regime shift in key economies around the world will be critical for investors hoping to protect and grow their wealth in a Code Red world.

The bible to read on hyperinflation is Peter Bernholz's *Monetary Regimes and Inflation*. Bernholz examined 12 of the 29 hyperinflationary episodes where significant data existed. Every hyperinflation looked the same. "Hyperinflations are always caused by public budget deficits which are largely financed by money creation." But even more interesting, Bernholz identified the level at which hyperinflations start. He concluded that ". . . the figures demonstrate clearly that deficits amounting to 40 percent or more of expenditures cannot be maintained. They lead to high inflation and hyperinflations. . . ." Interestingly, even lower levels of government deficits can cause inflation. For example, 20 percent deficits were behind all but four cases of hyperinflation.

It is extremely important to note Bernholz's conclusion: "Hyperinflations are not caused by aggressive central banks by themselves. They are caused by irresponsible and profligate legislatures that spend far beyond their means and accommodative central banks that lend a helping hand to governments."

What are the implications for the present day? For all our complaints about central banks, fiscal liabilities are the real threat that will lead to higher inflation if central banks continue to monetize government liabilities. But if they're going to monetize, governments with independently authorized central banks should disavow the overly convenient "slippery slope" option of paying their bills by directly printing new currency.

A government should either pay down its liabilities with currency already in circulation or else finance deficits by issuing new bonds and selling them to the public or to its central bank in order to acquire the necessary money. For the bonds to end up in the central bank, the central bank must conduct an open-market purchase. This action increases the monetary base. This process of financing government spending through the money creation process is called monetizing the debt. Monetizing debt is thus a two-step process where the government

issues debt to finance its spending, and the central bank purchases the
debt from the public. But even when monetization is performed correctly, the economy is left with an inflationary swelling of the base
money supply.

Inflation in the longer run is highly related to the growth in
unproductive government spending. While not all U.S. government
spending is unproductive, it is easily seen that the inflationary pressures
of the late 1960s and 1970s occurred in a period when government
spending was sharply expanding as a share of GDP. From this perspective, the recent explosion of government spending as a share of GDP is
a source of longer-term inflation concern.

Exiting QE will cause all sorts of problems, but the biggest problem will come if there is no exit at all. The dirty secret of central banks
is that they will likely not shrink their balance sheets at all. Many economists are already openly admitting this. Columbia Professor Michael
Woodford, a leading monetary theorist, says it is time for central banks
to come clean and state openly that bond purchases are forever, and the
sooner people understand this the better. He thinks that discussing exit

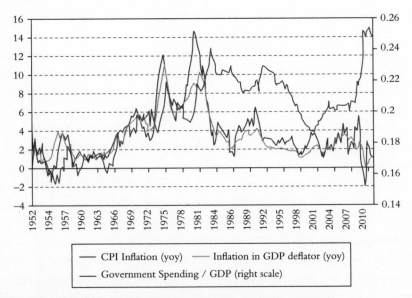

Figure 8.4   Growth of Government Spending Leads to Inflation
SOURCE: Hussman Funds

strategies is very counterproductive. If the idea of QE, LSAP, ZIRP, financial repression, and other Code Red policies is to raise inflation expectations and create negative real rates, then the more irresponsible the policy, the better. As Professor Woodford argued at a conference held at the London Business School, "If a we are going to scare the horses, let's scare them properly. Let's go further and eliminate government debt on the bloated balance sheet of central banks." Apparently, Professor Woodford thinks the motto of central banks should be "When in doubt, go nuts." It's what Paul Krugman calls "credibly promising to be irresponsible."

As we will see in the next chapter, everything, including irresponsibility, will be on the table. For many countries, there will be no good choices.

The irony is that we think the most probable outcome will be a period of even more volatility in markets and economies. The proximate causes will not be the same as in 2008, but the volatility will be just as wrenching. As we saw in Europe, a small country or problem (such as Greece) can have far-reaching consequences.

You need to understand that there is no playbook for what is coming. Any investment plans that rest on the assumption that current policy and economic environments will not change will be proven wrong. The best plan is to assume volatility.

Despite the cries against austerity, budgets are going to have to be cut in ways that none of us can now imagine possible, or monetary policies are going to be pursued that will make today's efforts seem tame. Either path will be problematic, probably in the extreme.

The lesson from history is rather clear. Things go along fine until the *Bang!* moment. Right up until that event there are innumerable politicians, economic pundits, and other voices in the mainstream media who go right on saying all is well. And then everyone is greatly surprised when the red balloon pops. You won't be. And the good news is that you have time to prepare.

Before we jump into our final section on how to invest, please note that we are not part of the "doom and gloom" crowd. We are quite bullish on human progress and markets, just bearish on governments. Ignore what governments are doing at your peril. Or "short" them to your advantage.

Key Lessons from the Chapter

In this chapter we learned:

- Central banks have expanded their balance sheets massively. If banks loan out the excess reserves they have parked at the Fed, money growth would surge and create very high levels of inflation.
- Exiting Code Red policies will require central banks to get the timing right. Unfortunately, most economists and central bankers have a very limited understanding of where the economy is or where it is going.
- Most central banks are likely to tighten too late because they are afraid that they will kill off any recovery. There are many reasons why central banks will unwind Code Red policies too late or will not do so at all.
- Governments around the world borrow money very cheaply from central banks. They will not like to see the biggest buyers of their bonds stop buying and start selling. Government borrowing costs would skyrocket.
- Central banks are holding trillions of dollars of bonds and will sustain large losses on paper when interest rates rise. Technically, central banks will likely be insolvent.
- Historically, the biggest source of inflation has not been central banks but governments that have forced central banks to finance them.

Chapter Nine

Easy Money Will Lead to Bubbles and How to Profit from Them

The difference between genius and stupidity is that genius has its limits.

—Albert Einstein

Genius is a rising stock market.

—John Kenneth Galbraith

Any plan conceived in moderation must fail when circumstances are set in extremes.

—Prince Metternich

E very year, the Darwin Awards are given out to honor fools who kill themselves accidentally and remove themselves from the human gene pool. The 2009 Award went to two bank robbers. The robbers figured they would use dynamite to get into a bank. They packed large quantities of dynamite by the ATM machine at a bank in Dinant, Belgium. Unhappy with merely putting dynamite in the ATM, they pumped lots of gas through the letterbox to make the explosion bigger. And then they detonated the explosives. Unfortunately for them, they were standing right next to the bank. The entire bank was blown to pieces. When police arrived, they found one robber with severe injuries. They took him to the hospital, but he died quickly. After they searched through the rubble, they found his accomplice. It reminds you a bit of the immortal line from the film *The Italian Job* where robbers led by Sir Michael Caine, after totally demolishing a van in a spectacular explosion, shouted at them, "You're only supposed to blow the bloody doors off!"

Central banks are trying to make stock prices and house prices go up, but much like the winners of the 2009 Darwin Awards, they will likely get a lot more bang for their buck than they bargained for. All Code Red tools are intended to generate spillovers to other financial markets. For example, quantitative easing (QE) and large-scale asset purchases (LSAPs) are meant to boost stock prices and weaken the dollar, lower bonds yields, and chase investors into higher-risk assets. Central bankers hope they can find the right amount of dynamite to blow open the bank doors, but it is highly unlikely that they'll be able to find just the right amount of money printing, interest rate manipulation, and currency debasement to not damage anything but the doors. We'll likely see more booms and busts in all sorts of markets because of the Code Red policies of central banks, just as we have in the past. They don't seem to learn the right lessons.

Targeting stock prices is par for the course in a Code Red world. Officially, the Fed receives its marching orders from Congress and has a dual mandate: stable prices and high employment. But in the past few years, by embarking on Code Red policies, Bernanke and his colleagues have unilaterally added a third mandate: higher stock prices. The chairman himself pointed out that stock markets had risen strongly since he signaled the Fed would likely do more QE during a speech in Jackson Hole, Wyoming, in 2010. "I do think that our policies have contributed to a stronger stock market, just as they did in March 2009, when we did the last iteration [of QE]. The S&P 500 is up about 20 percent plus and the Russell 2000 is up 30 percent plus." It is not hard to see why stock markets rally when investors believe the most powerful central banker in the world wants to print money and see stock markets go up.

Investors are thrilled. As Mohamed El-Erian, chief executive officer at Pacific Investment Management Company, said, "Central banks are our best friends not because they like markets, but because they can only get to their macro objectives by going through the markets."

Properly reflected on, this is staggering in its implications. A supposedly neutral central bank has decided that it can engineer a recovery by inflating asset prices. The objective is to create a "wealth effect" that will make those who invest in stocks feel wealthier and then decide to spend money and invest in new projects. This will eventually be felt throughout the economy. This "trickle-down" monetary policy has been successful in creating wealth for those who were already rich (and for the banks and investment management firms who service them) but has been spectacularly a failure in creating good jobs and a high-growth economy. The latest quarter as we write this letter will be in the 1 percent gross domestic product (GDP) range.

And to listen to the speeches from the majority of members of the Federal Reserve Open Market Committee, their prescription is more of the same. Indeed, when Bernanke merely hinted this summer that QE might end at some point, something that everyone already knows, the market swooned and a half-a-dozen of his fellow committee members felt compelled to issue statements and speeches the next week, saying, "Not really, guys, we really are going to keep it up for a bit longer."

We've seen this movie before. In the book *When Money Dies*, Adam Fergusson quotes from the diary of Anna Eisenmenger, an Austrian widow. In early 1920 Eisenmenger wrote, "Speculation on the stock exchange has spread to all ranks of the population and shares rise like air balloons to limitless heights. . . . My banker congratulates me on every new rise, but he does not dispel the secret uneasiness which my growing wealth arouses in me . . . it already amounts to millions." Much like after the initial Nixon Shock in the 1970s, stock prices rise rapidly when a currency weakens and money supply grows. Not surprisingly, the 1970s led to bubbles in commodities.

This chapter will show how to spot bubbles when they form, how to profit from them, and how to avoid the dire consequences when they burst.

Excess Liquidity Creating Bubbles

As we write *Code Red*, stock prices are roaring ahead. In fact, many asset classes are looking like bubbles from our cheap seats. (While we expect a correction at some point, when the Fed or the Bank of Japan creates money, it has to go somewhere.)

One area that stands out as particularly bubbly is the corporate bond market. Investors are barely being compensated for the risks they're taking. In 2007, a three-month certificate of deposit yielded more than junk bonds do today. Average yields on investment-grade debt worldwide dropped to a record low 2.45 percent as we write this from 3.4 percent a year ago, according to Bank of America Merrill Lynch's Global Corporate Index. Veteran investors in high-yield bonds and bank debt see a bubble forming. Wilbur L. Ross Jr., chairman and CEO of WL Ross & Co. has pointed to a "ticking time bomb" in the debt markets. Ross noted that one third of first-time issuers had CCC or lower credit ratings and in the past year more than 60 percent of the high-yield bonds were refinancings. None of the capital was to be used for expansion or working capital, just refinancing balance sheets. Some people think it is good there is no new leveraging, but it is much worse. This means that many companies had no cash on hand to pay off old debt and had to refinance.

One day, all the debt will come due, and it will end with a bang. "We are building a bigger time bomb" with $500 billion a year in debt coming due between 2018 and 2020, at a point in time when the bonds might not be able to be refinanced as easily as they are today, Mr. Ross said. Government bonds are not even safe because if they revert to the average yield seen between 2000 and 2010, ten year treasuries would be down 23 percent. "If there is so much downside risk in normal treasuries," riskier high yield is even more mispriced, Mr. Ross said. "We may look back and say the real bubble is debt."

Another bubble that is forming and will pop is agricultural land in many places in the United States (although agriculture in other countries can be found at compelling values). The bubble really started going once the Fed started its Code Red policies. Land prices in the heart of the Corn Belt have increased at a double-digit rate in six of the past seven years. According to Federal Reserve studies, farmland

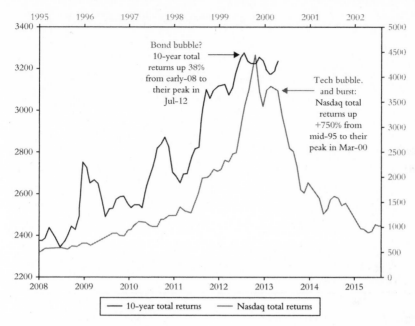

Figure 9.1   Bond Market Bubble
SOURCE: Goldman Sachs Global ECS Research.

prices were up 15 percent last year in the most productive part of the Corn Belt, and 26 percent in the western Corn Belt and high plains. Iowa land selling for $2,275 per acre a decade ago is now at $8,700 per acre. As you can see from Figure 9.2, the increase in farmland prices beats almost anything the United States saw during the housing bubble. A lot of banks in the Midwest will have problem with their lending.

Why are we seeing so many bubbles right now? One reason is that the economy is weak and inflation is low. The growth in the money supply doesn't go to driving up prices for goods like toothpaste, haircuts, or cars. It goes to drive up prices of real estate, bonds, and stocks.

Excess liquidity is money created beyond what the real economy needs. In technical terms, Marshallian K is the difference between growth in the money supply and nominal GDP. The measure is the surplus of money that is not absorbed by the real economy. The term is named after the great English economist Alfred Marshall. When the money supply is growing faster than nominal GDP, then excess liquidity tends to flow to financial assets. However, if the money supply is

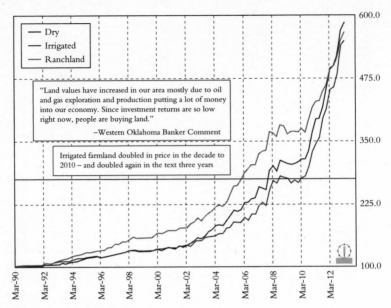

Figure 9.2 Farmland Bubble
Sources: KC Fed, Diapason.

growing more slowly than nominal GDP, then the real economy
absorbs more available liquidity. That's one reason why stocks go up so
much when the economy is weak but the money supply is rising.

It is also why stock markets are so sensitive to any hint that the Fed
might ease off on QE. Real players know how the game is played. You
can listen to the business media or read the papers and find hundreds
of "experts" saying that stock prices are rising based on fundamentals.
You can take their talking points and change the dates and find they
are essentially the same as 1999 and 2006–2007. (More on the implications of this in Part II when we talk about investing.)

The rise in real estate, bonds, and stocks does not count toward
any inflation measures. On the desk in his office at Princeton, Einstein
once had the words "not everything which can be measured counts,
and not everything which counts can be measured." Inflation happens
to be one of the things that counts but can't be measured (except in
very narrow terms). Excess liquidity flows from asset class to asset class.
As you can see from Figure 9.3, booms and busts around the world
happen whenever central banks tighten or loosen monetary policy.

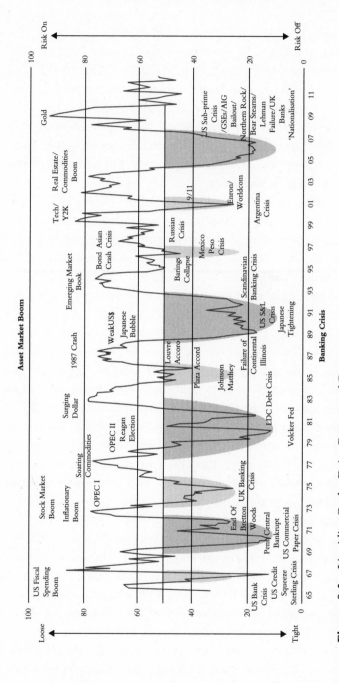

Figure 9.3 Liquidity Cycles Drive Booms and Busts

SOURCE: Crossborder Capital, www.liquidity.com/Docs/Global_Liquidity_Indexes_(GLI)_2012_Data.pdf.

Humans Never Learn

Financial bubbles happen frequently. In the 1970s, gold went from $35 to $850 before crashing. In the 1980s, the Japanese Nikkei went from 8,000 to 40,000 before losing 80 percent of its value. In the 1990s, the Nasdaq experienced the dot-com bubble and stocks went from 440 to 5,000 before crashing spectacularly in 2000. The Nasdaq lost 80 percent of its value in less than two years. Many housing bubbles over the past decade in the United Kingdom, United States, Ireland, Spain, and Iceland saw house prices go up 200 and even 500 percent and then lose over half their value in real terms.

The U.S. market has had frequent crashes: 1929, 1962, 1987, 1998, 2000, and 2008. Every time, the bubble was driven by different sectors. In 1929, radio stocks were the Internet stocks of their day. In 1962, the electronic sector crashed. The previous year, most electronic stocks had risen 27 percent, with leading technology stocks like Texas Instruments and Polaroid trading at up a crazy 115 times earnings. In 1987, the S&P had risen more than 40 percent in less than a year and over 60 percent in less than two years. In 1998, it was strong expectation on investment opportunities in Russia that collapsed. In 2000, the Internet bubble was so crazy that companies with no earnings and often no real revenues were able to go public, skyrocket, and then crash. Eventually, in all bubbles fundamental values re-assert themselves and markets crash.

Economists and investors have spilled a lot of ink describing bubbles, yet central bankers and investors never seem to learn and people get caught up in them. Peter Bernstein in *Against the Gods* states that the evidence "reveals repeated patterns of irrationality, inconsistency, and incompetence in the ways human beings arrive at decisions and choices when faced with uncertainty."

What is extraordinary is how much bubbles all look alike. The situations were similar in many ways. In the 1920s, the financial boom was fueled by new technologies such as the radio that supposedly would change the world. In the 1990s, the stock market bubble was driven by the rapid adoption of the Internet. Both technologies were going to fundamentally change the world. Stocks like RCA in the 1920s and Yahoo in the 1990s were darlings that went up like rockets. Figure 9.4 plots the two charts against each other. The similarities and timing of market moves are uncanny.

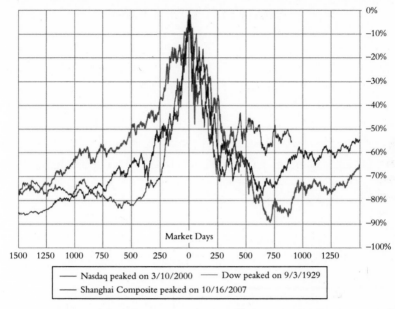

Figure 9.4   Almost All Bubbles Look Alike: 1920s Stock Bubble vs. Nasdaq
SOURCE: Dough Short, http://dshort.com/charts/bears/bubbles/bubble-overlay-3.gif

If you look at Figure 9.5, you can see the gold bubble in the 1970s. (Some academics have noted that the surge in gold prices closely followed the increase in inflation in the late 1970s, reflecting its value as a hedge against inflation. When inflation fell in the 1980s, gold prices followed. So it is an open question whether gold in the 1970s should be considered a bubble.)

Fast-forward 10 years, and you can see from Figure 9.6 that the bubble in the Japanese Nikkei looked almost exactly the same.

Bubbles happen again and again. The same basic ingredients are found every time: fueled initially by well-founded economic fundamentals, investors develop a self-fulfilling optimism by herding that leads to an unsustainable accelerating increase in prices. And each time people are surprised that a bubble has happened. As billionaire investor George Soros once said about financial cycles: "The only surprise is that we are always surprised."

For example, the corporate bond market appears to be in another bubble. "We have a hyper-robust bond market right now," Dallas Fed

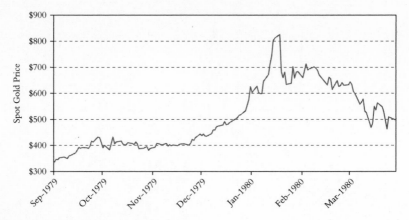

Figure 9.5   Gold Bubble in the 1970s
SOURCES: Mauldin Economics, S&P Capital IQ.

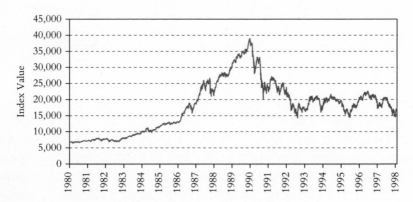

Figure 9.6   Japanese Stock Market Bubble in the 1980s
SOURCES: Mauldin Economics, S&P Capital IQ.

President Richard Fisher, a former investment manager, said in an interview. These robust markets are part of the Fed's policy intent, he said, but the credit market jump has put him on guard for a new destabilizing credit boom. "You don't sit on a hot stove twice."

Economists and investors, though, repeatedly sit on hot stoves. Economic researchers have managed to create bubbles in laboratories. Economist Reshmaan N. Hussam and his colleagues not only managed to create bubbles once, they managed to bring the same subjects back in for the same experiment and still managed to reproduce bubbles. It didn't matter if people were given fundamental information regarding what was available or not. It didn't matter how financially sophisticated the participants were either: corporate managers, independent small business people, or professional stock traders. No one was immune from re-creating bubbles.

It seems that everyone is born a sucker. As humans, we developed our instincts dodging lions and chasing antelopes on the African savannah over hundreds of thousands of years. Now it seems we chase asset prices. It is as if we are hard-wired to respond to movement in what market we are following. The conclusion from repeated experiments shows that it doesn't matter if people live through one bubble or even two, they'll likely fall for bubbles again. The smarter people learn from bubbles. But they don't learn to avoid them; they participate again and simply think they're smart enough to know when to get out. This has been showed many times in trading experiments conducted by Vernon Smith, a professor at George Mason University who shared in the 2002 Nobel Prize in Economics. As Smith said, "The subjects are very optimistic that they'll be able to smell the turning point. They always report that they're surprised by how quickly it turns and how hard it is to get out at anything like a favorable price."

Anatomy of Bubbles and Crashes

There is no standard definition of a bubble, but all bubbles look alike because they all go through similar phases. The bible on bubbles is *Manias, Panics and Crashes*, by Charles Kindleberger. In the book, Kindleberger outlined the five phases of a bubble. He borrowed heavily from the work of the great economist Hyman Minsky. If you look at Figures 9.7 and 9.8, you can see the classic bubble pattern.

Figure 9.7   Anatomy of a Bubble: The Kindleberger-Minsky model
SOURCES: Kindleberger, SG Cross Asset Research.

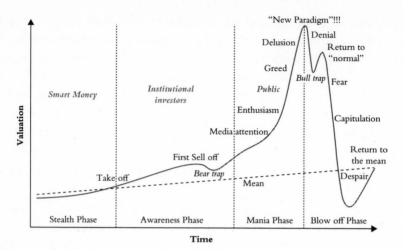

Figure 9.8 Anatomy of a Typical Bubble
SOURCE: Jean-Paul Rodrigue

(As an aside, all you need to know about the Nobel Prize in Economics is that Minsky, Kindleberger, and Schumpeter did not get one and that Paul Krugman did.)

Stage 1: Displacement

All bubbles start with some basis in reality. Often, it is a new disruptive technology that gets everyone excited, although Kindleberger says it doesn't need to involve technological progress. It could come through a fundamental change in an economy; for example, the opening up of Russia in the 1990s led to the 1998 bubble or in the 2000s interest rates were low and mortgage lenders were able to fund themselves cheaply. In this displacement phase, smart investors notice the changes that are happening and start investing in the industry or country.

Stage 2: Boom

Once a bubble starts, a convincing narrative gains traction and the narrative becomes self-reinforcing. As George Soros observed, fundamental analysis seeks to establish how underlying values are reflected in stock prices, whereas the theory of reflexivity shows how stock prices can influence underlying values. For example, in the 1920s people believed that technology like refrigerators, cars, planes, and the radio would change the world (and they did!). In the 1990s, it was the Internet. One of the keys to any bubble is usually loose credit and lending. To finance all the new consumer goods, in the 1920s installment lending was widely adopted, allowing people to buy more than they would have previously. In the 1990s, Internet companies resorted to vendor financing with cheap money that financial markets were throwing at Internet companies. In the housing boom in the 2000s, rising house prices and looser credit allowed more and more people access to credit. And a new financial innovation called securitization developed in the 1990s as a good way to allocate risk and share good returns was perversely twisted into making subprime mortgages acceptable as safe AAA investments.

Stage 3: Euphoria

In the euphoria phase, everyone becomes aware that they can make money by buying stocks in a certain industry or buying houses in certain places. The early investors have made a lot of money, and, in the words of Kindleberger, "there is nothing so disturbing to one's well-being and judgment as to see a friend get rich." Even people who had been on the sidelines start speculating. Shoeshine boys in the 1920s were buying stocks. In the 1990s, doctors and lawyers were day-trading Internet stocks between appointments. In the subprime boom, dozens of channels had programs about people who became house flippers. At the height of the tech bubble, Internet stocks changed hands three times as frequently as other shares.

The euphoria phase of a bubble tends to be steep but so brief that it gives investors almost no chance get out of their positions. As prices rise exponentially, the lopsided speculation leads to a frantic effort of speculators to all sell at the same time.

We know of one hedge fund in 1999 that had made fortunes for its clients investing in legitimate tech stocks. They decided it was a bubble and elected to close down the fund and return the money in the latter part of 1999. It took a year of concerted effort to close all their positions out. While their investors had fabulous returns, this just illustrates that exiting a bubble can be hard even for professionals. And in illiquid markets? Forget about it.

Stage 4: Crisis

In the crisis phase, the insiders originally involved start to sell. For example, loads of dot-com insiders dumped their stocks while retail investors piled into companies that went bust. In the subprime bubble, CEOs of homebuilding companies, executives of mortgage lenders like Angelo Mozillo, and CEOs of Lehman Brothers like Dick Fuld dumped hundreds of millions of dollars of stock. The selling starts to gain momentum, as speculators realize that they need to sell, too. However, once prices start to fall, the stocks or house prices start to crash. The only way to sell is to offer prices at a much lower level. The bubble bursts, and euphoric buying is replaced by panic selling. The panic selling in a bubble is like the *Roadrunner* cartoons. The coyote runs over a cliff, keeps running, and suddenly finds that there is nothing under his feet. Crashes are always a reflection of illiquidity in two-sided trading—the inability of sellers to find eager buyers at nearby prices.

Stage 5: Revulsion

Just as prices became wildly out of line during the early stages of a bubble, in the final stage of revulsion, prices overshoot their fundamental values. Where the press used to write only positive stories about the bubble, suddenly journalists uncover fraud, embezzlement, and abuse. Investors who have lost money look for scapegoats and blame others rather than themselves for participating in bubbles. (Who didn't speculate with Internet stocks or houses?) As investors stay away from the bubble, prices can fall to irrationally low levels.

Anatomy of Bubbles and Crashes

It would be unfair to compare humans to lemmings. Lemmings don't deserve such an awful comparison, and, and believe it or not, they don't actually commit mass suicide. But humans have a lot in common with locusts, fish, and birds.

While economists stick to traditional and orthodox (and generally boring) models for understanding how investors behave, academics in other disciplines have made great advances in understanding bubbles. The interdisciplinary work has shown that crowd behavior can shift from a highly unpredictable mass of individuals and look similar to large-scale collective wave like patterns. When these shifts happen, the whole is a lot more than the parts.

Biologists such as Iain Couzin, at Oxford University, have studied collective behavior of swarms, flocks, schools, and colonies of animals. What is amazing is that he has been able to re-create herding in laboratories.

Couzin would put groups of up to 120 [juvenile locusts] into a sombrero-shaped arena he called the locust accelerator, letting them walk in circles around the rim for eight hours a day while an overhead camera filmed their movements and software mapped their positions and orientations. He eventually saw what he was looking for: At a certain density, the bugs would shift to cohesive, aligned clusters. And at a second critical point, the clusters would become a single marching army. Haphazard milling became rank-and-file—a prelude to their transformation into black-and-yellow adults.

That's what happens in nature, but no one had ever induced these shifts in the lab—at least not in animals. In 1995, a Hungarian physicist named Tamás Vicsek and his colleagues devised a model to explain group behavior with a simple—almost rudimentary—condition: every individual moving at a constant velocity matches its direction to that of its neighbors within a certain radius. As this hypothetical collective becomes bigger, it flips from a disordered throng to an organized swarm, just like Couzin's locusts. It's a phase transition, like water turning to ice. The individuals have no plan. They obey no instructions. But with the right if-then rules, order emerges.[1]

You can see this in your own habits in traffic. If you are not careful, you will match the speed of your neighbors, often going over the posted limits. This shift is exactly what happens in financial markets with bubbles. At first, traders buy and sell according to their own interests. They're like locusts doing their own thing. But over time traders have a tendency to imitate their friends and colleagues. This tendency increases up until the market reaches the euphoria phase, and then the mass of traders may place the same sell orders at the same time, thus causing a crash.

By far the biggest advances in understanding the dynamics of bubbles comes from Didier Sornette, a French physicist turned financial economist. Sornette has developed mathematical models to explain earthquake activity, Amazon book sales, herding behavior in social networks like Facebook, and even stock market bubbles and crashes. In his brilliant book *Why Stock Markets Crash*, Sornette explains how bubbles form and how they burst. He found that most theories do a very poor job of explaining bubbles. The only explanations that make sense are cooperative self-organization, very much like schools of fish or flocks of birds that Couzin was studying at Oxford University. As he wrote, "A central property of a complex system is the possible occurrence of coherent large-scale collective behaviors with a very rich structure, resulting from the repeated nonlinear interactions among its constituents: the whole turns out to be much more than the sum of its parts."

Sornette found that log-periodic power laws do a good job of describing speculative bubbles with very few exceptions. Classic bubbles tend to have parabolic advances with shallow and increasingly frequent corrections. Eventually, you begin to see price spikes at 1-day, 1-hour, and even 10-minute intervals before crashes.

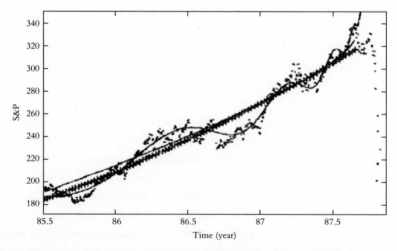

Figure 9.9   Log-Harmonic Oscillation of New York Stock Exchange before 1987 Crash
SOURCE: Didier Sornette.

After crashes, journalists often look for the cause of crashes. They'll blame something like portfolio insurance for the crash of 1987 or the bankruptcy of Lehman Brothers, rather than a fundamentally unstable market.

Most approaches to explain crashes search for possible mechanisms or effects that operate at very short time scales (hours, days, or weeks at most). We propose here a radically different view: the underlying cause of the crash must be searched months and years before it, in the progressive increasing buildup of market cooperativity or effective interactions between investors, often translated into accelerating ascent of the market price (the bubble). According to this "critical" point of view, the specific manner by which prices collapsed is not the most important problem: a crash occurs because the market has entered an unstable phase and any small disturbance or process may have triggered the instability. Think of a ruler held up vertically on your finger: this very unstable position will lead eventually to its collapse, as a result of a small (or absence of adequate) motion of your hand. The collapse is fundamentally due to the unstable position; the instantaneous cause of the collapse is secondary. In the same vein, the growth of the sensitivity and the growing instability of the market close to such a critical point might explain why attempts to unravel the local origin of the crash have been so diverse. Essentially, anything would work once the system is ripe.

Sornette's conclusion is that a fundamentally unstable system and human greed means that market bubbles and crashes won't disappear anytime soon.

Just as people imitate each other on the way up, causing markets to fluctuate in rising waves, when crashes happen, investors still take their cues from each other, and "anti-bubbles" form. For example, in Figure 9.10, Sornette has shown that the bursting of bubbles follows the same patterns as the buildup, but in a reverse wave-like oscillation.

The advances in the study of bubbles and crashes are progressing at a good pace. Some behavioral economists are doing great work in labs in recreating bubbles and finding what motivates people. Biologists are developing a greater understanding of the math behind group behavior and herding. And geophysicists like Didier Sornette are continuing to

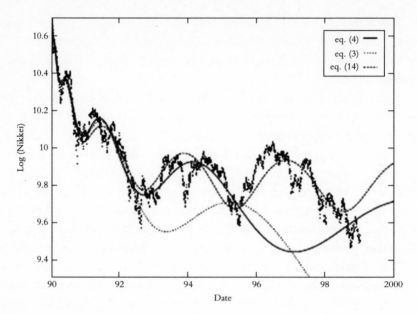

Figure 9.10   Bubbles Bursting Form Anti-bubbles and Wave-like Patterns
SOURCE: Didier Sornette.

publish new research. As an aside, he is now beginning to predict bubbles. It will be interesting to see how traders respond to his statements.

Keep Moving, There's Nothing to See

Horrible housing bubbles in the United States, United Kingdom, Spain, Ireland, and Latvia created severe banking crises that threatened the global economy. You might think that central bankers would be busy trying to figure out how to identify bubbles and how to prevent them from happening again or causing banking crises. Nothing could be further from the truth.

Central bankers have a dismal record of identifying bubbles. During the Internet boom, Alan Greenspan briefly complained about "irrational exuberance" and then made an about face and argued that a productivity miracle accounted for the stock market surge. When the housing bubble came around in 2004, Alan Greenspan, then the chairman, said the rise in home values was "not enough in our judgment to raise major concerns." In 2005, Bernanke argued that a housing bubble was "a pretty unlikely possibility." After all, as he said on CNBC in 2005, "We've never had a decline in house prices on a nationwide basis." As late as May 2007, once the bubble had already burst, he said that Fed officials "do not expect significant spillovers from the subprime market to the rest of the economy."

Today, Bernanke has noted "the practical problems with using monetary policy to pop asset price bubbles." Bernanke and many of his colleagues believe that monetary policy is a "blunt tool" and would prefer using regulation rather than interest rates to pop bubbles. Bernanke often points out that recognizing a bubble is hard. "It is extraordinarily difficult," he said during his Senate confirmation, "to know in real time if an asset price is appropriate or not."

(Interestingly, they show no hesitation to use their "blunt tool" to engineer asset price increases!)

Federal Reserve governor and vice chair Janet Yellen endorsed the Greenspan doctrine in September 2005: "The . . . decision to deflate an asset price bubble rests on positive answers to three questions. First, if the bubble were to collapse on its own, would the effect on the economy be exceedingly large? Second, is it unlikely that the Fed could mitigate the consequences? Third, is monetary policy the best tool to use to deflate a house-price bubble? My answers . . . are, 'no,' 'no,' and 'no.'" She could not have been more wrong.

In 2009, after the Great Financial Crisis, Yellen changed her mind: ". . . it is now patently obvious that not dealing with some bubbles can have grave consequences, . . . in my view, recent painful experience strengthens the case for using such policies, especially when a credit boom is the driving factor." She now says "monetary policy that leans against bubble expansion may also enhance financial stability by slowing credit booms and lowering overall leverage."

After reading statements like that, you might think that Yellen would want to call for an end to Code Red policies. Yet she is by far the most in favor of Code Red policies at the Federal Reserve. With central bankers, you always have to watch what they do, not what they say. And what she says and does may soon be important. As we write, she is the odds-on favorite to be the next chairwoman of the U.S. Federal Reserve.

Carry Trades and Bubbles

Recently, much of QE's effects have been felt in emerging-market countries. This is not just a response to the U.S. Fed, but from the Bank of Japan, the European Central Bank, and the Bank of England. Unlike the sick, indebted developed world, many emerging-market countries are growing and doing well. We have not seen a lot of borrowing in the developed markets. Instead, growth of credit and lending to private borrowers is happening in emerging markets. Emerging markets have been a popular target of excess capital for a number of reasons: their overall ability to take on debt remains strong and relatively strong their balance sheets are still relatively healthy, and more important, investment yields have been high relative to sovereign competitors. This two-speed world presents enormous problems. Code Red type policies in the developed world are leading savers and investors to flee very low rates of return at home in favor of putting money into Turkey, Brazil, Indonesia, or anywhere that offers higher rates of return.

Code Red–type monetary policies are designed to produce investment and growth, and they are! Just not in the countries that central banks intended to help.

This is a major headache for governments in these countries. For them, it is like having loads of visitors drop by all of a sudden. It is flattering they like your house, but after a while, you'd rather they didn't show up unexpectedly. Hot money flows are like drunken guests. They create a very big party, they leave unexpectedly, and they leave a god-awful mess behind. Large hot-money flows have been behind most major emerging market booms and busts.

Whenever major developed central banks keep rates at very low levels and weaken their currency, they cause bubbles. Let's look at two recent bubbles and crashes that Code Red policies helped cause.

After the Japanese bubble burst in 1989, the Bank of Japan (BoJ) cut interest rates close to zero. By 1995 the dollar-yen exchange

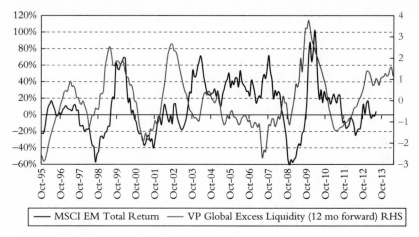

Figure 9.11   Global Excess Liquidity vs. Emerging Stock Market Returns
SOURCE: *Variant Perception*, Bloomberg.

rate weakened and the yen lost almost half of its value. The Japanese took money out of Japan and put money into Indonesia, Korea, Malaysia, Philippines, and Thailand. Investors in other countries borrowed money either directly in yen or through synthetic instruments. It was called the yen carry trade and was designed to take advantage of easy Japanese money to invest elsewhere. Everyone assumed that the yen would continue to go down making the terms of repayment easier.

Asia attracted nearly half of the total capital inflow to emerging markets, and the stock markets of South Korea, Malaysia, Singapore, Thailand, and Indonesia were soaring. The party didn't last forever. When the Thai currency came under pressure in June 1997, almost all Asian countries faced stock market crashes, capital flight, currency depreciations, and banking busts. The entire Asian episode perfectly fit the five stages of a bubble, but it was certainly much greater than it otherwise would have been given the policies of the BoJ.

Before the Great Financial Crisis, extremely loose monetary policy caused many bubbles. The main contributors to bubbles were the ultra-loose monetary policy of the BoJ from 2003 to 2006 when it engaged in massive quantitative easing, and the decision by Greenspan and the

Fed to keep interest rates at 1 percent for over a year. Investors again borrowed in yen and in dollars in order to invest abroad. These speculative money flows fueled commodity and real estate bubbles around the world. Oil, for example, increased 15-fold over less than a decade. Iron ore went up 10 times. Gold went up over 5 times. (More on commodity bubbles in Part II.) Very loose monetary policy precipitated real estate bubbles in the United States, United Kingdom, Spain, Ireland, Latvia, and other countries. When all the bubbles finally burst, the world experienced a traumatic crash in the fall of 2008 and the global banking system was close to collapse.

It should come as no surprise that bubbles happen when central banks bring rates too low. Researchers at the Federal Reserve are already warning about the problems of too low rates. William White is the chairman of the Economic Development and Review Committee at the Organization for Economic Cooperation and Development (OECD) in Paris and former chief at the Bank of International Settlements, about as establishment as you can get.

Writing for the Dallas Federal Reserve, he published a paper titled "Ultra Easy Monetary Policy and the Law of Unintended Consequences." His warnings were clear:

> Rate manipulation below the free market level distorts the investment calculation, systematically misallocating capital towards low yielding business ventures. The longer ZIRP [zero interest rate policy] lasts, the more the yield-starved investors desperately take reckless risks and the more capital flows into doubtful investments yielding ever lower returns. ZIRP thereby has the counterproductive consequence of eroding the productivity of capital as well as to slow down capital accumulation, with a prolonged and deepened recession as the final result.

The last time the Fed kept rates far below inflation and far below nominal GDP, the United States had a housing bubble. As you can see from Figure 9.12, currently the Fed Funds is far too low given current economic conditions.

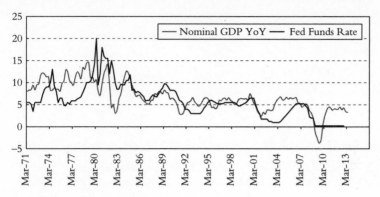

Figure 9.12   Nominal GDP vs. Fed Funds Rate
SOURCE: *Variant Perception*, Bloomberg.

The idea that ultra-low interest rates cause booms and busts is not new. Economists of the Austrian school, led by von Mises and Hayek, warned that credit fueled expansions lead to the misallocation of real resources that would end in crisis. In the Austrian theory of the business cycle, the central cause of the credit boom is the fall of the market rate of interest below the natural rate of interest. Investments that would not be profitable at higher rates become possible. The bigger the deviation of interest rates from the natural rate, the bigger the potential credit boom and the bigger the bust.

Like all bubbles, rapid price increases can rapidly reverse when interest rates return to normal levels. The greatest danger will then be to leveraged investors who bought farmland, corporate bonds, some emerging markets, and other bubbles with borrowed money. As you can see from Figure 9.13, whenever the Federal Reserve has announced QE stock markets have rallied very strongly, but when the central bank has paused QE, financial markets have experienced crashes. The first was the "flash crash" of 2010, and the second was the crash that happened in August 2011. You can bet money that leveraged investors chasing returns will be shocked when the Fed decides to exit Code Red policies. Expect more volatility and crashes.

Figure 9.13   QE Has Driven Stock Markets and End of QE Crashes
Sources: Mauldin Economics, S&P Capital IQ.

What You Can Do in Bubbles

While some bubbles have been very profitable for the few investors who bought at a low price and sold high at the peak of the bubble, most investors in bubbles arrive late, invest in the euphoria stage, and then see life-changing losses to their savings.

If you are fortunate enough to invest in the early displacement or boom phase of a bubble, pat yourself on the back. Don't chase gains into the euphoria phase. J. P. Morgan said he had made his fortune by selling too soon, and it is better to arrive early at an investment party and leave early rather than stay around for the euphoria phase and then the crash.

Do not get caught up in frenzies and avoid the euphoria phase of a bubble. Whenever something is on the front cover of magazines and constantly on CNBC, you can bet that it is a bubble. Avoiding urges to speculate or overtrade is critical. As Warren Buffett has said, "Investing is not a game where the guy with the 160 IQ beats the guy with the 130 IQ. . . . Once you have ordinary intelligence, what you need is the temperament to control the urges that get other people into trouble in investing." A great investor needs to be like Ulysses tying himself to the mast to avoid responding to the sirens calls of overvalued and over-stretched markets.

Smart people are often the ones most hurt by bubbles. Many investors think they can be heroes and trade the ups and downs well. Here's some news: you're not George Soros, and even a great trader George Soros can't always trade bubbles well. Let's look at how Soros's Quantum Fund traded the Nasdaq bubble, one of the greatest bubbles of all time. Soros correctly identified that Nasdaq was a bubble, and he was buying them in 1998, but many bubbles have severe corrections before they reach their peak. In 1998, his Quantum Fund was badly hit by losses as Nasdaq declined by 30 percent. Then the Nasdaq went up five times and Quantum was able to recover some gains. The fund returned 35 percent in 1999, but by not selling soon enough, Soros was involved in the dot-com crash in early 2000. For months, through late 1999 and early 2000, the weekly research meetings at Quantum focused on how to prepare for the inevitable sell-off of technology stocks. Soros himself would regularly phone his top managers, warning that tech stocks were a bubble set to burst. But when the crash happened, the fall was so quick, they were not able to get out fast enough. By April 2000, Quantum was down 22 percent. Soros had given back all the gains he made on the way up.

Moral of the story: When you see a bubble, don't try trading it at home. Even professional investors find it very difficult to trade. You might be able to light a match in a gunpowder factory and survive. But it doesn't mean you're not an idiot.

Once the bubble bursts, everyone tries to sell at the same time but can't. That is when you end up with crashes. Afterwards, many investors hang on to their shares at lower prices, hoping the stocks will go up again. If you recognize that you might be invested in a bubble that has burst and are in the crisis stage, you should sell. When stocks or property burst and are overvalued, they often have a very long way to fall. Remember that the Japanese Nikkei and the dot-com bubble both fell 80 percent and did not stop falling for a few years. They have never returned to their highs. Unfortunately, selling is easier said than done. No one enjoys admitting that they were wrong.

It is very difficult to sell because once investors have invested or bet, their confidence in their own abilities goes up. In *Influence* by Robert Cialdini, it is clear that his study of confidence has had a profound effect on the way he sees social interaction. In the book, Cialdini points out that once people bet on something they're far too confident. "A study done by a pair of Canadian psychologists uncovered something fascinating about people at the racetrack: Just after placing a bet, they are much more confident of their horse's chances of winning than they are immediately before laying down that bet."

Believe it or not, some of the very best investment opportunities you will ever find in your entire life are in the revulsion stage of a bubble. In the revulsion phase, when the markets have gone bust, investors no longer want to touch any investment associated with the boom years. Just as speculators were irrational during the euphoria phase, they become equally irrational during the revulsion phase.

Chasing bubbles higher involves buying things that are very irrationally *overvalued*. Buying after bubbles burst involves buying things that are irrationally *undervalued*. When things are too expensive, you have little to no margin of safety. When things are cheap, you can have ample margin of safety.

And therein lies the true secret to making money in bubbles. Simply patiently wait until they burst (they *always* do) and then invest when there is "blood in the streets." With this thought, cash is not simply money sitting idle. Cash should be seen as a call option on a future "blood event." Warren Buffett and other investors who follow the wisdom of Benjamin Graham make their money by patience and having the cash to buy when a true value opportunity presents itself.

Back in the days of the dot-com bubble, American Tower was one of the largest owners and operators of wireless towers. The company took on lots of debt building their towers. When the telecom and Internet bubble crashed, the stock traded at $1 in October 2002. That happens only when everyone is irrationally miserable. The irrationality doesn't last forever. As we write this today, it trades at over $80. American Tower had too much debt in 2002, but almost all the money the company had raised built a highly valued network of telecom towers. If any company wanted to re-create the network of towers, it would require billions of dollars of capital expenditures. Investors were throwing the baby out with the bathwater when they dumped all telecom-related shares. As it turned out, American Tower

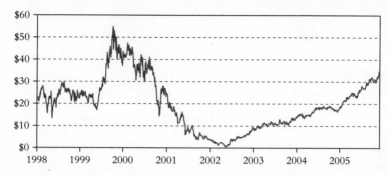

Figure 9.14   Some of the Greatest Investments Ever Happen in the Revulsion Phases of Bubbles
SOURCES: Mauldin Economics, S&P Capital IQ.

was able to lower its debt levels. When it did, the value of the stock skyrocketed. There are dozens of examples like American Tower after every bubble.

Global Crossing and other similar ill-fated ventures spent billions building fiber-optic networks across oceans based on Excel spreadsheets that promised massive Internet traffic. Up to 90 percent of that fiber went "dark" after the crash. But now, that fiber is extremely valuable. Savvy investors who bought that fiber for pennies on the dollar offered connective services at far lower prices and turned a profit. We got cheap international communications. The world should be grateful to investors who were willing to lose billions so we could have a cheap global Internet.

The same could be said for railroads in the United Kingdom in the mid-1800s and the United States in the 1870s. The companies went bankrupt, and the countries ended up with much cheaper transportation. As an aside, the only U.S. railroad company that did not go bankrupt was the only one that was totally privately financed. Again, cheap money from government sources created a massive bubble.

Looking back at 2002, the great investor Howard Marks said it was one the greatest opportunities for investment of his lifetime. Many stocks traded for less than the cash on their balance sheet. The same was true during the Great Financial Crisis.

Opportunities to buy hated investments cheaply do not come around often. When they do, you must be ready to act. As Charlie

Munger once said, when asked about his extremely successful long-term investment activity, "It wasn't hyperactivity, but a hell of a lot of patience. You stuck to your principles and when opportunities came along, you pounced on them with vigor."

Key Lessons from the Chapter

In this chapter we learned:

- Central banks are trying to make stock prices and house prices go up. They would like to see them go up moderately, but instead we are seeing bubbles in various asset classes like corporate bonds, farmland and some emerging markets.
- Bubbles in financial assets happen regularly—whether it is gold in the 1970s, the Japanese Nikkei in the 1980s, Internet stocks in the 1990s, or house prices before 2007. Humans are suckers for rising prices, and people hate to see their neighbors get rich, so everyone gets involved in bubbles.
- Bubbles look the same because they go through five typical phases:
  - Displacement: A real technological advancement or economic change provides for investment opportunities.
  - Boom: Other investors wake up to the opportunity and lending and borrowing help finance purchases.
  - Euphoria: Everyone finally wakes up to the opportunity and everyone and their brother tries to get involved in the bubble. Prices shoot up and everyone piles in.
  - Crash: In the crash phase, insiders sell first and then everyone tries to head for the exits at the same time. Usually, banks that lent the bubble go bust in this phase.
  - Revulsion: Investors have almost all sold and do not want to see or hear anything relating to the bubble. Prices usually become extraordinarily cheap. Journalists and politicians investigate the bubble and uncover fraud and scams.
- Bubbles happen when crowds start to act like schools of fish or flocks of birds. At first traders all do their own thing, but when they start to imitate their neighbors, markets transition into self-organizing systems.

- Avoid participating in investment when values are no longer cheap. Bubbles are always marked by excessive valuations. Stocks will trade at very high price to earnings ratios or houses will trade at very high price to income ratios or extremely low rental yields.
- If you are patient and do your homework, you can often find the best bargains of your life in the revulsion phase of a bubble.

Part Two

MANAGING
YOUR MONEY

Believe it or not, we've written *Code Red* with cab drivers in mind. Many times as we've traveled, cabbies have asked us what we do. When we say that we analyze the economy, they usually have two questions. When will the economy get better? And then, what should I do with my savings? We hope the first part of the book has explained what is going on in the global economy in simple, under-standable terms. In the second part, we will do our best to answer how people should think about managing their money.

Code Red policies and financial repression make it difficult for savers and investors, and so it is no easy task to manage your money. We cannot tell you what to do with your specific investments. Only you can decide that for yourself based on your own personal circumstances. But what we can do is offer *a way to think* about how to invest.

In Chapter 10, we'll look at how to diversify your savings and build a robust portfolio that will withstand the ups and downs of a Code Red world. With that knowledge in hand, in Chapter 11 we'll explore what you should do if you know enough to actively manage your own investments and buy stocks. The chapter highlights our views on value investing and gets into how we pick companies. We'll look at who wins and who loses in a period of financial repression and inflation.

First, though, we want to share with you our general sense of the world. Even though central banks will create bubbles, booms, and busts, and governments will run up overwhelming debts, we are bullish on humanity. We're optimists by nature. We think the potential of new technologies to improve our lives is staggering. The simple drive in developing countries for a more modern lifestyle will create all sorts of opportunities and economic progress. Global markets, free trade, the Internet, and the competitive drive of our fellow humans to improve their own lifestyles make us optimistic about the future. We just want to make sure that we don't get run over by the out-of-control train run by central banks and governments.

We certainly do not advocate running for the hills with your freeze-dried food, gold, and guns. You will have plenty of good options if you take control of your own future.

We all possess one asset that is critical to investing success: time. Wall Street is obsessed with monthly returns and quarterly earnings, but you don't have to be. And that is your edge over Wall Street. You can be patient and wise while Wall Street is greedy and maniacally focused on the short term. Instead of fixating on daily, weekly, or even monthly market returns, you should focus on finding value, keeping your portfolio diversified, and controlling how much you spend and save. If you make time your friend, you will be successful.

Now, let's look at some principles for investing in a Code Red world.

Chapter Ten

Protection through Diversification

He who lives by the crystal ball will eat shattered glass.
—*Ray Dalio*

Diversification is a protection against ignorance.
—*Warren Buffett*

Any plan conceived in moderation must fail when circumstances
are set in extremes.

—*Prince Klemens von Metternich*

I nvesting is simple but not easy. The billionaire and great investor Howard Marks once remarked, "I keep going back to what Charlie Munger said to me, which is, none of this is easy, and anybody who thinks it is easy is stupid. It is just not easy. There are many layers to this, and you just have to think well." Warren Buffett makes investing look easy. Michael Jordan makes dunking look easy. Yo Yo Ma makes playing Bach's cello concertos look easy. But these are experts who have spent their lifetimes perfecting a skill. They've made things appear simple, but performing well and consistently is never easy.

If you have savings, you face a choice. You can manage the money yourself, or you can find others to help manage it for you. Our view is that if you know a great deal about investing, you should probably manage your own money and buy great companies that you understand very well. That works if you've got time, ability, patience, and confidence. You have to know how to properly value securities, to understand accounting, and to have a good feel for industries. But unless you are a superstar investor like Warren Buffett, Seth Klarman, or Eddie Lampert, it makes sense to diversify your investments and entrust your money to others.

Even with great skill in a specific area, it is hard to be an expert in all areas of a properly diversified portfolio. You could manage all your own money, but it probably makes sense to let someone else do it in areas where you don't have the time, expertise, or access to be successful. You probably have a day job and other things to do with your time. You could probably also read medical textbooks and learn how to perform operations—sort of, but it makes more sense to let a doctor do it.

We would not want to discourage you from acting as you own investment adviser, but if investing is not your day job, you will struggle. We want you to recognize that it is highly unlikely you will be successful if you are spending only a few hours per week at investing. Many of us know golfers who make the game look easy and no longer spend that much time on the course. While we would all like to be scratch golfers with minimal effort, we need to remember that at some point the best ones spent thousands of hours honing their skills.

Some of the best investors we know manage their own accounts or the portion of them where they have the skills. But they also spend a great deal of time on research, research, and more research. They read constantly, and they understand the intricacies of valuing stocks and bonds and know how to trade currencies. It is unlikely you're going to become a great investor by simply reading the *Wall Street Journal* or the *Financial Times*. There is a reason it takes thousands of hours to become a Chartered Financial Analyst and two years to get an MBA. And for most CFAs and MBAs, that is simply the first phase of their learning efforts. Investing is a lifelong discipline, and experience counts. If you are willing to put in the thousands of hours of practice to become an expert, we encourage you to do so. It will be a challenge, but it will be a rewarding one.

You might consider that your best investment may be the time you spend in understanding the environment in which your investment adviser operates, so that you can appreciate what he is doing in your account. That way you know the questions to ask. Our experience and the experience of many successful investors suggest that there is nothing better than a well-prepared mind in investing.

A Portfolio for All Seasons

As Warren Buffett once said, "Diversification is a protection against ignorance." He did not say that in a negative way. We're all ignorant about many things, and we're perfectly fine with it. We don't have the time to become experts in law, medicine, plumbing, or gardening. We let lawyers, doctors, plumbers, and gardeners do the specialized learning and work for us. In the field of finance, the best way to protect yourself is to diversify.

The average investor should not put all his or her eggs in just one basket. This is true whether you're a cab driver in London or the head of a multi-billion-dollar endowment like Yale University's. There is no magic bullet that will help you make money. There is no perfect portfolio. Diversification helps you avoid losses from any single asset class. Diversification is the only free lunch in investing, and it is available to anyone, anywhere in the world. But the average investor consistently fails to capture the long-term benefits of investing through a truly diversified portfolio.

In a world of financial repression and Code Red policies, as an investor you ultimately have three choices: (1) hold your wealth in cash and eventually lose your purchasing power to Code Red monetary policies, (2) pick a macro path and risk everything on that outcome, (3) buy stocks in great companies that you know well, or (4) diversify your holdings and have a plan for every plausible scenario as the story unfolds.

Diversification works because it helps you avoid catastrophic losses, not because it helps you make more money in any given year. The trick to increasing your capital is not making a killing in any one year, but avoiding losses. As Warren Buffett once said, "Over the years, a number of smart people have learned the hard way that a long list of numbers multiplied by a single zero is always zero." In the past 15 years, the

U.S. stock market has declined by 50 percent *twice*. If you were entirely invested in the stock market, in order to come back from a 50 percent decline, the market would have had to double. Many individual stocks have gone bust. If you had put all your money into IndyMac, Lehman Brothers, or Fannie Mae, you would have lost nearly all of it. (Sadly, we do know a few people who bought "cheap" banks during the crisis and lost most of their money.) You can't come back from that as an investor.

Great investors understand that they can't predict the future. That is why it is important to avoid betting your portfolio on only one outcome. As Howard Marks once wrote, "We don't know what lies ahead in terms of the macro future. Few people, if any, know more than the consensus about what's going to happen to the economy, interest rates, and market aggregates." And it's not just Howard Marks; George Soros can't predict the future, either: "The financial markets generally are unpredictable. So that one has to have different scenarios. . . . The idea that you can actually predict what's going to happen contradicts my way of looking at the market." If Marks and Soros can't predict the future, we'll bet money that no one can.

The good news is that we can show you a few portfolios that can help protect you against most outcomes and that have performed very well over the long run.

In his 1981 book *Inflation Proofing Your Investments*, Harry Browne proposed a simple portfolio that would do well no matter what was happening in the economy. He called it the Permanent Portfolio. The Permanent Portfolio design has stood the test of time. It is based on a very simple idea. Browne identified four major economic seasons—prosperity, inflation, deflation, and recession—and four corresponding asset classes (equities, gold bullion, bonds, and cash). With this portfolio structure, investors divide their money equally, putting 25 percent of the portfolio in each asset class and regularly rebalancing back to the target asset allocation.

Browne recommended dividing your portfolio up into four parts evenly:

- 25 percent in U.S. equities, which tend to do well when economic times are good. Also, equities are the best long-term asset class to own.
- 25 percent in gold and precious metals to protect yourself against inflation.

- 25 percent in Treasury bonds, which normally do well when the economy is slowing and in a recession.
- 25 percent in cash, which adds stability to the portfolio.

The Permanent Portfolio produced an average annual return of 9.6 percent from January 1971 through December 2012, with its worst annual loss of 4.1 percent in 1981. Stocks have performed almost as well as the Permanent Portfolio, but they've done so with a lot more volatility and very large drawdowns.

Ray Dalio and Bob Prince at Bridgewater Associates—arguably the largest and one of the top-performing hedge funds in the world, with over $120 billion in assets under management—offer an elegant solution with a similar four-economic-season framework. Although Bridgewater employs one of the finest macroeconomic research teams in the world, the entire firm is built on the simple and enduring truth that the future is always uncertain; so they set out to build an "All-Weather" portfolio capable of performing well in almost every economic season.

In the mid-1990s, Dalio and Prince figured out that markets are driven by three factors: growth, inflation, and sentiment (or the market's expectations about future growth and inflation). According to Dalio, the price of any asset is a function of its unique characteristics in light of the market's expectations for growth and inflation in the future.

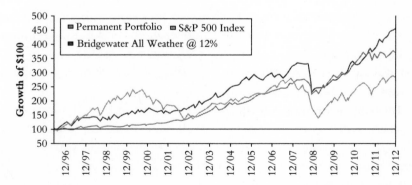

Figure 10.1 The Long-Term Returns of the Permanent Portfolio and All-Weather Portfolio
Source: http://markovprocesses.com/blog/wp-content/uploads/2013/02/bridgewater_gr_big.png

Dalio and Prince demonstrated that there are four combinations of growth and inflation that have repeated again and again throughout history: (1) rising growth, rising inflation; (2) rising growth, falling inflation; (3) falling growth, rising inflation; and (3) falling growth, falling inflation. In contrast to the Permanent Portfolio, they identified *a globally diversified basket of assets* that tend to thrive in each of the four economic seasons. But Dalio and Prince realized that allocating 25 percent of the portfolio to each regime could not achieve real balance, because each of the four regime subportfolios included a different mix of assets with very different risk profiles. They realized that, just as equities account for over 90 percent of the risk in the traditional 60/40 portfolio, the "rising growth" and "rising inflation" regimes would dominate the "falling growth" and "falling inflation" regimes in terms of risk, potentially leading to larger drawdowns in a crisis.

A multiasset portfolio that is balanced among all of the economic seasons, Bridgewater's All-Weather model dramatically improved performance over traditional approaches to asset allocation. It has returned nearly 4 percent in yearly outperformance versus the 60/40 since 1970 (which really adds up), and it has suffered smaller and shorter drawdowns in times of crisis.

While the strategy is difficult to implement and few investors can access Bridgewater's All-Weather funds, any investor—at virtually any level—can access the strategy through a growing number of mutual funds. But the strategy does come with its own set of risks. Since the portfolio is designed to balance the risk contribution from equity, credit, commodities, and safe-haven government bonds, there are inevitably much larger allocations to government bonds and credit and smaller allocations to equities and commodities. As the risk in each asset class and its correlations to the other classes changes, the model attempts to rebalance accordingly.

It is critical to pick a plan you can commit to over the long term, especially when you find yourself in difficult investing environments. If you are not comfortable with your portfolio design, you are more likely to get nervous and commit the cardinal sin of investing: buying high and selling low.

With that, let's end our core portfolio discussion with a few words of advice from Ray Dalio:

What I'm trying to say is that for the average investor, what **I would encourage them to do is to understand that there's *inflation* and *growth*. It can go higher and lower and to have four different portfolios essentially that make up your entire portfolio, that gets you balanced. Because in every generation, there is some period of time, there's a ruinous asset class, that will destroy wealth, and you don't know which one that will be in your lifetime.** So the best thing you can do is have a portfolio that is immune, that is, well diversified. That is what we call an All-Weather portfolio. That means you don't have a concentration in that asset class that's going to annihilate you. . . ."[1]

There is no portfolio nirvana. The world is always changing, but changes in your portfolio design should be thought out carefully in advance and then implemented cautiously. The one thing we do know is that jumping around to try and catch the latest hot streak will guarantee poor performance.

Avoid Making Mistakes

You can be your own best friend or your own worst enemy, based on the investing choices you make. Rather than try to be a genius, the best thing you can do is to avoid some common investing pitfalls.

Five mistakes in the investment process are easily preventable and straightforward to address, so avoiding or correcting them may be the simplest way to improve real returns. If you can identify any of these problems in your own portfolio—and most of us can—the gains from addressing them can fall right to your bottom line.

1. Trying to time the market.
2. Home bias in investing.
3. Overpaying fees.
4. Overexposure to stocks.
5. Borrowing money to improve your returns.

Let's look at each one in turn.

1. Trying to Time the Market

Everyone wants to beat the market, and most investors think they have some kind of special edge. It's only human nature. Behavioral economists have repeatedly found that 80 percent of people in most groups will rate themselves in the top 20 percent of almost any positive attribute from intelligence to kindness to a good sense of humor. In the same way, most people rate themselves as great drivers, and most parents think their kids are above average in intelligence.

False confidence can be a dangerous handicap in the investing process. Unfortunately, individual investors tend to buy high and sell low, consistently destroying value. They try to get the returns they read about in the financial press or hear about on TV.

A yearly study by Dalbar, an investment consultancy, measures the average investor's returns based on mutual fund flows and highlights the very human tendency to buy high and sell low. Over past 20 years, while the S&P 500 returned 8.2 percent annualized and the Barclays Aggregate Bond Index returned 6.3 percent, the average equity mutual fund investor received only 4.3 percent, and the average asset-allocation mutual fund investor made only 2.3% annualized.[2] That is roughly 400 basis points of easily preventable underperformance for the equity investor, compounded year after year for 20 years. Over time, that is a lot of money.

Dozens of academic studies show that investors who try to time the market underperform. The message from Dalbar's yearly analysis has been consistent since the company's first study in 1994:

> No matter what the state of the mutual fund industry, boom or bust: *Investment results are more dependent on investor behavior than on fund performance. Mutual fund investors who hold on to their investment are more successful than those who time the market.*
>
> *This is true not only for individual investors; it is also true for large institutions. Market timing for the vast majority of investors simply does not work. As Charles Ellis wrote, "There is no evidence of any large institution having anything like the ability to get in when the market is low and get out when the market is high."*

Lee Partridge is the chief investment officer at Salient Partners, former deputy chief investment officer at the $100 billion Teacher

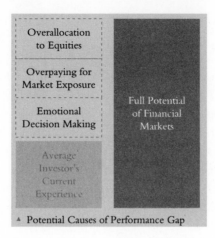

Figure 10.2 Three Opportunities to Improve the Average Investor Experience

Retirement System of Texas, and winner of *Institutional Investor*'s 2012 Small Public Fund Manager of the Year award for his turnaround of the $9 billion San Diego County Employees Retirement Association. You may not know him yet, but Lee is one of the leading institutional voices for efficient and diversified portfolios as a first line of defense against economic deleveraging, financial repression, and Code Red monetary policies. His research explains the yawning gap between the long-term returns historically available in global markets and the returns average investors typically receive. As you can see from Figure 10.2, investors tend to underperform the markets as a result of inefficient portfolio design and emotional decision making.

2. Home Bias in Investing

Another emotional mistake many investors make is called *home market bias*. It's a form of familiarity bias, where people know so much about a given subject that they start thinking they have an edge. Typically, investors tend to concentrate their wealth in their home country and their home currency, but there is a whole world out there with markets waiting to be exploited. Many investors have started to include modest allocations to foreign stocks and bonds in their portfolios, but not enough to really matter.

Many investors are like drunks who search for their keys under a lamppost. They are not looking there because their keys are there but simply because that is the only place with light. Germans invest in Germany, Greeks invest in Greece, and the Irish invest in Ireland. The only place they know is their own stock market. By not investing abroad and not diversifying their investments out of domestic stocks, they are often exposed to enormous losses of wealth. When Greece restructured its debt, Greek investors lost over 60 percent of their money. When Irish banks went bust, Irish investors lost almost 80 percent from the peak to the trough. You hardly want to follow in their footsteps.

Michael Kilka and Martin Weber wrote a paper called "Home Bias in International Stock Return Expectations." They compared German and U.S. investors. Each group felt more competent about their home markets and stocks, and each group assessed probable future returns for their home stocks to be higher than those for the foreign stocks. Simply because they were more familiar with a stock, they thought it was more likely to go up than another stock that they knew less well. Rationally, how could you make such a statement if you do not know much about the other stock? What is your basis in fact for making such a comparison? The fact that they knew nothing about the foreign stocks did not deter them from making judgments.

Think this only applies to the small guy? Think again. The study shows that the same bias seems to apply for institutional investors.

In 2002, Daniel Kahneman won a Nobel Memorial Prize in Economics for his work on irrational behavior. Kahneman's research colleague Amos Tversky would have won one as well if he had not died. (Unfortunately, they don't give the prizes posthumously.) Tversky noted in his research that ". . . people on average prefer to bet on their own judgment over an equally probable chance event when they consider themselves competent about the event being judged. Otherwise, they prefer betting on the chance event."

This is why local horses at racetracks generally get better odds from the local bettors than they do when they are out of town. It is why the bookies know local citizens will bet more on the hometown team. People read and study the papers every day, learning more and more about "their" team. Since they know more about it, they judge it more likely to win. Of course, you don't have to be from Dallas or

Munich to be sucked into such irrationality. The same phenomenon occurs all over the world.

This is not just a German or U.S. issue. Another study has shown exactly the same home bias response from institutional investors with regards to Japan and the United States. Yet another study showed that the more we know about a stock, the more likely we are to be optimistic and the more likely we'll judge ourselves competent and trust our analysis.

Familiarity with stocks breeds overconfidence, and overconfidence can breed market losses. Taking a global view and equally weighting foreign and home markets can be particularly valuable in a Code Red world where extreme economic shifts are bound to happen but very difficult to predict. The idea is to build in as many separate return streams as possible to harvest more persistent, more durable global risk premiums—and do it asset class by asset class.

3. Overpaying of Fees

In the world of finance, there are two rival groups. One group thinks it is impossible to beat the market. The people who believe this apply the fancy name *Efficient Market Hypothesis* to their ideas. One of their leaders is Professor Burton Malkiel at Princeton University. The other group believes that you can indeed beat the market. They tend to be followers of Benjamin Graham and practice "value investing." Their biggest proponent is Warren Buffett. The two groups disagree on almost everything, but you won't be shocked to learn that they do agree on one thing: investors pay too far too much to their money managers.

In a recent editorial in the *Wall Street Journal*, Professor Malkiel pointed out just how much the average investor paid the financial services sector and just how little there was to show for it.

From 1980 to 2006, the U.S. financial services sector grew from 4.9% to 8.3% of GDP. A substantial share of that increase represented increases in asset-management fees.

Excluding index funds (which make market returns available even to small investors at close to zero expense), fees have risen substantially as a percentage of assets managed. In my judgment, investors have received no benefit from this increase in expense ratios.

The increase in fees could be justified if it reflected increasing returns for investors from active management, or if it improved the efficiency of the market. Neither of these arguments holds. Actively managed funds of publicly traded securities have consistently underperformed index funds—by roughly the differential in fees charged.

Passive portfolios that held all the stocks in a broad-based market index have substantially outperformed the average active manager since 1980. Therefore, the increase in fees likely represents a deadweight loss for investors.

Every dollar matters in a world of financial repression, but most investors unnecessarily give up value by overpaying for market exposure. Make sure you find index funds that have very low fees. The whole idea of a diversified portfolio is to participate in global markets over long periods of time, to accept whatever returns are available in different economic seasons, and to collect the benefits of efficient diversification. Unfortunately, if you're overpaying for diversification, it will cost you a lot of money in the long run.

Today, you can buy and maintain passive exposure to equity, credit, commodity, and safe-haven government bond markets for very low implementation costs, which means you can capture more of the markets' returns rather than lose value in unrewarded fees. Moreover, there are cheap, passive, and systematic mutual fund options that allow you to buy a well-diversified, regularly rebalanced core portfolio for very reasonable fees.

4. Overexposure to Stocks

Most investors put almost all their money in stocks. In the long run, stocks have performed better than all other asset classes, but it is very dangerous to put all your money in only one asset class. The best-performing U.S. university endowment is Yale University's, and its manager, David Swensen, is legendary for his consistently high returns. He has achieved stably consistent returns by not concentrating his assets in equities. As Swensen wrote in *Pioneering Portfolio Management*—considered the bible on portfolio management for large institutions: "Even though market return studies indicate that high levels of equity market exposure benefit long-term investors, the associated risks come through less clearly. Significant concentration in a single asset class poses extraordinary risk to portfolio assets."

We should note that Swensen has an extraordinarily high percentage of his portfolio in so-called alternative investment strategies, which would be difficult for the average investor to duplicate. But the principle demonstrates the need for diversification.

Equities typically produce positive real returns if the inflation rate is between 1 percent and 6 percent. If inflation runs too low, giving way to deflation and recession, equities prices tend to fall, resulting in negative nominal and real returns. If inflation rates run above 3 percent, nominal returns on equities may be positive, but real returns during high-inflation periods are almost always negative. So equities are essentially a bet on growth with low inflation. Unfortunately, it is often the case that growth is poor and inflation is high.

When traditional approaches to portfolio design call for more than 50 or 60 percent of a portfolio in stocks, most investors have no idea that they may be concentrating over 90 percent of their risk in the equity markets. Stocks have been roughly three times more volatile than bonds over the long term. The traditional 60/40 portfolio approach may appear balanced in dollar terms, but in risk terms it is not diversified at all.[3] As a result, the overallocation to equities consistently results in lower risk-adjusted returns over the long term and leaves the average investor more vulnerable to recession, high inflation, and dramatic swings in investor sentiment. As you can see from Figure 10.3, the 60/40 portfolio tends to closely track the equity market with little respect to movements in the bond market—meaning the success or failure of the average investor depends almost entirely on one asset class and a positive-growth, moderate-inflation investment climate.

The dilemma is that diversifying away from equities within a traditional asset-allocation model has often resulted in a portfolio with lower risk but also lower expected returns; so rather than reduce their reliance on equities, many investors attempt to tactically adjust their asset allocation based on market timing views. This is where the investing process gets dangerous, because it is virtually impossible to identify the optimal portfolio ahead of time. We have little idea what will happen in the economy or how each market will perform—especially in a Code Red world—and investors who attempt to actively time the market

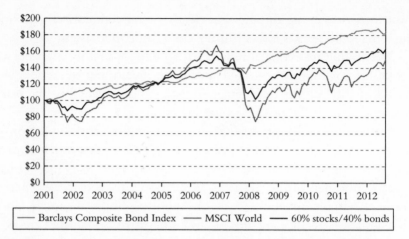

Figure 10.3 Equity Risk Dominates in the Traditional 60/40 Portfolio
SOURCE: Salient Partners, www.salientpartners.com/static/pdfs/rpf/Fund_Documentation/Salient%20
Risk%20Parity%20Fund%20Presentation%202013%20%28print%29.pdf

tend to underperform due to emotional decision making and higher trading costs.

Instead of concentrating risk in one asset class or one country, investors can boost returns and achieve more balance by taking a global view, broadening the mix of asset classes, and weighting their return streams to achieve balance across potential economic outcomes, rather than by trying to predict the future.

Since stocks and corporate bonds are essentially a directional bet on positive economic growth and benign inflation, you have a lot to gain from diversifying into other asset classes, including commodities (but in a tactical way, as we outline later), which thrive when expected inflation is rising; and nominal safe-haven government bonds, which thrive in bad times.

5. Borrowing Money (Leverage) to Improve Your Returns

As a general rule, with few exceptions, you should not borrow money to invest. Leverage magnifies outcomes but doesn't add value. Leverage will never make a bad investment better, but it can make you abandon a good investment if prices move against you. Many investors find a good idea, borrow too much, and are forced to sell their good idea if the price goes down at all. It is far better to avoid leverage in investing if you can. As Warren Buffett once said about leverage, "If you're smart you don't need it, and if you're dumb you shouldn't be using it."

That's all you need to know about leverage.

Betting on Tail Risks

We believe opportunities exist in every market around the world— in some more than others—for active managers to exploit inefficiencies and anticipate market shifts. That is especially true in a Code Red world where anything can happen, depending on where you live— inflation or deflation, growth or recession. And as dramatic swings in sentiment prove, markets are anything but efficient today. Depending on the actions and reactions of central banks and governments, some countries will see deflation and depression; others will experience rapid inflation; and against all odds, a lucky few may enjoy stability in the midst of chaos.

Both in *Endgame* and in *Code Red* we've offered views on what we think will happen in the European periphery, Japan, the United States, and Australia. We've posited that Japan will have a weaker yen and higher inflation. We've argued that Australia will see a real estate bust and that the European periphery will experience a long, painful debt-deflationary slowdown.

Once you have a built a truly balanced, cost-efficient, and globally diversified portfolio, you may be able to improve your experience by expressing a macro view or hedging against extreme economic and market risks. We stress that the process we will describe next will work only for *some* investors because you are now entering into the realm of a perilous but potentially rewarding set of games where there are always winners and losers.

Fortunately, a well-diversified portfolio gives you "permission" to take some of these risks at the margin, and you don't have to do it alone. If you really think you have the competitive edge to outperform a market dominated by skillful, hardworking, and competitive players who may have far better information than you do, then go right ahead and overweight one of your economic regime portfolios or tilt your portfolio toward a basket of themes; but most investors should just make active allocations at the asset-class or strategy level and hire a team of expert guides—active managers—to invest for them within each niche.

With the help of a qualified financial advisor you can build your own version of the All-Weather portfolio with a global view, but ultimately you have to decide how you will allocate the asset classes in your core markets portfolio, and you have to have a plan for how you will react or rebalance in every plausible outcome. You have a lot to gain from diversifying as broadly as possible, eliminating costs, reducing your reliance on equity risk, and reining in the emotional mistakes that often lead investors to dramatically underperform. Remember, in a Code Red world, every basis point counts and anything can happen.

Key Lessons from the Chapter

In this chapter we learned:

- Unless you are a superstar investor, it makes sense to let professional managers help you manage your money and diversify your investments.
- Diversification is the best protection against uncertainty and ignorance. Diversification works because it helps you avoid catastrophic losses. All investors, from retail investors to large institutional endowments, should be properly diversified and should invest outside of their home equity markets.
- There is no portfolio silver bullet and no perfect portfolio, but diversification helps protect you from big losses.
- Harry Browne's Permanent Portfolio combined two important elements: diversification and buy and hold. It recommended 25 percent stocks, 25 percent government bonds, 25 percent precious metals, and 25 percent cash. Bridgewater's All-Weather portfolio improved on Browne's diversification model.
- Investors are often their own worst enemies. Avoid common investment mistakes:
    - *Avoid being emotional.* Too many investors buy high and sell low. Don't attempt to time the market. Studies show that retail inves-

tors and even larger, supposedly smarter, institutional investors have no ability to time the market. Invest for the long term.

- *Avoid home bias.* Investors typically allocate too much money to their own country's stock market.
- *Avoid overpaying for market exposure.* Many investors pay excessive fees in order to invest in the market. Find funds with low management costs. Over time, fees add up and eat away at your capital.
- *Avoid overinvesting in stocks.* Many investors allocate almost all their money in equities and miss out on the benefits of having other asset classes in their portfolio.
- *Avoid borrowing money to invest.* Leverage is a bad idea.

Chapter Eleven

How to Protect Yourself
Against Inflation

I do not think it is an exaggeration to say history is largely a
history of inflation, usually inflations engineered by governments
for the gain of governments.

—*Friedrich August von Hayek*

By a continuing process of inflation, government can confiscate,
secretly and unobserved, an important part of the wealth of
their citizens.

—*John Maynard Keynes*

I f you look at photographs from the 1930s, you will see images of
things that now appear wildly out of date. For an economist, the
most interesting details in these photographs are often the prices in
ads and store windows. One of the first pictures in Walker Evans'
American Photographs is of a barbershop. Amazingly, you could get a haircut in the 1930s for 25 cents. Another photographer took a similar picture just 20 years later in the 1950s. Saul Leiter's beautiful *Early Color*
depicts a sign advertising haircuts for 75 cents. The two photographs tell
us that in just 20 years the price of a haircut had tripled. Today, the cost
of a haircut has gone up to around $15. That is about 20 times as much

as a haircut cost in the 1950s and 60 times as much as in the 1930s. That is inflation for you.

The comedian Sam Ewing once said, "Inflation is when you pay 15 dollars for the 10-dollar haircut you used to get for 5 dollars when you had hair." He had no idea how right he was.

As a simple haircut shows, inflation is the great destroyer of purchasing power. A saver experiencing inflation is like a frog plopped into a pot of water brought slowly to a boil. From one year to the next, the inflationary change, like the change in temperature in the pot, is very gradual, but over a few years it will boil you alive. The faster inflation rises, the quicker the dollar in your pocket loses its purchasing power.

Inflation makes saving extremely difficult. Investing and saving is not merely about making your money grow. If your savings grow, but only as fast as inflation, you're just treading water. If you actually want to make any money, your wealth needs to grow *even faster* than inflation. With inflation, as a saver you're always running just to stand still.

Inflation devastates savings, but it is great for debtors. If you found a dollar someone stuffed under a mattress back in 1973 and tried to spend it today, the dollar would have lost about 80 percent of its original value. That is clearly very bad news for savers. However, if you had borrowed money and had to pay it back 40 years later, you would have had to pay back less than one fifth of the principal in real terms.

We've shown in the earlier chapters how central banks want to create inflation today via Code Red policies. They want to accelerate the process by which the value of a dollar goes down. The faster that happens, the quicker the value of debt denominated in dollars falls, and the lighter the debt burden will be on borrowers. We also showed how, under a system of financial repression, governments are able to borrow at low interest rates while they drive up inflation and thereby reduce the real value of government borrowing. When governments are busy reducing the value of bonds, you need to think through your investments in stocks and bonds.

A quick preface to our discussion. It may seem strange to some to focus on inflation in a deleveraging world that is largely dominated by deflationary impulses, but there are three main reasons to do so. For many readers in many countries, inflation will in fact be the dominant theme. And in countries where deleveraging and the accompanying deflation are taking place, this period will pass. In fact, one of the problems investors face is that Code Red policies are in fact less-than-subtle means to ensure that eventually inflation does come back. And finally, even though inflation is currently low in the United States, Europe, and Japan, it is still present. *It doesn't take much inflation to damage your portfolio. Even at a mere 2 percent, buying power is eroded by 25 percent every 10 years.* Inflation is most definitely not your friend.

In a Code Red world, central bankers fear deflation even more than they do inflation. While the deleveraging process can take longer than most observers think, it will pass, and the process of exiting unconventional monetary policies will not be smooth. The forecast for most countries in most periods of the future will be for inflation. In this chapter, we offer investment principles that will serve investors long after *Code Red* is published. One of our real concerns is that central bankers may take their Code Red policies too far, so that inflation spikes unexpectedly. That said, a properly positioned portfolio can not only withstand inflationary periods but take advantage of them.

Indeed, inflation is a significant component of long-term nominal returns. The challenge investors face in a Code Red world is to make sure that their investments are designed for real returns in a period of financial repression. We offer these insights into investing in periods of inflation for those countries and times when inflation is the overriding paradigm.

Inflation and Taxes Are Toxic for Investors

Inflation on its own is very bad, but inflation and taxes together are disastrous. The worst part about inflation is that it forms a toxic combination with taxes. The government taxes you based on the value of your wages, stocks, and bonds. If you bought a stock in 1973 and sold it today for five times the value, you'd have a very large tax bill. The government would say you made a lot of money. But had you? Given inflation, in real terms your stock would be worth no more today than it was in 1973. You'd have to pay tax nonetheless. As you can see, inflation increases everyone's tax bill on investments, even if your investments are just keeping up with inflation and you are no wealthier in real terms.

With inflation at work, no new laws are necessary to raise your income taxes. As Milton Friedman once said, "Inflation is taxation without legislation." Inflation helps government take in more taxes through what is called "bracket creep." Most governments tax the wealthy more heavily than the middle class, and the poor generally pay almost no taxes. In an inflationary world, if the government doesn't change tax rates, as your salary rises in line with inflation, you could go from being a middle-class person to being "rich," so that you find yourself taxed at a higher rate.

Inflation moves people from lower tax brackets to higher ones, even though they are no wealthier or better off. Let's look at how it happens. For example, in 2012 the median household income was $50,000. To enjoy the same purchasing power in 1973, you would have had to earn only $9,430. In fact, that was about the median household income back then. By comparison, if you earned $50,000 in 1973, you would have been very well off. That income would be equal to over $250,000 in 2012 dollars. As you can see, inflation and taxes are an awful combination that manages to raise taxes without any new laws.

Tax bracket creep is a depressing movie we've seen before. For example, the alternative minimum tax (AMT) in the United States was passed in 1969. Despite rampant inflation in the 1970s, the threshold was not changed for decades. Originally, the AMT was designed to punish a handful of wealthy tax dodgers. In 1967 there were 155 taxpayers who earned over $200,000 and yet paid no income tax. Today, the AMT has transmogrified into a tax that affects more than 3 million taxpayers. (It would affect an additional 30 million had it not finally been indexed as part of the deal that reversed the Bush tax cuts on higher-income households.)

A tax similar to the AMT was incorporated into Obama's health care reform. Obamacare imposes a 0.9 percent tax surcharge on the amount by which individuals' earned income exceeds $200,000 this year and a 3.8 percent surcharge on some or all of the investment income of single households with an adjusted gross income of more than $200,000 and married households with an adjusted gross of $250,000 and up. With a little inflation, middle-class people will be affected by those taxes in a few years.

Another example of what happens with bracket creep is the tax that some Social Security beneficiaries pay on up to 50 percent of their benefits. This tax was created in 1984 as part of the grand bargain, enacted in 1983, that increased Social Security taxes and raised the retirement age. The threshold was fairly high 20 years ago—single taxpayers with $25,000 of income, married taxpayers with $32,000 of income (in both cases including half their Social Security). Approximately 15 percent of Social Security beneficiaries paid this tax when it first took effect. Now, however, about 35 percent pay because incomes and benefits have risen a lot since 1984, but the cutoff points haven't moved.

When central banks succeed at creating inflation, they will start moving you from lower tax brackets to higher tax brackets. You won't be any wealthier, but you'll certainly be paying higher taxes.

Benjamin Franklin once said, "In this world nothing can be said to be certain, except death and taxes." In this chapter, we'll tell you how to protect your savings, but unfortunately there is very little we can do to help you with death and taxes. (If we figure out those two, we'll write another book about it.) There are strategies that you can use to mitigate taxes, and a good adviser can help you find ones that work for you. In fact, just about the best investment return you can get is to shelter your taxable income. Given the fact that our readers come from a hundred countries and have a very wide range of incomes, we can't get into taxes, but tax strategy should be one of your real areas of focus when you talk to your financial advisers.

Inflation: Who Wins, Who Loses

So who are the biggest losers in the savings game when inflation erodes wealth? Old people. They typically don't work anymore, so they can't even get wage increases to match the increase in inflation. Any retirees who have bought fixed annuities, which provide a regular income for life, will see the value of their pensions reduced significantly over time. The longer they live, the poorer they become, as the real value of their fixed pensions goes down because of inflation. And given advances in medicine, it now looks as if people are going to live a lot longer than they expected to when they originally bought their annuity.

The Fed apparently sees retirees as "rentier" capitalists (*rentier* is a French word) whose savings should be expropriated by keeping short-term interest rates below inflation. What's a rentier capitalist? According to Vladimir Lenin, a rentier capitalist is someone who "clips coupons, who takes no part in any enterprise whatever, whose profession is idleness." As active as the older generation is, that term would generally define retired people as well, as they no longer work for an income but live on their savings and pensions instead. In a very real sense, the Fed has decided to wage an undeclared war on them. Oh, not the kind of war that you declare publicly, as in "the war on poverty" or "the war on drugs," but a de facto war that arises as an unintended consequence of their desire to have investors and savers take more risk. From our perspective, this is immoral, cruel, and stupid.

Older people we talk to are terrified of outliving their savings. Most people are going to need to work past what we used to think of as retirement age, and their decision to continue working will primarily be a financial one, not one they make because they don't want to retire. Not surprisingly, people are retiring later and later. The average retirement age in the United States hit a low of 62 in the mid-1990s, but today it is 64 and climbing. (Talk about progress. We're going back in time. For example, in the United States, the average retirement age was 74 in 1910.) In fact, since the Great Financial Crisis, older people are filling most of the job openings, as they have to work to pay their bills. Retirement is simply not financially possible for most people.

In fact, in the United States in the past six years, people 55 years of age and older have seen their employment levels rise every year, while younger people have seen the opposite. "Boomers" are taking market share in terms of employment from younger generations. This is a new phenomenon and is especially difficult on people in their 20s. If you ask economists who agree with the current easy monetary policies what they have against young people, they will look at you with a blank stare and tell you that young people are the future or something along those lines. They will see no connection between their monetary policy and the employment rate among twenty-somethings. Or thirty-somethings. But the connection is clear and obvious to anyone who studies the data. With interest rates so low and inflation eroding their income as the cost of living rises, older people cannot afford to retire and are often beating out younger jobseekers in the job market because they have more experience and are willing to work as hard as young people.

Most politicians are rightly opposed to inflation, at least in theory, but firmly in favor of the policies that produce it. Inflation is a lot like sin. Every government is against it, but every government practices it. Now politicians may be hypocrites, but they are not complete idiots. Congress has made sure that their pensions are indexed to cost-of-living changes after retirement. That's a far better deal than retirees get in the private sector. We should note that many public pensions of government workers are also indexed to inflation. Politicians are not above buying a few votes.

If you don't have the luxury of being in Congress or otherwise participating in a retirement system where your pension is indexed, you'll have to make sure that you put your money in the right place. In the next section, we'll look at what investments have done best during inflationary periods, as well as what investments have done well for the very long term, in periods of inflation and deflation.

Specifically, we will delve into the relative opportunities offered by annuities, stocks, and bonds. Then we will show you how to buy companies that thrive, comparatively speaking, even when inflation is chewing up profit margins in many other sectors. We'll teach you how to identify companies that have defensive "moats" of one kind or another that keep the competition at bay and enable those companies to maximize profits. And we'll examine what constitutes a good defensive moat and what doesn't, so that you aren't fooled into thinking that a company is better positioned than it actually is. And finally, most important of all, we'll sound the cautionary principle that should guide all your investments, not only in Code Red times, but all the time: don't just buy the right companies; buy at the right time, when the price relative to value is right.

Annuities, Stocks, and Bonds

The last time we saw governments fighting currency wars and devaluing their currencies against each other was in the 1970s. The last time we saw government deficits financed by central banks was the 1970s. And, though moderate inflation is normal in wealthy countries like the United States, the only time high inflation has plagued the United

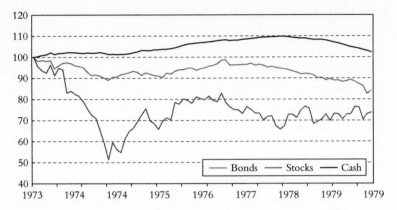

Figure 11.1 Real Returns to Cash, Equities, and Bonds in the 1970s
SOURCE: Society Generale.

States was in the 1970s. So if you want to understand what investments will do best in a time of higher inflation, say over the next decade, you have to go back to a time of bell bottoms, big collars, and shiny disco balls to see what asset classes did well.

If, in 1970, you had invested $100 in stocks or bonds, or simply put it in a savings deposit, any of these moves would have lost you money over the next 10 years. The biggest loser category by far was bonds. Right behind was cash. Stocks did better than bonds or cash did, but you still would have lost money. There are few winners under inflation.

Let's look beyond the 1970s to now. Surprisingly, the picture is not very different.

The conclusion that stocks beat both bonds and cash holds true even outside of the 1970s. Let's look at Table 11.1, which has the long-term returns for stocks, bonds, and cash. Over the long term, the evidence clearly shows that stocks beat longer-term and short-term bonds as well as cash. Table 11.1 shows the returns going back 1 year, 5 years, 10 years, 25, 50, 75, and 80 years.

The very clear message from Table 11.1 is that stocks outperform bonds over the very long term. Stocks are more volatile and can deliver stomach-wrenching moves in the short run, but they are clearly the winners in the long run. Some investors can't live with the volatility of stocks. For example, within our lifetimes, we've seen the crash of 1987,

Table 11.1   Stock and Bond Returns

	1 Year	5 Years	10 Years	25 Years	50 Years	75 Years	80 Years
S&P500							
Compound Return	15.5%	6.2%	8.4%	13.4%	10.6%	11.5%	10.4%
Standard Deviation	5.5%	12.3%	15.3%	14.8%	14.4%	18.5%	19.2%
SmallCap							
Compound Return	16.2%	15.2%	13.5%	14.0%	14.5%	15.8%	12.9%
Standard Deviation	13.3%	17.3%	22.0%	19.1%	20.5%	28.7%	29.4%
T-bond							
Compound Return	1.2%	7.2%	7.8%	11.1%	6.8%	5.6%	5.4%
Standard Deviation	8.7%	10.3%	9.1%	10.0%	9.5%	8.1%	7.9%
T-bill							
Compound Return	4.8%	2.3%	3.6%	5.3%	5.4%	3.8%	3.7%
Standard Deviation	0.1%	0.4%	0.5%	0.7%	0.8%	0.9%	0.9%

SOURCE: Ibbotson.

the Nasdaq meltdown, and the enormous crash after the bankruptcy of Lehman Brothers. Many investors pulled money from stocks after these events, promising not to return. But even though short-term ups and downs have scared people away from stocks, stocks are a far better bet in the long run than bonds.

There is one caveat about the generalization that stocks beat bonds. You can certainly find periods in which bonds have outperformed stocks. For example, if beginning in 1966 you had invested annually in 20-year U.S. treasuries, in 2012, at the end of 46 years, bonds would have slightly outperformed stocks. Forty-six years for most people is definitely the long run! But the data render that result only because we picked just the right starting year to do the analysis, ensuring that our 46-year period spanned two secular bear markets.

Given that example, what do we think about the future? We are reasonably confident that we are entering a period where stocks will outperform bonds over the long term. Why? Because bonds are either at or close to the end of a 30+-year secular bull market. Rates are generally so low they have little room to go anywhere but up. And we have been in a secular bear market for equities for almost 14 years. The average secular bear market lasts about 17 years, so we are getting close to the end of a normal life span for the current secular bear market. While stock market valuations are relatively high as we write this book and risk premiums are as low as they have ever been, these are not phenomena we would expect to persist for much longer. Transitions are always difficult for investors, but a generational transition certainly looks as if it could be close to making an appearance.

Stocks and Mutual Funds

Most investors assume that stocks perform much better than bonds when inflation is high. Decades ago, the conventional wisdom regarded stocks as an inflation hedge because stocks represented a claim on companies and real assets. The decade of the 1970s destroyed this idea. Most companies during that decade saw their costs go up much faster than they were able to raise prices on their customers, and they were always one step behind inflation. The U.S. stock market traded sideways throughout the entire decade of the 1970s. After you considered inflation, the stock market was worth a lot less. Only when Paul Volcker killed inflation in the early 1980s did the market rebound.

From 1968 to 1982, stocks traded sideways in nominal prices, but in real, inflation-adjusted terms, stocks declined. As you can see from Figure 11.2, the difference over time is enormous, and the gap between real returns and nominal returns can be very large. In fact, if you invested one dollar in the stock market in 1966, it was 26 years later, in 1992, before you finally saw an inflation-adjusted real return.

Bonds

Anyone who owns government bonds will lose money in a rising inflationary environment. Bonds are fixed-income assets, and the

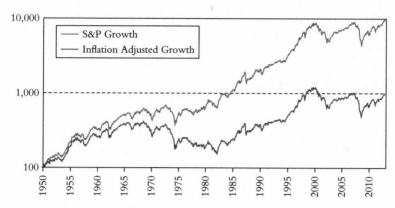

Figure 11.2 Real vs. Inflation–Adjusted S&P 500
SOURCE: *Variant Perception*, Bloomberg.

amount you will be repaid is fixed, as are the coupon payments. The value of the regular coupon payment doesn't go up with inflation. There is no mystery at all about the problems bondholders confront in an era of inflation. When the value of the dollar deteriorates month after month, a security with income and principal payments denominated in those dollars isn't going to be a big winner. You don't need a doctorate in economics to figure that out.

In the 1970s, at least bond yields went up, but today central banks are capping bond yields in a concerted attempt to achieve financial repression. We can already see this happening. Government bond yields are now trading below inflation, guaranteeing that any investor who holds the bonds until maturity will lose money. As inflation rises, real yields will only become more negative.

A little over a decade ago, in 1997, the U.S. government started issuing bonds indexed to inflation. The problem is that we have yet to meet individual investors who actually own them. But seriously, the bonds and traders do exist, although the supply of these bonds is very, very small. An indexed bond is better than a regular bond, but unfortunately not everyone who might want to buy them can do so. Also, if inflation does rise, the price you have to pay to get your hands on these indexed bonds will go up to reflect expected future inflation, offsetting somewhat the effects of indexation.

Annuities

The guaranteed lifelong payments made by annuities are fixed by contract and do not keep up with inflation. Since annuities are intended to provide income for life no matter how long beneficiaries live, this is a serious problem. Until recently, inflation-indexed annuities were unknown in the United States. There are some today, but they are still uncommon. In Europe and South America, however, inflation-indexed annuities have been offered for years. Unfortunately, they tend to pay out very little in the early years and pay out more later only if inflation rises.

Money Market Funds and Savings Accounts

Believe it or not, before 1979 a Federal Reserve regulation prevented the payment of interest on bank demand deposits and restricted interest rates paid on savings. When short-term interest rates skyrocketed into double digits and approached 20 percent, no one wanted to keep money in savings accounts that didn't pay interest. Today, financial institutions can raise short-term interest rates to compensate savers. However, the interest on bank accounts almost always lags behind inflation. Still, current practices are better than in the bad old days when people were paid no interest at all.

Buy Companies That Benefit from Inflation

We now know that stocks beat bonds and cash. We also know that when inflation really takes off, stocks don't do that well. The big question is what kinds of stocks do best. This may sound blindingly obvious, but when inflation is rising, you want to buy companies that can raise prices on their customers. That is easier said than done, but it is not impossible.

Again, please note that inflation may not be obvious for some time and in all countries. But Code Red policies more than open the door for potential inflationary problems. And if, as seems likely now, central banks do not pull back on the throttle in time, the world may be shocked by how quickly inflation can take off. We offer this analysis on what is a very possible future world of inflation.

Not all companies can raise prices on their customers. For example, one of the worst industries over the past 100 years has been the airline industry. The main cost for many airlines is their fuel bill. When oil has risen and jet fuel has gone up, airlines have been hit with enormous bills. Sometimes the price of oil will double. But are airlines able to double their prices? Hardly. When the price of oil goes up, usually a few airlines go bankrupt, and the rest lose money. As Warren Buffett once said about the invention of aviation, "If a farsighted capitalist had been present at Kitty Hawk, he would have done his successors a huge favor by shooting Orville down."

Investors often assume that commodity-producing companies (the gold miners, oil drillers, copper miners, etc.) are the best companies to own when inflation is rising. There is some truth to this. However, commodity producers rarely do as well as the commodities themselves. Commodity companies go through boom and bust cycles. They do very well when prices go up and often go bankrupt when firms start competing with them and commodity prices go back down. Even more important, though, these commodity-producing companies often fail to make money. They fail to produce good returns for shareholders because the cost of mining or extracting gold, oil, or copper rises faster than the price of the commodities themselves. For example, in the past few years, the price of gold has skyrocketed, reached a peak of over $1,900 in 2011, and then fallen over $600. It has since treaded water (as of our writing deadline). However, gold miners' costs do not follow the price of gold. Mining costs went up even faster than the price of gold did, and they did not fall when the price of gold plummeted. You can make money with commodity companies, but the proposition is difficult and uncertain. Gold mining companies don't control their costs, and competitors can dig mines, too.

As we have suggested, the very best kind of business to own is a business where you can raise prices no matter what is happening around you. These kinds of companies have *pricing power*. Not many businesses are like this, but they do exist. If you buy these kinds of businesses, you will be able to protect your wealth in good and bad times. We'll show you how.

Warren Buffett wrote a letter to Berkshire Hathaway shareholders and identified various types of business that would withstand higher

Table 11.2   Sector Performance during Inflation

High Avg. % Change and Freq. of Market Outperformance	Low Avg. % Change and Freq. of Market Outperformance
Aluminum	Airlines
Containers(Metal & Glass)	Auto Parts & Equipment
Foods	Automobiles
Gold & Precious Metals Mining	Computers (Hardware)
Metals Mining	Consumer Finance
Natural Gas	Electric Companies
Oil & Gas (Drilling & Equipment)	Household Furnishings & Appliances
Oil (Domestic Integrated)	Retail (Department Stores)
Oil (International Integrated)	Truckers
Tobacco	Trucks & Parts

Sources: Standard & Poor's; www.forbes.com/2007/11/06/inflation-stocks-funds-pf-ii-in_jl_1106newsletterwatch_inl.html

inflation. At the time, inflation was running in the mid-teens in the United States, and finding business that could not only survive but thrive in such an inflationary environment was critical. Buffett wrote that a good business that resists inflation (1) has pricing power and (2) doesn't require constant spending just to keep business going.

The last time we had a currency war was in the early 1970s. In 1971, Nixon closed the gold window and started to devalue the dollar. Soon, almost every other country followed. At the time, Warren Buffett recognized that he was entering into a different kind of world. He said that he anticipated "a world of continuous inflation." He put his money where his mouth was and bought a company called See's Candies a year later, in 1972.

See's Candies makes candy and chocolate in the American West. A great brand like See's Candies was able to increase prices on its chocolate as inflation rose, and customers kept on buying chocolate all the same. And unlike airlines or steel mills, chocolate companies don't require enormous amounts of investment to make chocolate. It was Buffett's dream business.

You're probably wondering how the purchase turned out. It was extraordinary. Buffett bought the business for $25 million in 1972, when the company had earnings of $2 million. Thirty years later, See's Candies earned $60 million. More important, over that period the amount of money that See's Candies sent to Buffett's Berkshire Hathaway topped $1.35 billion. Now that's a great, inflation-proof business.

In the next section, we'll show you how to find companies like See's Candies.

Build a Moat around Your Stocks

Companies that can raise prices along with inflation usually have economic "moats." In days of old, many castles were protected by a moat. The wider the moat that circled it, the more easily a castle could be defended from marauders. A business is like a castle, as it is constantly under attack by competitors, and the "moat" is the competitive advantage the company has. The best moats are wide ones full of alligators and snakes. Obviously, companies cannot literally surround themselves with wide waters teeming with wild animals, but there are some things they can do to keep competitors at bay.

The main reason moats are important is that no matter how great or innovative the company or the industry, it will face competition. The business world is based on the survival of the fittest. One competitor is enough to ruin a business running on small margins. Warren Buffett described the idea behind moats for *Fortune* magazine in 1999:

> The key to investing is not assessing how much an industry is going to affect society, or how much it will grow, but rather determining the competitive advantage of any given company and, above all, the durability of that advantage. The products or services that have wide, sustainable moats around them are the ones that deliver rewards to investors.

No matter how good your company's product is or how quickly the industry is growing, if there is no moat, competitors will invade your castle and burn it down. That is why snakes and alligators are important.

While constructing and stocking a new moat is difficult, expensive, and time consuming, maintaining an existing moat is much easier and much less costly. One need only keep it in good repair and feed the alligators. Businesses with moats can raise prices on customers, but they don't need to reinvest enormous amounts of cash into their business to keep them going and keep them competitive. Generally, as inflation rises, the difference between what they can charge their customers and what they must spend on their own business keeps growing.

There are five principal kinds of moats. In the following section, we will explain each one and give examples of companies in each category. Each moat protects companies in its own way from competitors and helps them increase prices and lock in customers. We'll also give you a short list of companies to buy. Most of the companies are American, but quite a few are foreign.

Important Note to the Reader

Before we discuss specific companies, please read this warning carefully. Do not read this book and follow it blindly. (Do not read and follow anything blindly. That is how cults start.) Do your own homework. Think for yourself. Read the annual reports of the companies we talk about and study their investor presentations, research them, and find out as much as you can. If you can't or won't do your own homework, please put this book down and leave it on a park bench.

Even great businesses stumble and fall. We are highlighting companies that have economic moats and earn high returns on invested capital as we write. As you read this section, keep in mind that there is no guarantee that the world will not change and take these companies down.

Further, we mention these companies primarily for illustrative purposes. There is no way to know if these specific companies will still represent reasonable value when you read this chapter. At any point, doing your homework can help you find companies that do meet our criteria and do represent good value at what will be the current price.

Moat 1: Intangible Assets (Brand Value, Patents, Government Licenses)

Though they are not physical in nature, intangible assets are critical to doing business and keeping competitors at bay. There are three main kinds of intangible assets. Let's look at each one.

Brands. The most common intangible asset of any business is its brand. A great company normally has strong brand value. Many a consumer would prefer a Coca-Cola any day to a generic cola. Coca-Cola can charge a fortune for sugared water, while generic colas cannot charge high prices for very similar drinks.

In the American West, See's Candies was a brand name that people trusted and liked. As prices rose in the 1970s, See's Candies had no problem raising prices on its customers. Chocolate lovers and those who bought with chocolate lovers in mind would choose See's any day over a generic chocolate from a competitor.

The fact that you have a moat doesn't mean you don't need to feed the alligators and snakes. Companies that aren't continually widening their brand moats suffer. One brand rarely stays on top for long. For example, Kodak was once the number one film company in the world, but when Fuji advertised at the Olympics and spread their brand, Fuji's sales started to outpace Kodak's. Brand names may temporarily be valuable, but companies must continually protect and position their brands in order to retain market share. That is one reason why Coca-Cola and McDonald's almost always sponsor the Olympics.

Patents and Copyrights. Benjamin Franklin was a prolific inventor who gave us bifocals, the Franklin stove, and a simple odometer. Even though Franklin never patented any of his own inventions, he promoted inventors' rights and was responsible for inserting into the U.S. Constitution an article guaranteeing limited terms for patents and copyrights. Many other countries have similar laws.

If you have a patent and a highly desirable product, the government grants you exclusive ability to make and market your technology. Patents on great products are a license to print money, as they provide monopoly conditions. Consider, for example, drug companies like

Pfizer, Merck, GlaxoSmithKline, or Novartis and the intellectual patents they hold on the drugs they have developed.

Many technology companies have patents that provide a strong moat. For example, Qualcomm sits on thousands of patents, many of which are standard for 3G communications. They are leaders in the code division multiple access (CDMA) 3G protocol and have a large number of technology licensing agreements. Worldwide, Qualcomm's extensive patent portfolio boasts more than 3,000 United States patents and patent applications for CDMA and other technologies. Thousands and thousands of companies have to pay royalty and licensing fees to use their patents.

Patents are great moats, but they do not last forever. Patents also expire, so watch out for single-patent companies. Many pharmaceutical companies haven't discovered new drugs, and their old patents are now running out. Patents can also be challenged in court, so you should make sure that the company you invest in has good patents and good defenses, since patent lawyers love suing other companies.

Copyrights of brands and characters are very powerful. Disney still owns the copyright to Mickey Mouse and loads of other cartoon characters. No one can create new toys, films, or anything relating to Disney characters without paying Disney a licensing fee. Disney knows its copyrights are a gold mine. That is why Disney also bought Pixar, Marvel, and George Lucas's *Star Wars* characters. (Disney also fights to extend patent laws. A law that delayed the expiry of patents, the Copyright Term Extension Act of 1998, was known as the Mickey Mouse Protection Act.) James Bond? Harry Potter? Marvel Comics? Who wouldn't want to own those franchises?

Regulatory Approvals. Ratings agencies like Moody's and Standard & Poor's may have done a terrible job during the subprime crisis, but they still are about the only companies that are allowed to rate bonds. All bond issuers need to get their bonds rated before many pension funds, insurance companies, and even banks can buy them. The government has made it extremely difficult for companies to act as ratings agencies, so Moody's and Standard & Poor's operate within a government-run oligopoly. There are some smaller ratings agencies, like Egan Jones, but they are not allowed to rate all bonds.

Examples of Companies with Moat 1

Great brands: Disney, Coca-Cola, Hershey, Tiffany, Harley Davidson, Louis Vuitton, and Luxottica, which owns Ray-Ban, Oakley, Persol, and other major brands.

Patents: Pfizer, Merck, GlaxoSmithKline, and Novartis. Almost all pharmaceutical companies have patents on their medicines. For example, Viagra was a cash cow. Some companies have dozens of patents and are well protected. Beware of pharmaceutical companies with only one patent. As soon as the patent expires on their medicine, their moat is gone.

Licenses and government approvals: Moody's, S&P.

Copyrights: Disney.

Moat 2: Network Effect

The network effect describes how the value of a service grows as more people use a network. Networks can be payment networks like Visa and MasterCard, or social networks like Facebook and Twitter, or auction platforms like Sotheby's or eBay. The more people that use any of these businesses, the harder it is for anyone else to compete with them.

The rule for analyzing networks is that with each additional person in the network, the number of potential connections in the network grows exponentially.

What would the value of eBay be if you were the only person on it? Zero. You need a buyer and a seller. With two people, the value would not be much. With 100, the possibilities get interesting. With a million people, it is hard to compete with eBay. Sellers want to go where all the buyers are, and buyers want to be where all the sellers are. The more buyers and sellers there are, the greater the value of eBay as a platform. The same is true for Skype. If almost no one is on Skype, you can't call anyone, but the more people there are, the more people you can call. PayPal doesn't work well if only a few people use it, but if everyone accepts it, you can pay for almost anything with it. The more people that use eBay, PayPal, Skype, Twitter, or Facebook, the less likely it is that they will face competitors.

Various mathematicians and computer scientists have come up with mathematical formulas to ascribe value to networks. They show that the value of a network is a function of the number of users.

Among these are Sarnoff's Law, Metcalfe's Law, and Reed's Law. The increase in value isn't arithmetic (3 + 3 = 6); it is much more exponential (3 × 3 = 9). The bigger, the better.

Examples of Companies with Moat 2

Payment networks: MasterCard, Visa, PayPal.
Auctions with large numbers of buyers and sellers: eBay, Sotheby's.
Large numbers of buyers and sellers: Financial exchanges such as CME Group, the New York Stock Exchange, the London Stock Exchange, and Deutsche Börse.
Social networks: Facebook, LinkedIn.
Ecosystems: Apple iOS, Google's Android. Developers of applications want to develop only for strong networks. They do not want to code for dozens of platforms. Apple via iTunes and Google via Android have created very strong network effects for their users and for the developers of applications.

Moat 3: Low-Cost Producer

Some businesses simply work more efficiently a very large scale. Larger business can buy in bulk, negotiate discounts, and centralize costs easily. Small businesses will always struggle to get lower prices for some things. The bigger the business is, the greater its efficiency. Think about Walmart compared to a mom-and-pop store. Walmart was so efficient, it even drove old, respected brands out of business, like the Great Atlantic & Pacific Tea Company (one of us is old enough to remember going to an A&P). Tesco has done the same in the United Kingdom, and Aldi and Lidl have done the same in Germany. You don't want to compete with a low-cost juggernaut. The bigger they get, the more efficient they get.

Low-cost producers are able to create a sustainable moat around their business because few competitors have the resources to start out big and offer the same economies of scale and scope. Even if you had dozens of billions of dollars to invest, it would still be hard to create a company like Aldi or Walmart.

Another type of business that favors the low-cost producer is a business that requires complex distribution networks. It is very difficult to deliver goods and packages cheaply if you have only a few customers. However, if you have many customers, you can centralize distribution centers and efficiently reach a very wide area. This is why UPS and FedEx have driven smaller delivery companies out of business.

Some companies are the low-cost producers because they simply happen to own mines or wells in places where it is extremely cheap to extract minerals or oil. Not all mines are created equal, and a miner that has extremely high grades of copper or gold easily accessible near the surface will incur much, much lower extraction costs than competitors do. However, as we have explained, we would not generally recommend commodity stocks for the long run, given that commodity stocks tend to skyrocket when things are good and are liable to crash when commodity prices go down.

Examples of Companies with Moat #3

Economies of scale: Walmart.
Distribution: UPS, Sysco, and Amazon.
Manufacturing: Intel.
Low-cost resource base: Compass Minerals, Freeport McMoran.

Moat 4: High Switching Costs

The big fear of most businesses is that if they raise prices their customers will simply walk away and go to a competitor. However, some businesses know that their customers can't leave them easily. Even if they did want to go to a competitor, the headaches involved (in terms of time, money, and the interruption to their business) would make it very difficult to jump ship.

Companies that provide critical support are hard to leave. All large modern businesses rely on powerful databases for accounting, inventory tracking, and so on. Ripping out an existing system and implementing a new one would be extremely difficult and pose big operational challenges. If the transition didn't go well, it would leave customers stranded or disappointed by poor service. No company wants that.

Likewise, companies that rely on integrated software like data processing, tax, or accounting solutions know that changing providers would interrupt a key part of their business. No manager wants that.

We all know that time is money. Banks have been able to charge extortionate fees to their customers because it would require too much time for customers to switch: changing bank accounts means changing all the direct debits, changing payroll details, changing most credit cards, and so on. Most people would prefer to have their fingernails pulled out slowly one by one to going through the hassle of changing all those things.

Examples of Companies with Moat 4

Integrated software: Oracle, Autodesk, and Microsoft.
Critical business processes: ADP, Jack Henry, Fiserv, Intuit, and Sage.

Moat 5: Efficient Scale

Competition is what drives reduces profits, but a market may be small enough or closed enough that when a company serves it, new competitors may not have an incentive to enter. Established businesses generate profits, but viable new competitors would cause returns for all players to fall well below cost of capital.

Some industries have natural geographic monopolies. Transportation costs are extremely expensive for some things. Heavy, cheap products are best suited to local monopolies, as competitors can't ship in products economically. That is why quarries and local garbage companies almost always operate without much competition. Getting permits for new quarries or landfills is difficult, and once a company serves a given area, they pretty much dominate the local business.

Other kinds of geographic monopolies include things like airports, racetracks, and stadiums. Airports have the benefit of network effects. The more flights that come in and leave, the more likely it is that airlines will want to connect through the airport as a hub. It is very difficult to establish a smaller airport next to a big, successful one. Only very large cities like New York and London can support more than one airport profitably.

Companies You Could Buy

Natural geographic monopolies: quarries, airports, racetracks, NASCAR company, pipelines.
Niche markets: defense companies, Lubrizol, Graco, Alexion, and the like; rational oligopolies like Canadian, U.K., and Australian banks.

Table 11.3 How Wide Is Your Moat?

Moat Sources:	Intangible Assets	Switching Costs	Network Effect	Cost Advantage
Wide Moat	**Coca-Cola:** It's just sugar water, but consumers pay a premium.	**Oracle:** Switching from Oracle's tightly integrated databases could cause massive disruptions.	**Chicago Mercantile Exchange:** Its clearing-house function keeps volume captive.	**UPS:** Ground delivery network has low marginal costs and high returns on capital.
Narrow Moat	**Dr Pepper Snapple:** Good brands, but a lack of scale hurts returns.	**Salesforce.com:** A popular product, but switching costs are low for users.	**NYSE Euronext:** Equity volume is interchangeable, and competitors have been stealing share.	**FedEx:** The high fixed-cost air express segment is still a large proportion of revenue.
No Moat	**Cott Corporation:** Private-label beverages are a commodity, with no brand loyalty.	**TIBCO:** High-end software "plumber" seeing competition from all-in-one solutions.	**Knight Capital Group:** Few network benefits from being an order-taker or market-maker.	**Con-way:** Trucking industry is very fragmented, making it tough to build scale and dig a moat.

SOURCE: Morningstar.

The lists above are by no means exhaustive or comprehensive. If you use your head and do a little research, you'll definitely come up with companies we haven't mentioned. Happy hunting!

Beware of False Moats

There are other business characteristics that present themselves as advantages, but they are false moats. Beware of companies that promote their great management, great execution, great products, big market share, catchy advertising campaign, or hot fashion trends. These attributes may produce temporary advantages, but they are likely to erode over time or to be duplicated by competitors. None of these in and of themselves offer any long-term sustainable moat.

If a company doesn't have a moat, no matter how popular a product is, it will eventually face competition and disappear. Companies generating high economic returns will always attract competitors willing to take a smaller but still decent return. The more mouths there are to feed in any industry, the lower the returns will be for everyone in the industry in general.

Investors who underestimate the competition will be forced to learn a painful lesson. Charlie Munger put it best: "Over the very long term, history shows that the chances of any business surviving in a manner agreeable to a company's owners are slim at best." The tech sector is littered with examples. For example, Palm pioneered the personal digital assistant (PDA). In the late 1990s, the Palm Pilot was extraordinarily popular and was the must-have gadget. Investors were so thrilled with the company that Palm's market value sky-rocketed to around $30 billion in the fall of 2000. But it didn't take long for rivals like Handspring, Sony, and Hewlett-Packard to introduce their own versions of the PDA. Eventually, PDAs were made completely irrelevant by the iPhone and other smartphones. And if you look at smartphones, the iPhone was the king of the hill for five years, until Samsung and other Android phone makers came along and started selling phones that were strongly competitive options. In technology, almost nothing lasts forever. That's called progress.

Buy at the Right Time

As Warren Buffett once observed, "It's far better to buy a wonderful company at a fair price than a fair company at a wonderful price." Finding companies that have a moat around their business is half the battle, but that is just the start. The key difference between making money and not making money is buying things at a good price. We want to emphasize a general principle that should be part of every investment decision you make: your profits when you sell are going to be determined by the price when you buy.

If you buy desirable companies at a very expensive price instead of a fair one, it is very difficult to make money. Earlier, we mentioned Walmart as a company that has a strong moat as a low-cost producer. Even if you know that is true, if you overpay for Walmart stock, it is hard to make money.

Let's look at Walmart over the past 15 years (Figure 11.3). When the market was going crazy with the dot-com boom in 1999–2000, Walmart traded at 40 times its price-to-earnings ratio, and the company was valued at over $250 billion. No matter how good a company is, 40 times earnings for a very large company is expensive. Indeed, over the next decade, Walmart continued to grow, earnings went up, dividends went up, and everything went well for the company. But

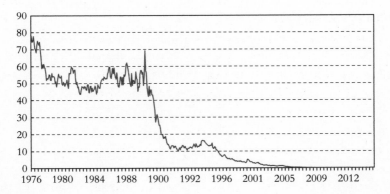

Figure 11.3   Walmart Stock since IPO

today, the stock is right back where it was 10 years ago. People had overpaid for growth and bought it too expensively.

It's easy to lose money on high-quality assets; people have been doing it for years. Buying high-quality assets at high prices and hoping that prices will go higher is not the best prescription for long-term success. Hope is not a strategy.

Let's consider a more rational approach instead. One of the things that makes investments safe and profitable is a good price relative to value. If you don't overpay for a stock, the chances for making money are highly skewed in your favor.

Let's look at Table 11.4. As you can see, the lower the price you pay for a stock, the higher your potential return. The table shows that if you buy the stock market at a reasonable price-to-earnings ratio, on average you will make money. If you're buying the stock market at anything above 24 times price-to-earnings, you're pretty much guaranteed not to make money. Moral of the story: never overpay for stocks.

The good news about successful investing is that you don't need to be a genius. Warren Buffett has repeatedly discounted the importance of a big brain. "Investing is not a game where the guy with the 160 IQ beats the guy with a 130 IQ," he has observed. "Once you have ordinary

Table 11.4 Stock Returns by Price-to-Earnings Ratio

S&P 500 P/E Entry Level	Subsequent Average Annualized S&P 500 Price Returns (%)				
	1 Yr	2 Yr	3 Yr	5 Yr	10 Yr
<8	13.6	10.6	8.5	10.2	11.1
8–10	8.3	10.9	12.3	12.0	9.0
10–12	12.3	12.9	11.5	8.0	8.3
12–14	8.9	8.8	6.7	6.2	7.4
14–16	11.4	7.3	6.5	6.8	6.5
16–18	3.3	1.8	2.3	3.1	2.6
18–20	3.5	3.4	3.5	4.0	3.1
20–22	2.4	5.8	7.4	8.2	6.2
22–24	−4.8	4.2	7.2	2.4	2.0
>24	−3.3	−2.5	−2.9	−0.7	−1.2

P/E = Price-Earnings Ratio
Sources: Henry McVey; KKR, www.kkr.com/company/insights/global-macro-trends-1.

intelligence, what you need is the temperament to control the urges that get other people into trouble in investing." The biggest problem people have is not their minds but their emotions. Investors chase fads and swing wildly from greed to fear and from euphoria to panic. They pay too high a price when markets are going up, and they sell most of their shares when markets go down. As the great investor Howard Marks pointed out, "The biggest investing errors come not from factors that are informational or analytical but from those that are psychological." Being a better investor is not about being smarter, it is about being less emotional.

Most people are thrilled when stock markets go up and panic when they go down. It takes a great deal of calm and perspective to do the opposite. You should be happy when the stock market goes down if you are a long-term investor. Stocks are claims on real businesses. When prices go down at Walmart, people who are thrilled with the discounts buy good socks or a flat-screen TV. Likewise, when the equity market goes down, you should be thrilled and buy good stocks. You aren't trading pieces of paper or lines on a screen when you trade shares; you're buying and selling pieces of real businesses—Oracle, Coke, and UPS—at lower prices. Think of stock market sell-offs like a discount at Walmart. Lower prices are better. Higher prices are worse.

Chances to buy stocks cheaply don't come around very often. Low price-to-earnings ratios and cheap stocks usually happen only during crises, when investors are panicking. The best times to buy stocks over the past 40 years have come during downturns: in the depth of 1973 downturn after oil prices spiked; in 1982 when people were burning Volcker in effigy on the steps of Capitol Hill; in 1992 when Clinton said, "It's the economy, stupid"; in 2002 when the dot-com bubble had burst and no one wanted to touch stocks; and in 2009 after Lehman Brothers had gone bust and people feared another Great Depression.

To understand these rare opportunities, it helps to know that stock markets move in very long cycles called secular bull and secular bear markets. On average, the cycles are about 17 years. During these cycles, markets go from high valuations to low valuations and then start back up to high valuations again. Each long-term secular market can see numerous bull and bear cycles, with breathtaking volatility. In a secular bear cycle, bullish advisers (usually those who want you to buy their funds) will tell you the bear market is over. And it is—until the next crisis.

It typically takes about three good bear markets to take valuations all the way down to single-digit numbers; but when they do get there, oh my, the following cycle is nothing but fun and roses. Everyone is a genius for the next 17 years (on average). Go back and look at the charts from 1949 or 1982. Those were wonderful times to be in the stock market. Every correction was met with a continuation of the secular bull until valuations simply got too high. Then the markets went sideways for about 17 years, the way it did starting in 1966 or early 2000. Even though stock markets are making new all-time highs as we write, we have not yet made the perilous trip to low valuations. Maybe this time is different, but we suspect there is one more good correction in our future before we see a return to a secular bull-market cycle. Notice in Table 11.4 that if you buy in the periods when valuations are low, your returns over time are quite high. Think of cash as a call option waiting for good valuations, just as Warren Buffett waits for good valuations to buy the companies in his portfolio.

The prospect of a further correction does *not* mean we suggest avoiding stocks. Far from it! There is always a bull market somewhere, and many stocks will make new highs in a secular bear market. That said, secular bull and bear markets require somewhat different approaches. Success in a bear takes more work and requires something more akin to a rifle approach than a shotgun approach. But take heart: this secular bear (if we are right) is almost over, and a fabulous bull market is just around the corner. We will all get to be geniuses one more time.

Bull and bear cycles are the subject for a whole different book (indeed, John has written two on the concept), so we won't go into detail here. But we will offer a few free links on www.thecoderedbook .com for you to read.

In the meantime, successful investing is all about value, value, value. And that means adopting a different attitude than most investors encounter on TV and in the financial press.

The bad news is that Code Red policies will lead to a lot more economic volatility and upheavals. Central bankers will get things wrong, and we will have more crises. The good news is that if you are patient, you will be able to buy stocks at bargain-basement prices when the next crisis happens. It almost makes us want to send central bankers a thank you note.

Key Lessons from the Chapter

In this chapter we learned:

- Inflation makes you poorer. It doesn't do this overnight, but over the years your money will easily halve in value, even with a modest inflation rate. Your savings have to add up faster than inflation can whittle them away in order for you to preserve your purchasing power.
- Inflation harms savers, but it works very well at getting rid of debt.
- Inflation hurts bonds and cash more than it does stocks. Bonds and cash get paid coupons and interest rates using dollars that lose their value. Stocks, however, represent claims on real assets. Also, companies can raise prices when there is inflation.
- Stocks are better than bonds, but not all stocks do well when inflation rises. Some companies face rising costs that erode their margins.
- Buying stocks that have moats around their business is critical. Moats are competitive advantages that sustainably allow companies to keep competitors at bay and to charge higher prices to their customers. Companies with moats are able to earn above-average returns on their invested capital.
- The five principal moats are Intangible Assets, Network Effects, Low-Cost Advantage, High Switching Costs, and Efficiency of Scale.
- Don't overpay for a good company. Pay a fair price for a good stock, not a high price. Even great companies can be bad investments if you overpay.

Chapter Twelve

A Look at Commodities, Gold, and Other Real Assets

But if inventions have increased man's power over nature very much, then the real value of money is better measured for some purposes in labor than in commodities.

—Alfred Marshall

A mine is a hole in the ground with a liar standing next to it.

—Mark Twain

There's a joke about a tourist in Ireland who asks one of the locals for directions to Dublin. The Irishman replied, "Well sir, if I were you, I wouldn't start from here." The same could be said for investing in commodities and other real assets today.

On the principle that central banks cannot print corn, oil, or copper, commodities can be among the very best places to be when central banks are implementing Code Red policies. Commodities have been phenomenally good investments in times of inflation and currency debasement. There are loads of academic studies that back up the case for investing in commodities when inflation is rising. For example, a study by Gary Gorton of Wharton University and Geert Rouwenhorst of Yale University found that "commodity futures are positively correlated with inflation, unexpected inflation, and changes in expected inflation."

Unfortunately, like much in life, a lot depends on where you start. Investors today are in a very difficult spot as they try to invest in almost any asset class. This is certainly true for investing in commodities. Normally, commodities are a slam-dunk when you see Code Red policies. And the returns can be phenomenal. For example, the last time the world had a currency war, sugar went from 1.4 cents to 66 cents from 1966 to 1974. But commodities today are a lot less attractive than they were 10 or even 15 years ago. The year 2013 was not at all like 1999. If we had written this book 10 years ago, we would have written this chapter very differently. (Indeed, John did write about them in his first book, in 1999. He was in love with commodities and long treasuries back in the day. My, how times of changed!)

You might be shocked that a book warning you about financial repression is not gung ho about commodities and gold. We'll explain when they're good investments, when they're bad investments, and what you should do with gold and commodities in your portfolio.

The Commodities Supercycle Is Dead

Whenever you invest your money, you should always be aware of what the smartest people in the investing world are doing. You want to find the people who are consistently right and who have seen bubbles and crashes before they happen.

By far one of the smartest investors is Jim Rogers. He's a legend. Rogers started the Quantum Fund with George Soros and has been investing successfully since the 1970s. He has the kind of experience that is almost impossible to match. Not only has Rogers been a great source of market insight over the years, he also provides a very long-term view.

Let's take a look at what he tells us about investing in commodities.

In 2004, Rogers wrote a book called *Hot Commodities* and argued that the world had entered into a commodities bull market. Then, Rogers was far ahead of everyone when it came to commodities. He even created his own commodity indices people could invest in, so he's an expert who knows what he's talking about. He had been writing about the coming commodities boom on the pages of the *Wall Street Journal*, *Barron's*, and other publications since 1998. In his book he wrote, "We know that history and simple economics are on our side: supply and demand have conspired to create a historic bull market in commodities, and that means commodities should rise at least until 2015." By the time he wrote that, commodities had increased 190 percent over the previous five years. Commodities then kept on rising for the next four years and proved that he was spectacularly right.

In the book *Hot Commodities*, Rogers pointed out that the twentieth century saw three long commodities bull markets (1906–1923, 1933–1953, 1968–1982), each lasting an average of a little more than 17 years. Notice that two of those bull markets coincided with currency wars. The 1933–1953 period started with the currency war of the 1930s, and the 1968–1982 period coincided with the currency wars of the 1970s. Even during the Great Depression, while economic growth was poor, commodities went up as currencies devalued and governments stoked inflation to fight deflation.

Not only did Rogers correctly call the beginning of the new-century commodities boom, he also pointed out what investors should look for when it ends. How would investors know the party was over? He wrote:

> When you see headlines about the discovery of new oil reserves or wind farms popping up outside major cities, when you see new mines coming on line, when you discover stockpiles of all kinds of commodities are rising, those are fundamental shifts – then it is time to get your money out of commodities. The bull market will be over.

He then went on to write, "Those days, in my opinion, are a decade away, at least." He wrote that in 2004. Almost 10 years have gone by since Rogers's book appeared, and a lot has changed. Today it's 2013, and by the time this book is in bookstores and you read it, it may well be 2014. *Even though Code Red policies are almost always very good for commodities, the current boom is in its final stages* (with one caveat we will explore in a moment!).

The latest commodity bull market started in 1999, so the current commodity supercycle is 14 years old, and commodities on average have more than doubled in price. The analysts at Ned Davis Research have pointed out that the average historical bull has lasted 16 years and gained 205 percent. Fifteen years ago there were shortages of many commodities, because there were almost no new mines and no new oil field discoveries. Today, the problem is that too many mines have started operating; and there is too much iron ore, copper, aluminum, and steel stockpiled as inventory in places like China. Meanwhile, much of Europe is dotted with wind farms, solar panels, and other energy-conserving technologies. The United States has been massively fracking many thousands of new wells each year, with more slated to come online. Where there were previously shortages and low prices, now higher prices have brought the new supplies of oil, iron ore, coal, and alumina online. That is how markets are supposed to work.

Have commodities peaked? If you look at the 10-year moving average of commodities going back two centuries, present valuations are stretched to extreme levels. You can see from Figure 12.1 that we're near the normal historical peak of commodity cycle returns. When the returns over a 10-year period are very stretched, we tend to be near a commodity peak and the end of a commodity bull market.

The boom and bust cycle of commodities is well documented. Professor David Jacks has shown in his research that commodities go through long periods of booms and busts. Depending on what kinds of commodities you look at, you can find long-run trends, medium-run cycles, and short-run boom/bust episodes. He likes commodities as investments, but as he points out, "[T]he accumulated historical evidence on super-cycles suggests that the current super-cycles are likely at their peak and, thus, nearing the beginning of the end of above-trend real commodity prices in the affected categories."

All of this leaves investors in a difficult position. Normally, commodities are one of the best investments to protect wealth against Code Red policies, but as we write this book, almost all commodity cycles have passed their peak and will not offer good returns over the next few years. The party is just about over; the guests are drunk and are heading home. When commodity bubbles burst, it can get ugly.

Let's look for a second at how commodity cycles start and finish. In most markets, if prices rise or fall, supply adjusts very quickly. For example, if people suddenly want to buy more copies of *Code Red*, it is

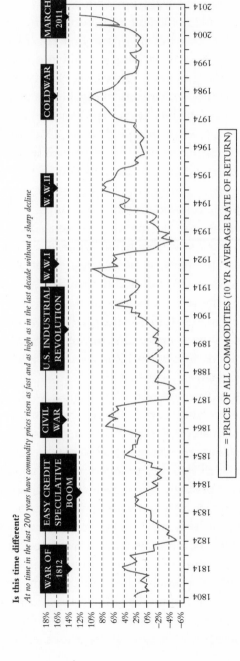

Figure 12.1 Long–Term Commodity Returns Have Been Very High

SOURCE: Hackett Financial Advisors, Macleans, http://hackettadvisors.com.

305

a trivial matter for Wiley to print more books. Doing another printing doesn't take many weeks.

For commodities, it takes a lot longer for supply to come online, sometimes even years. Take the example of iron ore. In 2000, the prices for iron ore were so low that not many mines were digging it up. But as China continued to grow, the Chinese could not buy enough iron ore. Prices skyrocketed, but supply could not keep pace. It takes years to find more iron ore deposits, get permits to dig, build railroads to get the iron ore to port, and launch ships to get the iron to customers. Global supply failed to keep pace with Chinese demand. Over the next decade, the price of iron ore went up 10 times. The increase in the price of iron ore outpaced the biggest bubbles of the past few decades: gold in the 1970s, the Nikkei in the 1980s, and the Nasdaq in the 1990s.

If you have not been reading all the breathless articles telling us why the price of iron ore can do nothing but rise due to Chinese and other Asian demand, then you have been living in a cave. It is part of the narrative of every bubble that people insist that this time is different. There are always good stories and reasons given in support of the argument that what made us money in the past is going to make us even more money in the future. And that is especially true when the writer is someone who is embedded in the industry being written about. It is difficult for people to imagine their prosperity going away. It's just the way we humans are hardwired.

That was the boom phase in iron ore, but now we'll get to the bust phase. The higher prices encouraged the biggest mining companies to boost output by a crazy amount. This past year, the world's biggest iron ore producers were planning a whopping $250 billion investment in new mines. That's on top of all the new production that has come online in the past decade. Not surprisingly, prices have already crashed, and dozens of projects are being put on hold. As with any bubble that has expanded tenfold, the crash will be very nasty. Many iron ore mining companies will go bankrupt, and lots of mines will shut down as prices fall.

As the case of iron ore shows, with commodities it is critical to invest at the beginning of a supercycle, not toward the end. Given the boom-and-bust pattern of commodity cycles, the long-run returns are very poor. Our good friend Dylan Grice, who was a highly rated strategist at Société Générale and is now at Edelweiss Funds, has written

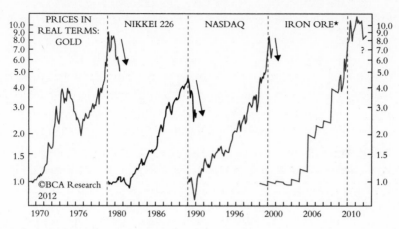

Figure 12.2 Iron Ore Increased by a Factor of 10
SOURCE: Bank Credit Analyst.

extensively about commodities. He makes the very good point that there is no reason why commodities should go up over the long term:

> Why should commodities provide investors with a real risk premium? Shouldn't prices actually decline in real terms over time? A bushel of wheat, a lump of iron-ore or an ingot of silver today is identical to a bushel of wheat, lump of iron-ore or ingot of silver produced one thousand years ago. The only difference is that they're generally cheaper to produce because over time, human innovation has lowered the cost of production. When you buy commodities, you're selling human ingenuity. Past performance is no guarantee of future results, obviously, but human ingenuity has a good track record of overcoming nature's constraints so far. A commodity bull market is really just a bottleneck and as a species we've succeeded in bottleneck removal. Historically, most bull markets have ended up where they started.

As Grice points out, betting on commodities implies betting against human ingenuity. As prices go up, humans find ways to grow more grain, dig more mines, and get their hands on commodities that previously couldn't be extracted.

You can see in Figure 12.3 that commodities from 1870 to today have offered a very poor long-term return. While commodities have

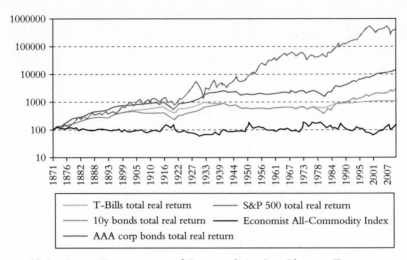

Figure 12.3   Long–Term returns of Commodities Are Close to Zero
SOURCE: Dylan Grice, Société Générale.

risen sharply during bull markets, in the very long run they do not offer value to investors.

Beyond the dynamic of boom and bust, there is a more important problem with commodities. Benjamin Graham, the father of value investing, defined investment and speculation as follows: "An investment operation is one which, upon thorough analysis, promises safety of principal and a satisfactory return. Operations not meeting these requirements are speculative." Commodities are inherently speculative.

Commodities do not produce a yield or pay interest to investors. You can really buy commodities only if you think prices are going up. As Warren Buffett once wrote:

> The problem with commodities is that you are betting on what someone else would pay for them in six months. The commodity itself isn't going to do anything for you . . . it is an entirely different game to buy a lump of something and hope that somebody else pays you more for that lump two years from now than it is to buy something that you expect to produce income for you over time.

If you invest in a company like Coca-Cola, you own a piece of a real business, and you can receive dividends from the company. (As we write this, Coca-Cola's dividend yield is 2.6 percent. That, by the way, is significantly higher than the yield on a 10-year U.S. treasury. Welcome to the Code Red world.)

If you're a speculator and really know your commodity markets, you can trade oil or copper and make a lot of money. People like Marc Rich, Andrew Hall, Michael Farmer, and David Lilley have made hundreds of millions of dollars doing it. But that is what they do for a living. They know the markets for oil, copper, and grain inside out. Most of us don't have the time, energy, and access to figure out the changes in supply and demand of most commodities. You should be an investor with your money, not a speculator. Choosing that path will bring you less stress and let you sleep better at night.

The fact that commodity prices may not be rising does not mean that commodities are not a very good asset class to have in your portfolio. But you should let the experts manage those investments. Don't try it at home. There is a whole industry devoted to trading commodities on the futures market. In general, we can refer to this as the managed futures industry.

Managed futures funds trade commodities not only from the long side of the market but also from the short side. Typically, these are trend-following funds, and they quite frankly don't care whether the market is going up or down, they just want it to move. The biggest funds trade on multiple dozens of markets in multiple dozens of commodities. If it moves, they trade it. They have scores of PhDs in math and physics sitting around trying to come up with better trend-following systems.

There's a great deal of research showing that managed futures does not correlate with stocks or bonds. Indeed, simply looking at the graphs will tell you that managed futures zig when other markets tend to zag. Trying to chase the hot commodity fund is not only futile but can be costly. It is much better to pick a few managers you feel comfortable with and stick with them.

The Biggest Buyer Stumbles

In *Endgame* we wrote a chapter on Japan titled "A Bug in Search of a Windshield," and it is hard to top a title like that. We've struggled to find something equally colorful to characterize China. Every boom eventually turns to bust, and after two decades of spectacular growth, China is bound to hit a wall. It may be happening as this book comes off the presses. And this is a big problem for commodities. The huge commodities supercycle is likely to move into reverse when China has to slow its commodities consumption.

China is by far the biggest customer in the world for commodities. The level of demand has been unprecedented. For many commodities like iron ore and soybeans, over half of all global exports have gone to China. The world has never seen anything like China's hunger for everything from copper to steel to cement.

China's growth story is well known. With a population of over a billion people, China had a lot of catching up to do in order to raise its gross domestic product (GDP) per capita. With hundreds of millions of workers to employ, China embarked on a strategy of driving its growth via exports to Europe, the United States, and its Asian neighbors. As the Chinese economy industrialized, hundreds of millions of workers moved from the countryside to large cities on the east coast. The process of industrialization and urbanization has been bigger and faster than anything the world has ever seen. The need to create bridges, railways, power stations, buildings, and factories made China the biggest buyer of commodities in the world. It needed copper, iron ore, alumina, and cement for all its construction. And it needed loads of soybeans, corn, and wheat to feed its workers.

The problem is that China's growth and investment boom is so extreme that it is unsustainable. Pivot Capital, a macro hedge fund, wrote a comprehensive report titled "China's Investment Boom: The Great Leap into the Unknown." They noted, "[B]oth in its duration and intensity, China's capital spending boom is now outstripping previous great transformation periods (e.g., postwar Germany and Japan or South Korea in the 1980–90s)." Pivot showed that China's growth is exaggerated and unbalanced. Even worse, a large debt bubble has fueled most of it, and that bubble is now bursting.

A few charts can tell the story of just how literally off the charts China's growth has been. Let's take a look at Figure 12.4. China's investment share of GDP has reached levels close to 50 percent in recent years. This far exceeds the peaks that we've seen before, when

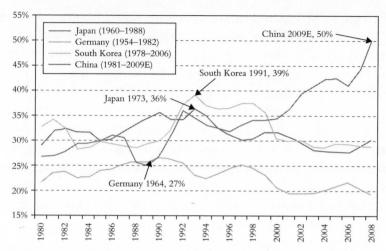

Figure 12.4   China's Investment Boom Is Unprecedented
SOURCE: Pivot Capital.

countries like Japan, Germany, or South Korea industrialized. While China does need bridges, factories, and ports, you can have too much of a good thing. Most countries have a more balanced growth pattern, with household consumption keeping pace with infrastructure investment. China, however, has relatively little domestic consumption. It is about as deformed as a bodybuilder with big biceps and spindly legs.

China has built too much, too quickly, and is unlikely to need to buy the same quantities of commodities in the future (with the obvious exception of food!). As China rebalances, lower commodity prices will result. Michael Pettis, a professor at Peking University's Guanghua School of Management and an astute observer of the Chinese economy, has observed,

> Almost all the increase in demand in the past twenty years, which in practice occurred mostly in the past decade, can be explained as the consequence of the incredibly unbalanced growth process in China. As China's economy rebalances towards a much more sustainable form of growth, this will automatically make Chinese growth much less commodity intensive.

In Figure 12.5 you can see just how much of every commodity China has bought. For some products, like iron ore and soybeans, Chinese demand is over 65 percent of global trade. China buys over half of the world's cotton and a third of the world's copper.

Over the past decade, Chinese commodity purchases have outstripped domestic needs and are now creating rapidly growing inventories. The Chinese have accumulated so much copper, iron ore, and other key commodities that it's likely they'll soon have to dump inventories onto their local markets, which will of course affect prices on global markets. This tendency is already causing the prices of industrial metals to fall, and it is unlikely that when prices rebound they will return to their previous peaks.

The most worrisome part of China's boom is that much of it was based on out-of-control credit growth. Financial crises that are built on debt are like houses built on quicksand. Many analysts, including Jim Chanos, Michael Pettis, and Patrick Chovanec, argue that China's debt bubble has passed the point of no return. For example, according to Standard & Poor's (S&P), China's corporate debt-to-GDP ratio

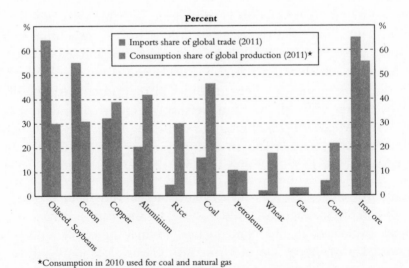

*Consumption in 2010 used for coal and natural gas

Figure 12.5 China Is the Biggest Buyer of Most Commodities
SOURCE: EIA; UN Comtrade; AME; U3 Department of Agriculture; NAB.

stands at 134 percent, compared to 78 percent in the United States, 87 percent in Japan, and 71 percent in Australia. It is difficult to know what the total debt level is in China, but Fitch estimates that if you include "shadow banking," credit may have reached 198 percent of GDP at the end of 2012. Shadow banks are entities that borrow money for the short term and invest it in long-term assets. These entities are not depository institutions and are not regulated. (This reminds us very much of the shadow banking system in the United States that encountered problems in 2007.) Chinese government debt is not high, at 49 percent of GDP by the end of 2012, according to Fitch. But countries like Spain had lower debt before their property bubbles burst, only to see debt skyrocket once the crisis arrived.

The commodity supercycle is likely over. The main buyer of commodities is stumbling. As an investor, you should not chase commodities, with the exception of managed futures, which can actually benefit from falling prices, as we mentioned earlier.

What Really Moves Gold Prices

It is impossible to write a book about currency wars and a Code Red world without writing about the price of gold. And no matter what we write, we're going to make a lot of people mad. Gold is like a religion: people either believe in it or they don't. We're going to get hate mail. (Please direct all letters to our publisher so they can shred them. The exception to that policy is if your letter is particularly colorful. We enjoy fun reads just as much as the next guy!)

The world is divided into two kinds of people. On one side you have gold bugs, who think that money can only be honest and pure if it is backed by gold. They still pine for the days of the gold standard. They think one of the greatest tragedies ever was the move to paper money that is backed only by a government's good faith and credit.

On the other side you have the people who scorn gold bugs and cannot see any use for the "barbarous relic." Neither side likes the other at all. (A friend who is a journalist at one of the world's major financial newspapers told us that articles on gold consistently generate the most comments and the most shares via Twitter and Facebook. Almost no one has a moderate opinion about gold.)

Gold can seem like a ridiculous investment. Warren Buffett once said, "Gold gets dug out of the ground in Africa, or someplace. Then we melt it down, dig another hole, bury it again, and pay people to stand around guarding it. It has no utility. Anyone watching from Mars would be scratching their head."

Buffett's comment is too clever by half. You could make a similar observation about money: "Trees get cut down in Oregon, or someplace. Then we pulp them, turn them into dollar bills, put them in ATMs, and trade them. They have no utility." Money itself has no utility, but it functions as a means of exchange, a store of value, and a unit of account. Money is valuable only insofar as you can trade it for something else of value. Gold may be irrational, but there is a fundamental need for a medium of exchange. Early civilizations used pebbles or shells. Prisoners have used cigarettes. And for thousands of years societies have used gold. But today we use dollars, euros, and yen. Gold has value only insofar as you can trade it for something else of value. If you can trade your gold for companies that will grow and produce cash, all the better.

In a world of Code Red policies and currency wars, we like to think that gold is effectively a form of "central bank insurance." We have health insurance, fire insurance, life insurance, and so on. We dearly hope we never have to use any of them. But we keep buying insurance anyway, because we don't know the future. In a perfect world, gold would be a collector's item, shiny jewelry, or an industrial metal. But this is not a perfect world. Central banks can print money and debase currencies. Gold rises and falls in relation to any given currency, in line with general concerns about the long-term viability of the obligations of the government issuing the currency. If you are in the United States, you might want only a small portion of your portfolio in gold. If we were in Japan right now, we would be buying gold or dollars or anything not denominated in yen. If you are a trader, buying gold in terms of yen might make a great deal of sense. If you live in Argentina, owning anything that is not physical pesos makes sense.

What drives the price of gold? The best predictor of the price of gold is the change in the real interest rate you can earn on your savings. As an investor, you have the choice every day as to whether to keep your money in cash or own a shiny metal. What influences that decision is whether you are getting any real return on your savings. If you are, you're unlikely to buy something like gold that gives you no yield and pays you nothing. However, if inflation is higher than the going interest rate, then you're earning a negative return by keeping your money in cash. Owning a real asset like gold suddenly doesn't seem so dumb.

This very clear relationship between real interest rates and the price of gold has held for the past few decades. There is a simple rule of thumb called Gibson's Paradox. Investors expect a real return on their cash of 2 percent. The rule states that for every percentage point the real interest is below 2 percent, gold returns 8 percent year-on-year *times that multiple*. So if real rates were 4 percent, then gold would *decline* by 16 percent. If real interest rates were 0 percent, then gold would *rise* by 16 percent. This rule has held true for over 40 years. Figure 12.6 shows the very tight correlation between real interest rates and the price of gold.

As we write this, gold has fallen over 30 percent from the highs it reached in the summer of 2011. It is worth asking whether the bull market in gold is over. Many investors have been spooked by the fall in the gold price. Within less than a year, traders have gone from being wildly optimistic about gold's potential to incredibly negative. Speculators are now shorting gold futures. However, while gold futures have fallen, the demand for physical gold has been extremely

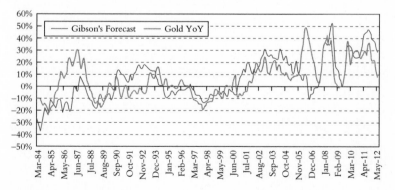

Figure 12.6 Gold Prices Can Be Explained by Changes in Real Interest Rates
SOURCE: *Variant Perception*, Bloomberg.

strong. According to GFMS in its 2012 "Gold Survey," net official central bank gold purchases were the highest in almost 50 years. Many emerging-market countries have been doubling their gold holdings. Also, all across the world, even as gold futures fell, buyers of physical gold hoarded gold coins and bars. Almost all government mints ran out of coins. Many investors are confused—what are they to think about these conflicting developments?

The bottom line is that as long as real interest rates are negative, gold will continue to go up. If we had to bet, we would say it is highly likely gold will keep appreciating. Central bankers have already told us they plan to keep real interest rates negative for the foreseeable future. As our friend Christopher Wood at CLSA has written, "Central banks worldwide continue to compete to become even more unconventional. Under such a scenario, gold is indeed the purest form of 'money' available, not contaminated by the current fiat paper system." His target for the price of gold in a few years is $3,500. Before you shudder, consider that Wood is one of the most highly regarded macro strategists, and he was far ahead of everyone in warning about the subprime and banking crises, before any central bankers even knew what a subprime mortgage was.

Gold has gone down, but nothing goes up in a straight line. Even big bubbles where prices went up over 10 times in a decade had major

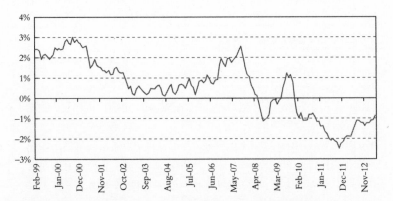

Figure 12.7   Global Real Policy Rate (Official Central Bank Rates Minus Inflation)
SOURCE: *Variant Perception*, Bloomberg.

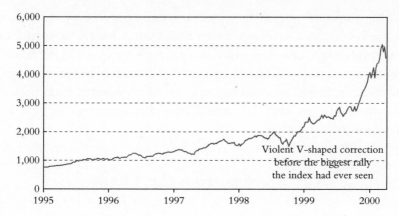

Figure 12.8   The Nasdaq Bubble
SOURCE: Bloomberg.

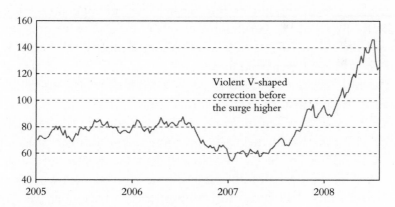

Figure 12.9   Spot Price of Light Crude Oil, 2006–2007
SOURCE: Bloomberg.

corrections. For example, the Nasdaq went from 400 to 5,000 in the 1990s. However, in 1998, it declined almost 40 percent before then rising almost five times. You can see that in Figure 12.8. Another bubble that had an almost 40 percent correction was oil when it declined from $80 in 2006 to $50 in 2007. Everyone thought the bull market in oil was over, but it then rallied from $50 to $148. It is highly likely gold has had a major, significant correction that will lead to a bigger boom ahead. Gold will probably be like Nasdaq in 1998 and oil in 2006.

This book will appear in your hands before we know whether the bull market in gold is over. Our view is that as long as central bankers are pursuing Code Red policies, gold will do well. However, if real interest rates become positive and central bankers decide to contract their balance sheets and tighten rates, gold will suffer. Sadly, the day that central bankers reverse Code Red policies appears to be a long, long way off.

Key Lessons from the Chapter

In this chapter we learned:

- Short-term returns of commodities can be good when central banks print money, but this rarely lasts. Buying commodities for the long term implies betting against human ingenuity. Humans always find ways to get things out of the ground or to grow more crops. If you want to invest in commodities today, the best way to do it is through managed futures.
- The real, inflation-adjusted prices of commodities rise or fall based on the supply that is mined or grown. In the short run, commodities can go up a lot when there are bottlenecks and supply shortages. In the long run, though, new supplies come online at higher prices.
- Commodities go through boom and bust cycles that last for years, caused by the cycles of investment in new mines or the cultivation of new fields. The cycles for mining tend to be longer because it takes time to dig new mines. The cycles for agriculture are shorter because farmers can grow more or less corn, wheat, or soy from one year to the next.
- The price of gold is most closely tied to the change in real interest rates. When inflation is above the interest rate that you can get on the cash in your bank account, gold goes up. When inflation is below the level of interest you can earn for your cash, gold will go down.

Conclusion

When we set out to write *Code Red*, we wanted to write a book that anyone could understand. Albert Einstein once said, "Make things as simple as possible, but not simpler." We tried to do that with this book.

Our hope is that you have enjoyed *Code Red*. We hope it has made you better informed and able to understand what is happening in the global economy. We wanted to leave you with some personal parting nuggets of wisdom, but we recognize that we are not the wisest people you could listen to. We are not fund managers or billionaires. We try to be curious, to write well, and to explain complex ideas as simply as possible. But that is as far as our talents take us.

We recognize what we're good at and what we aren't. Given our limitations, we thought it was best to leave you with the advice of two legends of the investing world. Both are billionaires with decades of investing experience, and they can offer a lot more wisdom than we could. We'll leave you with parting thoughts from Warren Buffett and Howard Marks. If you learn from them, this book will have been worth reading.

Warren Buffett needs no introduction as one of the greatest investors of all time. Others have produced slightly better returns, but no one has invested for as long and as consistently has Buffett has. You usually find him explaining his views on individual companies, but when he offers his views on global macro investing, it is worth paying close attention to what he says. In his 1994 Berkshire Hathaway shareholder letter, he wrote about investing in a rapidly changing world of inflation, deflation, and wars. No matter what was happening around him, it wasn't about to change the fundamental way he invests:

> We will continue to ignore political and economic forecasts, which are an expensive distraction for many investors and businessmen. Thirty years ago, no one could have foreseen the huge expansion of the Vietnam War, wage and price controls, two oil shocks, the resignation of a president, the dissolution of the Soviet Union, a one-day drop in the Dow of 508 points, or treasury bill yields fluctuating between 2.8% and 17.4%.
>
> But, surprise—none of these blockbuster events made the slightest dent in Ben Graham's investment principles. Nor did they render unsound the negotiated purchases of fine businesses at sensible prices. Imagine the cost to us, then, if we had let a fear of unknowns cause us to defer or alter the deployment of capital. Indeed, we have usually made our best purchases when apprehensions about some macro event were at a peak. Fear is the foe of the faddist, but the friend of the fundamentalist.
>
> A different set of major shocks is sure to occur in the next 30 years. We will neither try to predict these nor to profit from them. If we can identify businesses similar to those we have purchased in the past, external surprises will have little effect on our long-term results.

What Buffett is saying is that he can't forecast the future, and even when the world changes, as long as he is patient and willing to buy stocks cheaply when others are panicking, he'll do well. That is possibly the best advice you will ever get. The hard part is not letting your emotions control you.

The greatest investors never pretend they know the future. They're humble and agnostic. They build investment strategies that are robust in the face of uncertainty.

Buffett enjoys reading the memos Howard Marks of Oaktree sends out. You would not be surprised that they share the same philosophy. One of our favorite pieces Marks wrote is titled "What We Can Do for You." You can find it on Oaktree's web site. We highly recommend that you read it carefully. He makes the following point regarding what we cannot know:

> **The main thing we can't do is see the future, and particularly the macro future**. That simple statement has serious ramifications. It means a lot that we'd love to know is beyond us:
>
> We can't know what the economies of the world will do,
> We can't know whether markets will go up or down and by how much,
> We can't know which market or sub-market will do best, and
> We can't know which securities in a given market will be the top performers.

If you know that you don't have a crystal ball and can't foresee the future, it leads you to manage your investments differently. As he writes:

> The more you acknowledge you don't know what the future holds:
>
> The more you should diversify, spreading your bets to make sure you don't miss the winners or, more importantly, overload on losers,
> The less you should attempt to augment performance through adroit short-term market timing, and
> The less leverage you should employ.

You don't need to know the future to be a good investor. You should make sure that your strategy is robust in the face of an uncertain future by diversifying, by being patient and long-term-focused, and by not employing leverage.

Does this mean that reading *Code Red*, a book about the future we face, has been a useless exercise? Not at all. Many people think that value investors are supposed to ignore the macro news, forget about the bigger picture, and look at companies only from the bottom up. That hardly makes sense. You have to understand the economic, political, and social environment you live and invest in.

In the coming months and years, central banks and governments will be offering us many opportunities for investing. As an extreme example, if you live in Japan, you might want to seriously consider diversification outside your country. Sovereign debt has been a generally safe investment for many decades, but a number of countries are going to have problems. It is important that you understand the local environment in which you are investing. Understanding the macroeconomic environment is particularly useful for choosing the currencies in which you want your portfolios to be denominated, as well as helping you determine which asset classes you might want to be underweight or overweight, or in some cases simply avoid.

Designing a portfolio based solely on past performance leads to problems. It's the classic problem of the turkey and Thanksgiving. Right up until Thanksgiving the turkey is very happy with the farmer. What a wonderful person, who feeds him and makes sure all of his needs are met. Past performance indicates to the turkey that life is pretty good.

For the vast majority of our readers, using macroeconomics to fine-tune their investment portfolios will be problematic, but macroeconomics can be useful in making the larger calls about allocation and valuation. And really, those are the areas that, if you get them right, everything else seems to fall into place.

Be patient. Buy things of quality at cheap prices. Always think for yourself and do your own homework. That is how you will be able to stay clear of the crowd. When the next crisis happens—whether it's due to Code Red policies being pushed too far or being halted too quickly—those who have the patience and courage to go against the crowd will make money.

Being patient is boring and not as much fun as watching CNBC or Bloomberg. It is not as much fun as watching the financial markets football game play out every day. But boring is far safer, and it's effective. Getting rich slowly is less exciting than getting rich quickly, but it is much more certain.

We truly wish all our readers the very best. If you like our thinking, you can see our latest updates at www.thecoderedbook.com.

John has written a free weekly letter for the past 14 years that you can subscribe to at www.mauldineconomics.com. Jonathan and colleagues publish their research for institutional clients, family offices, and hedge funds at www.variantperception.com.

Afterword: A Few Thoughts from John

Life invests itself with inevitable conditions, which the unwise seek to dodge, which one and another brags that he does not know, that they do not touch him; but the brag is on his lips, the conditions are in his soul. If he escapes them in one part they attack him in another more vital part. If he has escaped them in form and in the appearance, it is because he has resisted his life and fled from himself, and the retribution is so much death.

Ralph Waldo Emerson

Only one fellow in ten thousand understands the currency question, and we meet him every day.

Kin Hubbard, American humorist, 1868–1930

I've been watching the sun set over Flathead Lake in Montana as summer draws to a close, reading the entire manuscript of *Code Red* for one last time before it goes to press. In the midst of the permanence of the Rocky Mountains and the peacefulness of the lake, I have found the perfect place to reflect on the volatility that we believe will soon once again roil the markets. My co-author, Jonathan Tepper, has graciously allowed me to add a few thoughts of my own to close the book.

We Can't Take a Chance

What would it have been like to be in the decision maker's seat at a central bank at the height of the 2008–2009 financial crisis? You'd know that you won't have the luxury of going back and making better decisions five years down the road. Instead, you have to act on the information that's coming at you from every quarter today, and none of it is good. Major banks are literally collapsing, the interbank market is almost nonexistent, and there is panic in the air. Perhaps you feel that panic in the pit of your stomach. Imagining what it was like might help us to understand how the next crisis will play out.

We can actually get a good idea how central bankers were feeling in that crucial moment by listening in on a debate that happened this past summer between bond maven Jim Bianco and former Bank of England Monetary Policy Committee member David Blanchflower. It was held at the annual August gathering of economists and money managers at "Camp Kotok" in Grand Lake Stream, Maine. Bianco is simply one of the most respected bond and interest rate gurus in the world. Blanchflower is currently a professor at Dartmouth and has one of the more impressive resumes you will find. He is not afraid to be contrarian and voted in the minority in 18 out of 36 meetings at the British equivalent of the Federal Open Market Committee (FOMC). Blanchflower's *The Wage Curve*, with 8 years of data from 4 million people in 16 countries, argued that the wage curve, which plots wages against unemployment, is negatively sloping, reversing generations of macroeconomic theory. "The Phillips curve is wrong; it's as fundamental as that," Blanchflower asserts.

The format for the debate between Bianco and Blanchflower was simple. The question revolved around Federal Reserve policy and what the Fed should do today. To taper or not to taper? In fact, should they even entertain further quantitative easing? Bianco made the case that quantitative easing has become the problem rather than the solution; Blanchflower argued that quantitative easing is the correct policy—fairly standard arguments from both sides but well reasoned and well presented.

It was during the question-and-answer period that we got the real lesson in how monetary policy might be decided in a future crisis. Bianco had made a forceful argument that big banks should have been allowed to fail rather than being bailed out. The question from the floor to Danny was, in essence, "What if the Bianco is right? Wouldn't it have been better to let banks fail and then restructure them in bankruptcy? Wouldn't we have recovered faster, rather than suffering in the slow-growth, high-unemployment world where we find ourselves now?"

Blanchflower pointed his finger right at Jim and spoke forcefully. "It wasn't the possibility that he was right that preoccupied us. *We couldn't take the chance that he was wrong.* If he was wrong and we did nothing, the world would've ended and it would've been our fault. We had to act."

That sentence is the key to understanding what will happen in the next crisis: "We couldn't take the chance that he was wrong." Whether or not you like the implications of what he said, the simple fact is that he was expressing the reigning paradigm of economic thought in the world of central bankers. And that mode of thinking will lead them to act in the next crisis with the same policy tools they have turned to in all recent crises: low interest rates, monetary easing, massive injections of liquidity, and financial repression.

A Few Impossible Things

Now, let's hold that train of thought for a few minutes as we intro-duce an essay by French geophysicist and complex systems analyst Didier Sornette, whom we met in Chapter 9. Sornette is Professor on the Chair of Entrepreneurial Risks at the Department of Management Technology and Economics of the Swiss Federal Institute of Technology Zurich.

Sornette's basic thesis is that a fundamentally unstable economic system, augmented by human greed, means that market bubbles and crashes won't disappear anytime soon.

I highly recommend all of his work but want to focus here on the recent paper he published with his colleague Peter Cauwels, entitled "The Illusion of the Perpetual Money Machine."[1] I'm going to quote a few paragraphs from the introduction. They begin with that marvelous exchange from *Alice in Wonderland*:

> "There is no use trying," said Alice. "One can't believe impossible things." "I daresay you haven't had much practice," said the Queen. "When I was your age, I always did it for half an hour a day. Why, sometimes I've believed as many as six impossible things before breakfast."

Chasing fantasies is not the exclusive pastime of little girls in fairy tales. History is speckled with colorful stories of distinguished scientists and highly motivated inventors pursuing the holy grail of technology: the construction of a perpetual motion machine. These are stories of eccentric boys with flashy toys, dreaming of the fame and wealth that would reward the invention of the ultimate gizmo, a machine that can operate without depleting any power source, thereby solving forever our energy problems. In the mid-1800s, thermodynamics provided the formal basis on what common sense informs us: it is not possible to create energy out of nothing. It can be extracted from wood, gas, oil or even human work, as was done for most of human history, but there are no inexhaustible sources.

What about wealth? Can it be created out of thin air? Surely, a central bank can print crispy banknotes and, by means of the modern electronic equivalent, easily add another zero to its balance sheet. But what is the deeper meaning of this money creation? Does it create real value? Common sense and Austrian economists in particular would argue that money creation outpacing real demand is a recipe for inflation. In this piece, we show that the question is much more subtle and interesting, especially for understanding the extraordinary developments since 2007. While it is true that, like energy, wealth cannot be created out of thin air, there is a fundamental difference: whereas the belief of some marginal scientists in a perpetual motion machine had essentially no impact, its financial equivalent has been the hidden cause behind the current economic impasse.

The Czech economist Tomáš Sedláček argues that, while we can understand old economic thinking from ancient myths, we can also learn a lot about contemporary myths from modern economic thinking. A case in point is the myth, developed in the past 30 years, of an eternal economic growth, based in financial innovations, rather than on real productivity gains strongly rooted in better management, improved design, and fueled by innovation and creativity. This has created an illusion that value can be extracted out of nothing; the mythical story of the perpetual money machine, dreamed up before breakfast.

To put things in perspective, we have to go back to the post-WWII era. It was characterized by 25 years of reconstruction and a third industrial revolution, which introduced computers, robots and the Internet. New infrastructure, innovation, and technology led to a continuous increase in productivity. In that period, the financial sphere grew in balance with the real economy. In the 1970s, when the Bretton Woods system was terminated and the oil and inflation shocks hit the markets, business productivity stalled and economic growth became essentially dependent on consumption. Since the 1980s, consumption became increasingly funded by smaller savings, booming financial profits, wealth extracted from house prices appreciation and explosive debt. This was further supported by a climate of deregulation and a massive growth in financial derivatives designed to spread and diversify the risks globally.

The result was a succession of bubbles and crashes: the worldwide stock market bubble and great crash of October 19, 1987, the savings-and-loans crisis of the 1980s, the burst in 1991 of the enormous Japanese real estate and stock market bubbles and its ensuing "lost decades," the emerging markets bubbles and crashes in 1994 and 1997, the Long-Term Capital Management (LTCM) crisis of 1998, the dot-com bubble bursting in 2000, the recent house price bubble, the financialization bubble via special investment vehicles, speckled with acronyms like CDO, RMBS, CDS, . . . the stock market bubble, the commodity and oil bubbles and the debt bubbles, all developing jointly and feeding on each other, until the climax of 2008, which brought our financial system close to collapse.

Each excess was felt to be "solved" by measures that in fact fueled following excesses; each crash was fought by an accommodative monetary policy, sowing the seeds for new bubbles and future crashes. Not only are crashes not any more mysterious, but the present crisis and stalling economy, also called the Great Recession, have clear origins, namely in the delusionary belief in the merits of policies based on a "perpetual money machine" type of thinking.

"The problems that we have created cannot be solved at the level of thinking we were at when we created them." This quote attributed to Albert Einstein resonates with the universally accepted solution of paradoxes encountered in the field of mathematical logic, when the framework has to be enlarged to get out of undecidable statements or fallacies. But the policies implemented since 2008, with ultra-low interest rates, quantitative easing, and other financial alchemical gesticulations, are essentially following the pattern of the past 30 years, namely, the financialization of real problems plaguing the real economy. Rather than still hoping that real wealth will come out of money creation, an illusion also found in the current management of the ongoing European sovereign and banking crises, we need fundamentally new ways of thinking.

And with that biting critique of central bank policy making, we come back to Blanchflower's fateful line: "We couldn't take the chance that he was wrong."

Without a fundamental shift in economic thought at the highest levels of central banking, there is little doubt that the response of any central bank during the next crisis—and there will always be a next crisis—will be more of the same. Central banks will again apply the limited tools they have: low interest rates, quantitative easing, a variety of bailout mechanisms—in short, they will resort to the financial repression of savers in the name of the greater good.

We have tried to make the case that savers should be rewarded, not punished; that financial repression should be practiced only *in extremis;* and that moral hazard should be respected. But the reality is that the people with their hands on the levers simply believe with all their hearts in a different theoretical economic framework and will not take a chance on being wrong. They will act just as they have in the past. Until such time as a different paradigm reigns, we should not expect any different policy actions.

I would argue, and I think Sornette would agree, that the current policies are simply increasing the instability of the entire system, leading up to another major dislocation in the not-too-distant future. In much the same way that everyone loved rising house prices in the middle of the last decade, we all find contentment in a rising stock market. For Bernanke and his kin, the markets simply confirm the correctness of their policies. The fact that savers and retirees are being crushed, that markets are being distorted, or that governments are being encouraged to spend beyond their means is lost on them.

As Sornette put it, "Each excess was felt to be 'solved' by measures that in fact fueled following excesses; each crash was fought by an accommodative monetary policy, sowing the seeds for new bubbles and future crashes."

How will it all end? Faith in central banks today is equivalent to faith in the term *dot-com* in 1999 or in the eternal rise of housing prices in 2006. With the support of a powerful narrative—that central banks can support asset prices and effectively backstop financial crises (eliminating tail risk)—sentiment is driving the markets higher in the face of cyclically improving but historically weak and unstable fundamentals (plagued by debt deleveraging and aging demographics).

Ultimately, the stability of the system depends on central banks' credibility sentiment and policy responsiveness to prevent minor drawdowns from becoming full-blown crashes. My friend Mohamed El-Erian has written extensively on the importance of the central bank "brand" and warned of the danger of a broken narrative. Markets tend to overshoot in both directions and will most likely fall even farther than fundamentals warrant when and if central banks lose control of popular sentiment.

It is not only the credibility of sovereign nations burdened with debt that can reach a *Bang!* moment. The credibility of and faith in central banks is just as fragile. Today, we see humorous images of dollar bills with Ben Bernanke's face on them, with the words "In Ben We Trust." But there is truth in that jest. Whether it is Mark Carney at the Bank of England (BoE) or Mario Draghi at the European Central Bank (ECB) or the future chairperson of the Fed, central bankers are in the hot seat when it comes to global stability. The world no longer worries first and foremost about the products corporations make or the services they perform. Rather, it is focused on the amount of easy money the central banks can dish out.

What happens when that amount is no longer enough and market forces turn? With central banks already in a hyper-easing mode, what can they do in the face of the next real crisis that will convince the markets they have things under control? And there are any number of potential trigger points for the next crisis. One that comes to mind is a political shock such as a southern European country refusing to submit to further austerity (if Italy or Spain is forced into early elections, that could do it) or a change in Germany's tune. What if the ECB actually has to follow through on its commitment to use OMT (outright monetary transactions) to buy unlimited amounts of short-term Italian, Spanish, and/or French bonds. Draghi simply cannot follow through without expanding the ECB's balance sheet, and it is not crazy to think that the German Constitutional Court could respond by limiting the size of OMT, as it did with the European Financial Stability Facility (EFSF). That kind of blow would mean game over for Draghi's sentiment-supporting bluff.

As if that is not enough, the era of financial repression will soon morph into currency war.

First Rule in a Currency War: Don't Say Currency War

We finished *Endgame* in early 2011. The book was not even out before we were already talking about our next book. But the physical fatigue of producing a book was fresh on our minds, so we were not ready to jump back into the trenches. Yet there was the clear implication in *Endgame* that we were headed into a world where easy monetary policies would have to be unwound.

The best way for a country to deal with the problems that had been and would be created is to *grow* its way out of the problems. That requires policies and economic conditions that increase exports. The easy way, the one that politicians and industrialists love? Debase the currency. Make the goods produced in your country cost less on world markets while temporarily holding down your costs. You get not only higher sales (and thus tax revenues) but also higher employment. What's not to like?

Especially when you are dealing with massive debts and leverage, fiscal deficits, slow growth or recession, and potential deflationary pressures, having your currency weaken a bit here and there can be seem like a good temporary solution (emphasis on temporary).

But back in 2011, that was all in the future. We decided we would write a book on currency wars and the end of QE. It would hit the shelves toward the end of 2014, well in time for the fun and games we expected in the latter half of the decade.

And then the darned Japanese fired the first shot in the next global currency war, in advance of our personal schedule, and we had to start writing madly.

All of which goes to say that your humble analysts are no more able to predict the future than anyone else.

What I now want to do is to develop a few scenarios as to how it all might play out. Given the multiplicity of the moving parts, it is unlikely I will get it right; but still, you have to think through how things might develop if you're to have any hope of positioning your business and investments properly. As facts change, you can change your plans, but reacting after the fact is almost always a bad idea. We will update our thoughts on scenarios at www.thecoderedbook.com from time to time as the situation warrants. (And, of course, I'll be thinking along these lines in my free weekly letter, *Thoughts from the Frontline*, as well!)

Let me emphasize that the following is speculation on my part. As Lord Keynes intoned, "When the facts change, I change. . . ." But here is what I see from the deck overlooking a lake in Montana.

There are four central banks that have the ability to unilaterally create significant mischief for the rest of the world: the U.S. Federal Reserve, the European Central Bank, the Bank of England, and the Bank of Japan. Because of the size of its economy, China would be a candidate, but its impact will be somewhat limited because its currency does not yet float. When they finally float their currency, they will expand the group mentioned above.

All other countries are basically bringing knives to a gunfight. While they can respond with their own attempts at quantitative easing (QE), the nature of their economies means that at some point the effects of QE will be more painful for their own citizens to bear than trying to adjust to a new level of currency valuation. In smaller economies, QE almost inevitably turns into significant inflation in a short amount of time.

It Begins with Japan

From the point of view of Japan, the yen is ridiculously strong. Back in the 1960s, it was over 350 yen to the dollar, but it topped out at 78 in late 2011—your basic 450 percent move. The Japanese had to learn to become ever more productive and competitive over that time, as they were up against a major headwind from currency valuation. They produced massive trade surpluses until just a few years ago and had the lowest interest rates of any developed country for the last 20 years. (Usually, low rates are associated with weak currencies, not strong ones.)

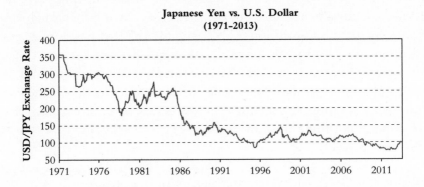

Japanese Yen vs. U.S. Dollar
(1971–2013)

They experienced one of the greatest bubbles in the history of the world, saw it burst in the late 1980s, and then suffered through 24 years of economic malaise, rather than the typical brief postbubble collapse. Of course, they were saddled with zombie banks, financial repression, and fiscal deficits on a scale not seen anywhere before.

But now the Japanese have come to the end of the journey. They have accumulated too much debt, have allowed their government spending to get too far out of balance, and have seen their trade surpluses turn into large trade deficits. The country is literally growing old and has run through the net savings of its citizens. Something has to give. As we detailed in Chapter 3, what will give is the valuation of the yen. Japan is going to try and export its deflation.

As we write, the yen is in the range of 100 to the dollar. While that is a 25 percent move in the last six months, from the perspective of history, it can't even be seen as an adequate correction by the Japanese.

Just for fun, take a look at the trade-weighted dollar from 1970 forward. The dollar rose early in the period and since then has fallen about 50 percent from its highs, to roughly where it was at the start of the period. What would U.S. exports look like if the dollar were three to four times stronger today than it was 30 to 40 years ago? Our politicians and unions write nasty letters to the U.S. secretary of the Treasury when they think a foreign currency is out of balance with the dollar by a mere 20 to 30 percent. What if the dollar had doubled in value and then doubled again? The howls in Congress and on K Street would be deafening!

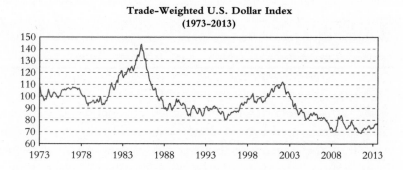

Trade-Weighted U.S. Dollar Index
(1973–2013)

As we wrote in Chapter 3, we think the yen is inexorably going to 120 and then 130 and then to 150 and beyond over the next three to five years. We expect nothing precipitous (if you can call a 15 to 20 percent annual move in a currency normal), but the erosion in the yen will become ever more clear over time.

There is not much the world will do about a yen at 120, other than carp and moan. But 135? 150? At some point it starts to bite; and nations, corporations, and unions will close ranks and demand the protection of "our jobs" and competitiveness.

The weakening of the yen is going to create real problems for the rest of Asia. Korea is especially vulnerable, since it competes directly with Japan in so many industries for the same export dollars. There is little the Koreans can do, as monetary easing on their part would bring inflation to their shores. They will have to become ever more efficient to maintain market share. Their dilemma could be compounded if North Korea collapses in much the same manner that the USSR imploded in 1988—a very real possibility. In 1986, few people thought there was the potential for the Iron Curtain to come down and for the Soviet empire to break up.

Vietnam, Taiwan, Indonesia, and the rest of Asia (ex-China) will have more or less the same problem with a weak yen. They will also have to be careful in managing foreign direct investment from Japan, as the Japanese will be looking to invest more and more of their savings outside of their own country. The natural human instinct will be to invest in assets close by, and for the Japanese that means the rest of Asia. That investment will tend to strengthen the currencies of these countries versus the yen at a time when there is already pressure on their exports.

Ironically, China is the one country in the world that has a potentially ready answer to a currency war. While members of the U.S. Congress complain about what they see as a weak Chinese currency, there is a large amount of money inside of China that is seeking a way to get out. What better way for the Chinese to respond to a currency war than to slowly (and I mean slowly, as in small baby steps all along the way) float their currency, allowing the pent-up Chinese demand for diversification overseas to express itself. That would serve the purpose of actually weakening the renminbi against the dollar, but would create yet more problems for the rest of Asia.

And the response of China? They would say, "We did exactly what you told us to do. You wanted us to float our currency and let the markets tell us the value, and we did. How can it be our fault if the markets say our currency was overpriced?" Watching Senators Schumer and Graham become even more apoplectic about China's currency valuation will be one of the few humorous moments in an otherwise serious situation.

Another real problem will be developing in Germany. As noted in Chapter 3, Germany, more than any other country, competes head-to-head with Japan. At some point, a falling yen will become intensely painful to a country that gets 40 percent of its GDP from exports.

Germany can, of course, become more productive as one way to respond. And that will initially be their only option, since as a Eurozone member they no longer have the ability to respond with monetary easing. Indulge me for a moment as I offer a very speculative but interesting scenario. German exporters would like to see a weaker euro, but Germany does not want to allow the ECB to print money. However, German leaders recognize that at some point, if the Eurozone is to maintain a currency union, it must also have a fiscal union. A breakup of the Eurozone would be disastrously expensive for everyone, but especially for Germany. There will be a live-or-die effort by all parties to maintain the euro. If Germany and the other fiscally sound members of the European Union can persuade the peripheral countries to adopt rules that require fiscal restraint in return for mutualization of debt, then that would allow the ECB to monetize deficits in the interim—and thus potentially weaken the euro.

This scenario would require members of the Eurozone to give up a great deal of their fiscal autonomy to Brussels. This will become the central question with regard to the existence of the euro within a few years. In an odd sort of way, the Eurozone is going to enter into its own internal currency war as the peripheral nations continue to have debt problems.

The situation will be exacerbated by the fiscal crisis that will soon engulf France. It will come precisely at the moment when Germany will be asked to allow the ECB to accommodate the French bond market, as it has done for Italy and Spain, and when France in turn will be asked to enter into a period of austerity, as both Italy and Spain have done (very painfully). It is at that moment that the ultimate survival of the euro will be decided.

While I do think the euro will likely survive, I have to admit that I'm not strongly convinced of it. The euro has never been a truly economic currency: it was created as a political statement and is a political currency. The problem for Europe is that a currency union ultimately requires a fiscal union. Just as the various states within the United States have to balance their budgets, that is what might be required of countries that are part of a European fiscal union. Given that most of Europe has entitlement-spending problems just as severe as—or worse than—those of the United States, there will not be a European fiscal union without a great deal of political contention.

Will Germany be willing to pick up the tab for the rest of Europe, given the serious fiscal constraint that will impose on its own budget?

Will France be willing to give up control of its budget process to Brussels? These are the questions on which the future of the euro experiment hinges. And those questions will come to the forefront precisely at the time that currency "tensions" come roiling out of Asia. The easy road for some European politicians will be to call for a return to their original currencies. Indeed, many members of the Eurozone are operating with their own de facto currencies today, as the populist Beppo Grillo of Italy has argued, since a euro in Cyprus, for instance, is no longer the same as a euro in Germany. And Grillo's movement did get 25 percent of the vote in the last election.

Britain has clearly signaled that it intends to continue to weaken the pound sterling over time. The pound is down 25 percent from its highs against the dollar, and I expect that trend to continue for the rest of the decade. Indeed, I've been saying for quite a long time that I think both the euro and the pound will go to parity against the dollar. Not next year, of course, but over time.

Turning to the commodity currencies, Canada and Australia will start to feel the pinch as well if their currencies rise too much. And both countries have housing bubbles that will burst at some point, allowing their central banks to lower interest rates and the value of their currencies.

And what of the United States? The U.S. dollar is the reserve currency of the world and is the medium of global trade. What would happen if the United States began to supply fewer and fewer dollars to world markets? Today, this seems like idle speculation, but as the United States becomes more energy independent, its need to buy oil will drop. And we expect an amazing thing to happen: the United States will actually become a net exporter of energy within a decade. Already, we are seeing sizable exports of energy-related products from the United States. The summer of 2013 saw the Port of Houston become the largest port in terms of exports in the United States, finally surpassing New York. Energy and chemical exports are the reason.

The shale boom in the United States is very real. Every quarter, new reports appear describing new or expanded oil fields in the United States. Every year or so, government agencies revise their estimates of the amount of energy contained in U.S. oil fields. Those estimates have been rising dramatically. Liquefied natural gas terminals that were being built to import liquid natural gas are now being converted to export it. With natural gas in the $4 range in the United States and $14 in Japan, it does not take a sharp accountant to see the arbitrage potential.

We are also witnessing a revival of manufacturing in the United States, for several reasons. China's relative wage advantage is beginning to evaporate, the cost of bringing Chinese products to the United States is rising, and new manufacturing tools and techniques are making it cheaper to produce products in the United States. A robot works for the same wages in the United States as it does in China, and you don't have to worry as much about logistics.

For these and other reasons, the potential for the U.S. dollar to become much stronger than the market currently expects is very real, in my opinion. That is not a critical problem in and of itself, but politicians, export businesses, and unions could turn it into one. The global recession of the early 1930s turned into the Great Depression because of trade protectionism. One country after another enacted protectionist laws, and other countries retaliated, soon stifling global trade. I have said for years that my biggest worry about the future is a return to a protectionist state of mind.

Protectionism will be seen as an easy fix for those who are so inclined when the Japanese yen rises above 150 and the Japanese government and central bank show no sign of slowing down. Those tensions will exist not just in the United States but in all countries affected by the Japanese devaluation. It is my sincere hope that cooler heads will prevail and forestall a protectionist movement and the very destructive outcome of a global trade war.

There are a hundred other potential paths we could take, and of course to explore them would require us to write another book. But rather than wait for another book, I invite you to sign up for my free weekly letter, where I try to piece together the puzzles that make up the global picture. You can subscribe for free at www .MauldinEconomics.com.

As businesspeople and investors, we have to be focused on the opportunities right in front of us while also keeping a watchful eye on the horizon for stormy weather. The proper attitude in today's environment is cautious optimism. And despite the fact that we've written about the likelihood of a difficult environment in the near future, I am actually quite optimistic. My optimism is for the overall human endeavor, based on how our individual desires for a better life for ourselves and our children translate into a better future for all of us. In trading terms, you might say that I am long on humanity but short government.

The future potential of biotechnology, robotics and automation, artificial intelligence, communications, nanotechnology, global trade, new forms of energy, and a whole list of new services and inventions that will transform our lives and those of our children and grandchildren is simply overwhelming once you really begin to dive deep into the possibilities. At the end of the day, I think all of that positive development will overwhelm the shortsightedness of governments and central banks. But getting to the other side of the Code Red environment will require more than the same-old same-old approach to business and investing.

You've taken the first step toward understanding what we are facing by simply reading this book and trying to put together a plan for yourself. Jonathan and I will continue to provide updates and course corrections at www.thecoderedbook.com. We look forward to learning what the future holds for us and sharing the experience with you.

Notes

Chapter 3

1. www.theglobeandmail.com/report-on-business/economy/economy-lab/japans-demographics-of-doom-trump-market-stimulating-tricks/article12092365/

2. www.ritholtz.com/blog/2013/05/it-takes-a-regime-shift/?utm_source=feedburner&utm_medium=email&utm_campaign=Feed%3A+The BigPicture+%28The+Big+Picture%29

Chapter 4

1. As Lacey Hunt of Hoisington Investment Management has pointed out, there are numerous studies that show that government debt slows down growth:

(1) In *Government Size and Growth: A Survey and Interpretation of the Evidence*, Swedish economists Andreas Bergh and Magnus Henrekson find a "significant negative correlation" between size of government and economic growth. Specifically, "an increase in government size by 10 percentage points

is associated with a 0.5% to 1% lower annual growth rate." (*Journal of Economic Surveys*, April 2011)

(2) In *The Impact of High and Growing Government Debt on Economic Growth, An Empirical Investigation for The Euro Area*, Cristina Checherita and Philipp Rother find that a government debt-to-GDP ratio above the turning point of 90 to 100 percent has a "deleterious" impact on long-term growth. Additionally, the impact of debt on growth is nonlinear. This means that as the government debt rises to higher and higher levels, the adverse growth consequences accelerate. (European Central Bank, Working Paper 1237, August 2010)

(3) In *The Real Effects of Debt*, Stephen G. Cecchetti, M. S. Mohanty, and Fabrizio Zampolli determine that "beyond a certain level, debt is bad for growth. For government debt, the number is about 85% of GDP." (Bank for International Settlements (BIS), Basel, Switzerland, September, 2011)

2. www.popmodal.com/video/2066/Vintage-pro-inflation-propaganda

Chapter 7

1. www.bwater.com/Uploads/FileManager/research/deleveraging/an-in-depth-look-at-deleveragings--ray-dalio-bridgewater.pdf

Chapter 8

1. www.treasurydirect.gov/govt/rates/pd/avg/avg.htm

Chapter 10

1. www.businessinsider.com/ray-dalio-average-investor-portfolio-2012-9#ixzz2YZ2FZHQe

2. www.moneynews.com/InvestingAnalysis/Dalbar-Harvey-individual-investors/2013/03/11/id/494045

3. Cliff Asness, *Where the Wild Things Aren't*.

About the Authors

JOHN MAULDIN is the president of Mauldin Economics, a research and publishing firm; president of Millennium Wave Investments, an investment advisory firm registered with multiple states; and a registered representative of Millennium Wave Securities, a FINRA-registered broker-dealer. Each week, over a million readers on multiple outlets turn to John Mauldin to better understand Wall Street, global markets, and the drivers of the world economy. John is a renowned financial expert, a *New York Times* best-selling author, a pioneering online commentator, and the publisher of one of the first publications to provide investors with free, unbiased information and guidance, *Thoughts from the Frontline*—one of the most widely read investment newsletters in the world. He is also a sought-after contributor to numerous financial publications, as well as a regular guest on multiple television outlets. His books have appeared on the *New York Times* business best-seller list four times. He is the father of seven children, five of whom are adopted, and he is now beginning to actively collect grandchildren. He is convinced that the dividends will be extravagant. He lives in a high-rise in uptown Dallas, Texas, and travels the world, speaking and seeking out opportunities.

JONATHAN TEPPER is the CEO of Variant Perception, a macroeconomic research group that provides economic and investment insights to hedge funds, banks, and family offices. Jonathan is the co-author, with John Mauldin, of *Endgame: The End of the Debt Supercycle*, a book on the sovereign debt crisis. Jonathan has worked as an equity analyst at SAC Capital, as a vice president in proprietary trading at Bank of America, and as a portfolio manager at Hinde Capital. Jonathan is a founder of Demotix, a citizen-journalism web site and photo agency. In 2012 he sold Demotix to Corbis, a Bill Gates–owned company. In 2012, Jonathan was a finalist for the Wolfson Economics Prize, an open challenge for economists to find the most efficient and least disruptive way to break up the euro. The prize is the second most lucrative prize for economists after the annual Nobel Prize. Jonathan is a Rhodes Scholar. He earned a BA with Highest Honors in History and Honors in Economics from the University of North Carolina at Chapel Hill, and an MLitt in Modern History from Oxford University.

Index